That Time I Got Reìncarnated as a SLIME

The Ways of the Monster Nation

1

Sho Okagiri Original Story: **FUSE** Character Design: **Mitz Vah**

Contents

Chapter 1 > **Food-Stall Takoyaki☆Three Stars!!** —————— 3

Chapter 2 > **Kimono Shop☆Three Stars!!** —————— 35

Chapter 3 > **Blacksmith Shop☆Three Stars!!** —————— 57

Chapter 4 > **Highway Wagon Trip☆Three Stars!!** —————— 79

Chapter 5 > **That Light Feeling of Inebriation☆Three Stars!!** —————— 107

Chapter 6 > **Dungeon Exploration☆Three Stars!!** —————— 127

Chapter 7 > **Dungeon Exploration☆Three Stars!!** (Part 2) —————— 145

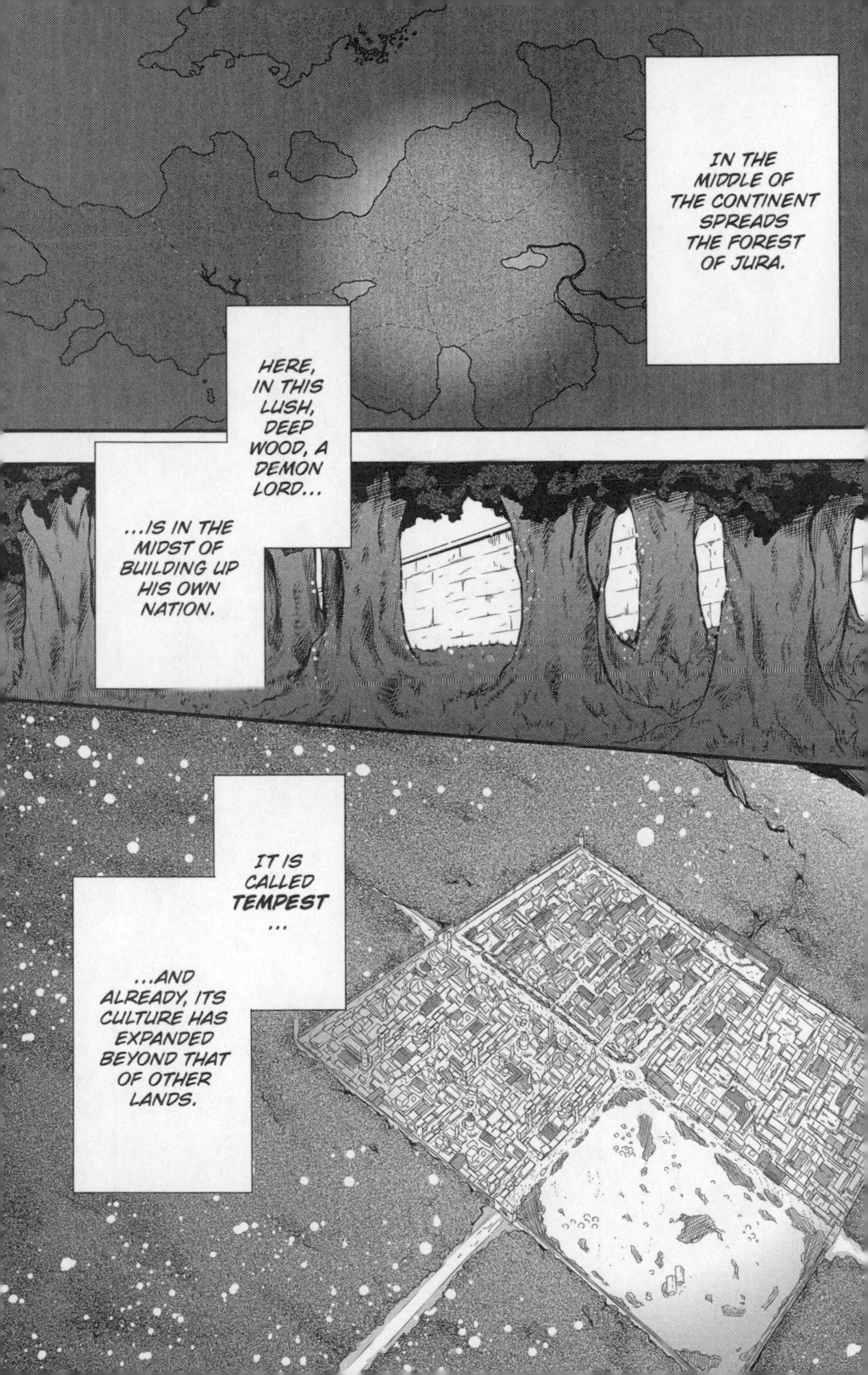
IN THE MIDDLE OF THE CONTINENT SPREADS THE FOREST OF JURA.
HERE, IN THIS LUSH, DEEP WOOD, A DEMON LORD...
...IS IN THE MIDST OF BUILDING UP HIS OWN NATION.
IT IS CALLED **TEMPEST** ...
...AND ALREADY, ITS CULTURE HAS EXPANDED BEYOND THAT OF OTHER LANDS.

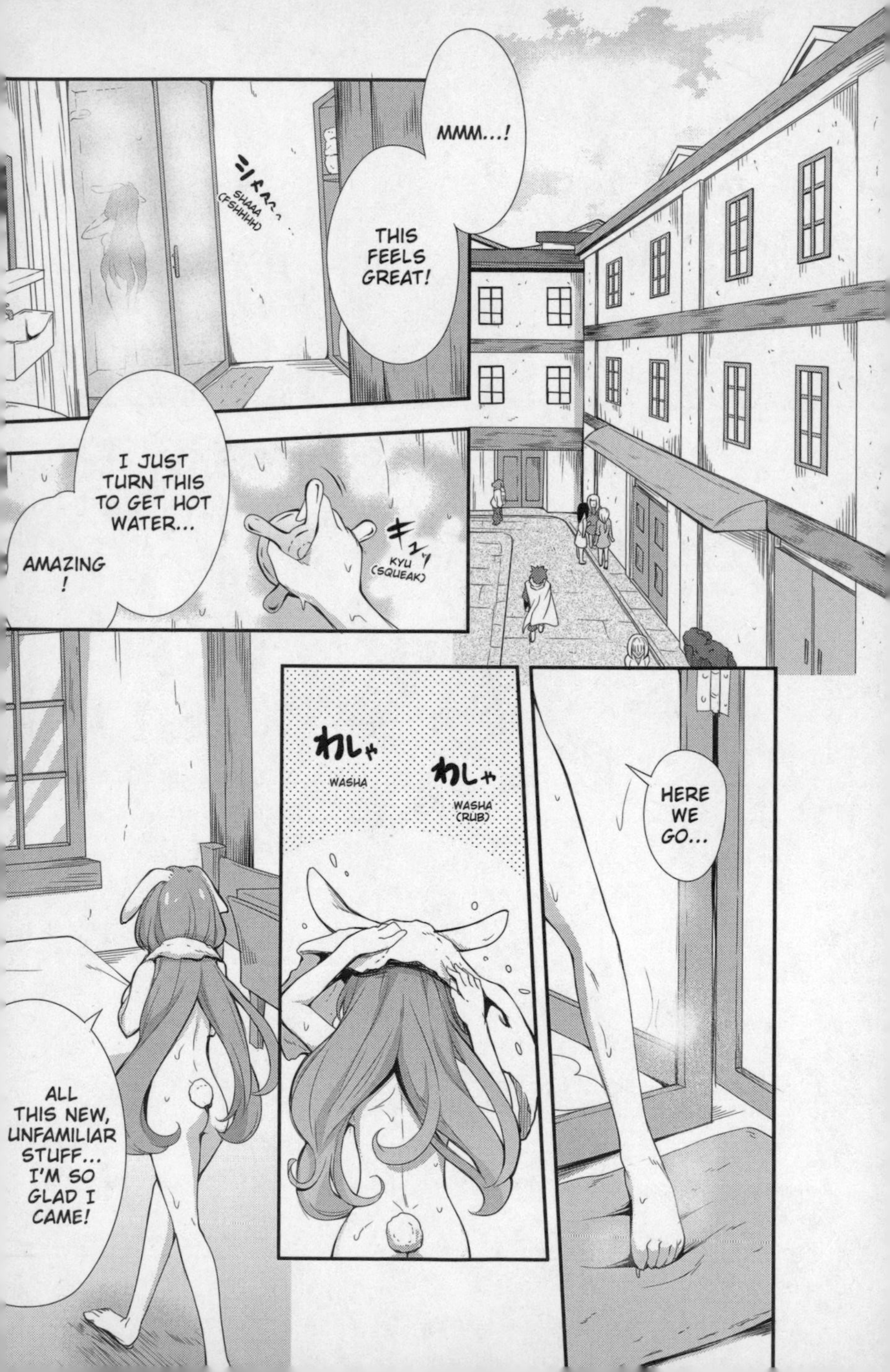
MMM...!
THIS FEELS GREAT!
シャー
SHAAA (FSHHHH)
I JUST TURN THIS TO GET HOT WATER...
AMAZING!
キュッ
KYU (SQUEAK)
HERE WE GO...
わしゃ
WASHA
わしゃ
WASHA (RUB)
ALL THIS NEW, UNFAMILIAR STUFF... I'M SO GLAD I CAME!

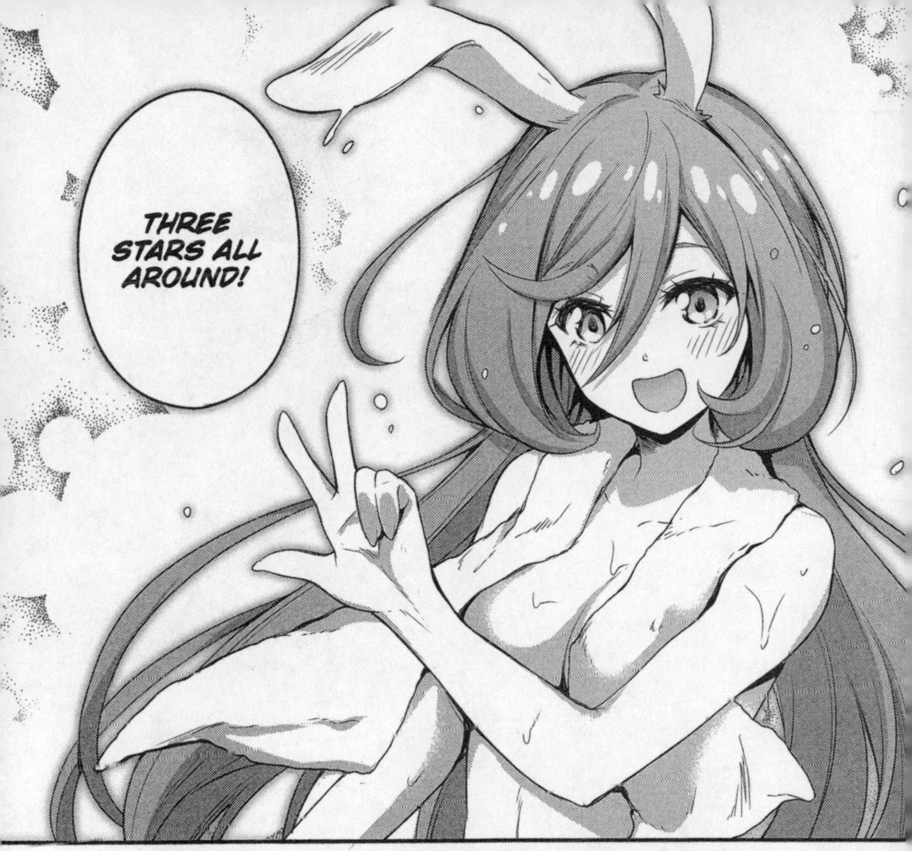
THREE STARS ALL AROUND!

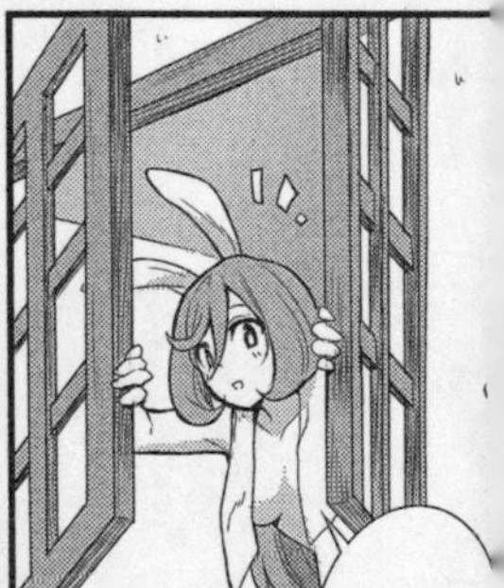
HMM?

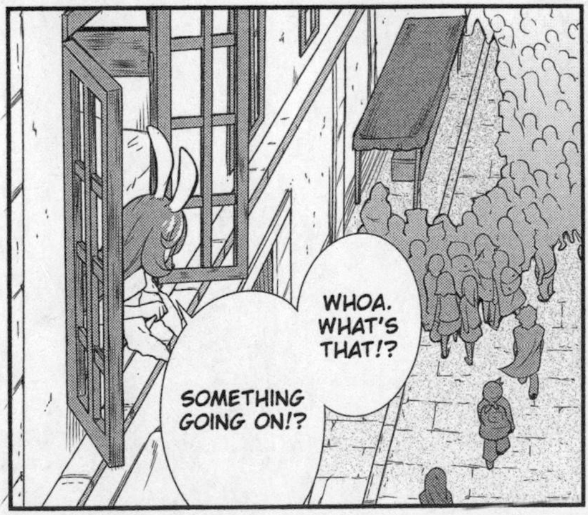
WHOA. WHAT'S THAT!?
SOMETHING GOING ON!?

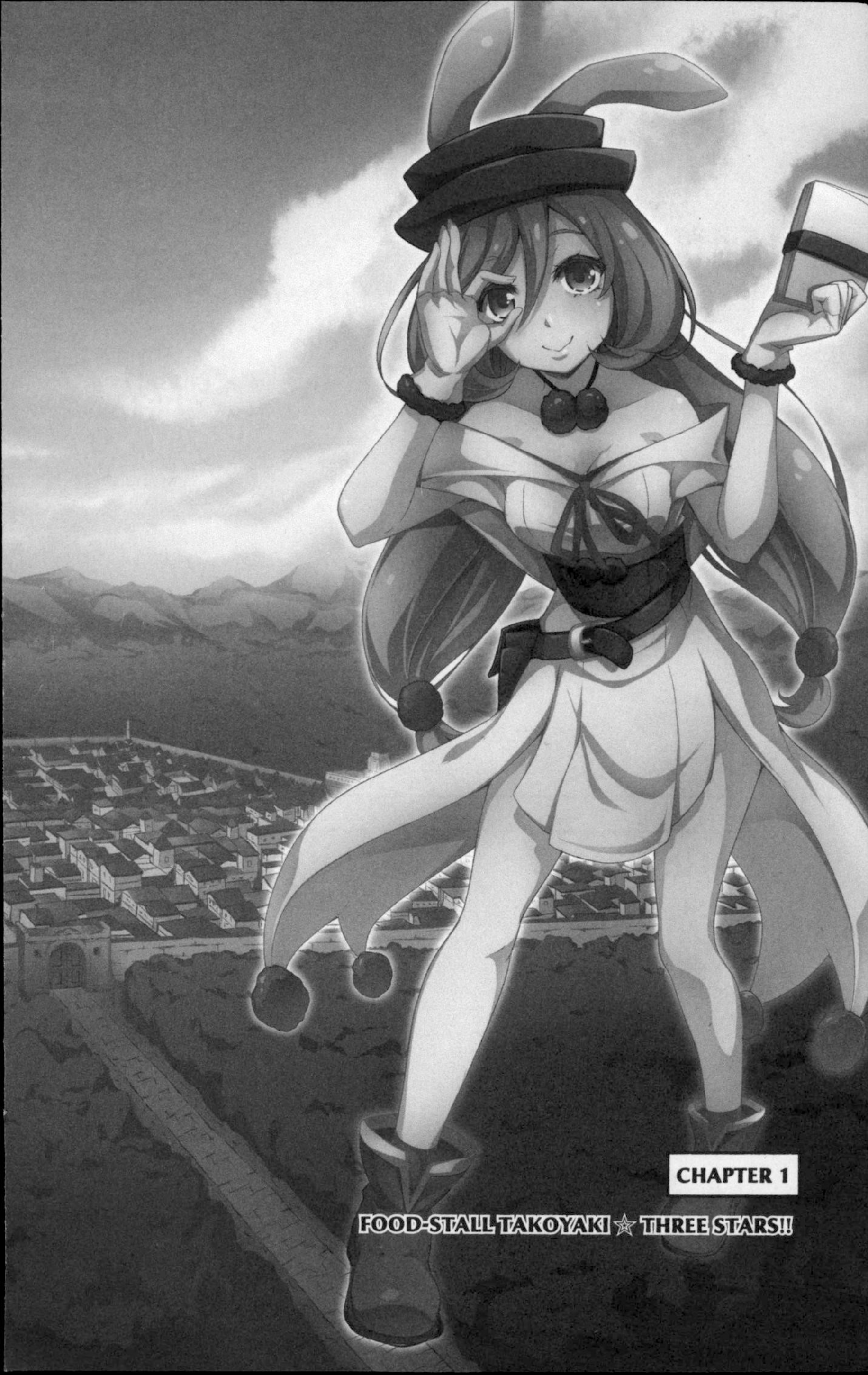
CHAPTER 1
FOOD-STALL TAKOYAKI ☆ THREE STARS!!

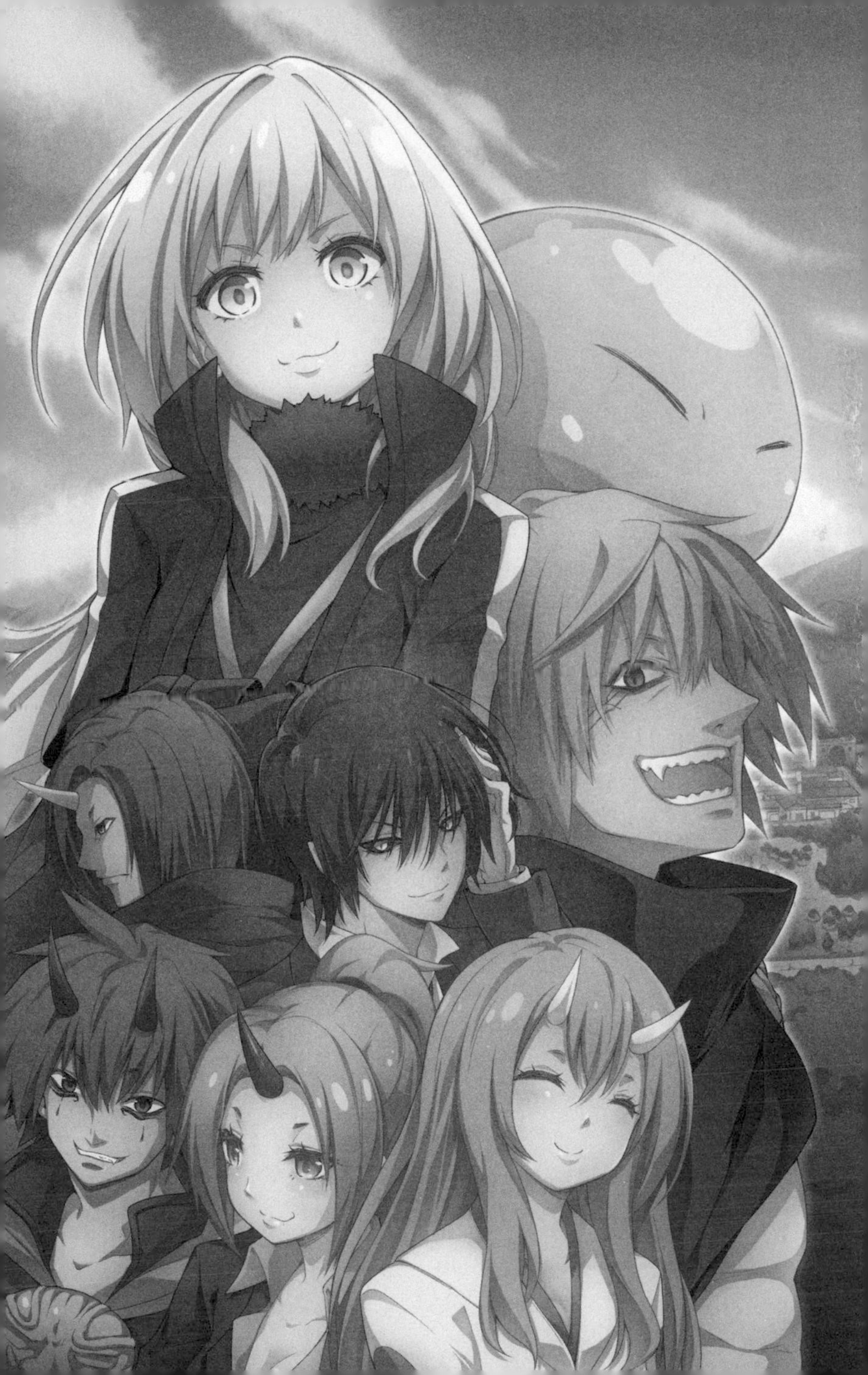

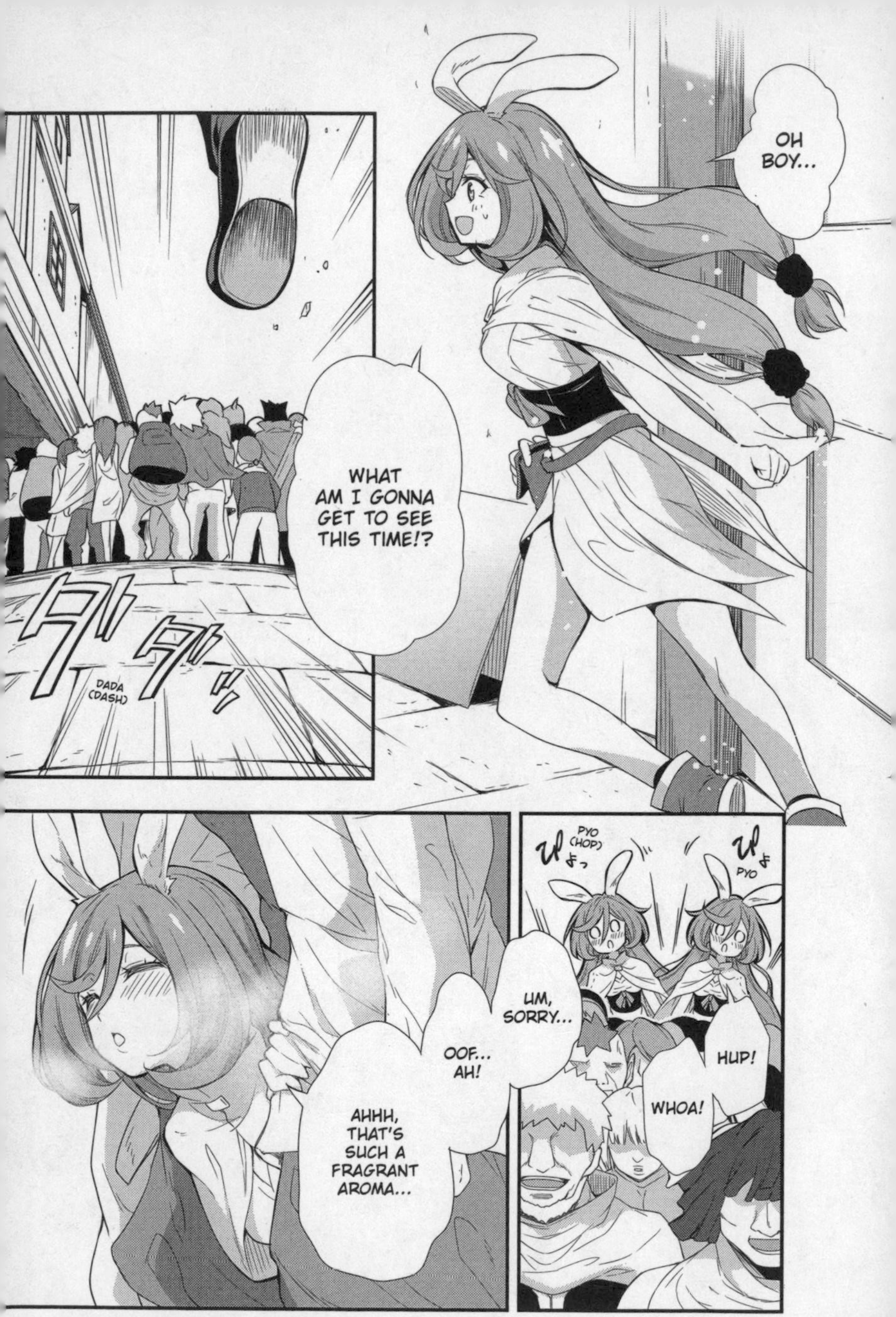
OH BOY...
WHAT AM I GONNA GET TO SEE THIS TIME!?
DADA (DASH)
PYO (HOP)
PYO
UM, SORRY...
HUP!
WHOA!
OOF... AH!
AHHH, THAT'S SUCH A FRAGRANT AROMA...

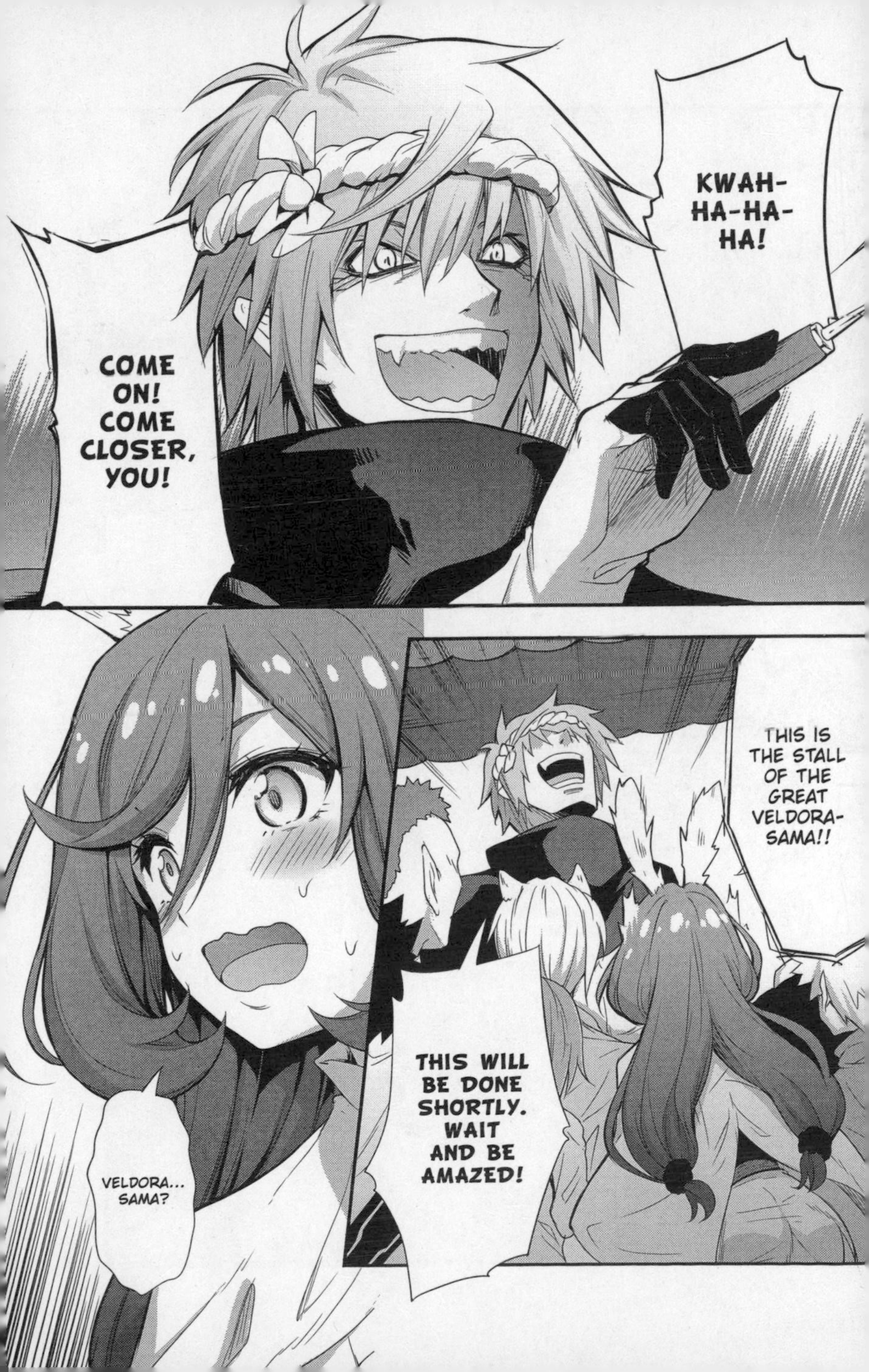
KWAH-HA-HA-HA!
COME ON! COME CLOSER, YOU!
THIS IS THE STALL OF THE GREAT VELDORA-SAMA!!
THIS WILL BE DONE SHORTLY. WAIT AND BE AMAZED!
VELDORA... SAMA?

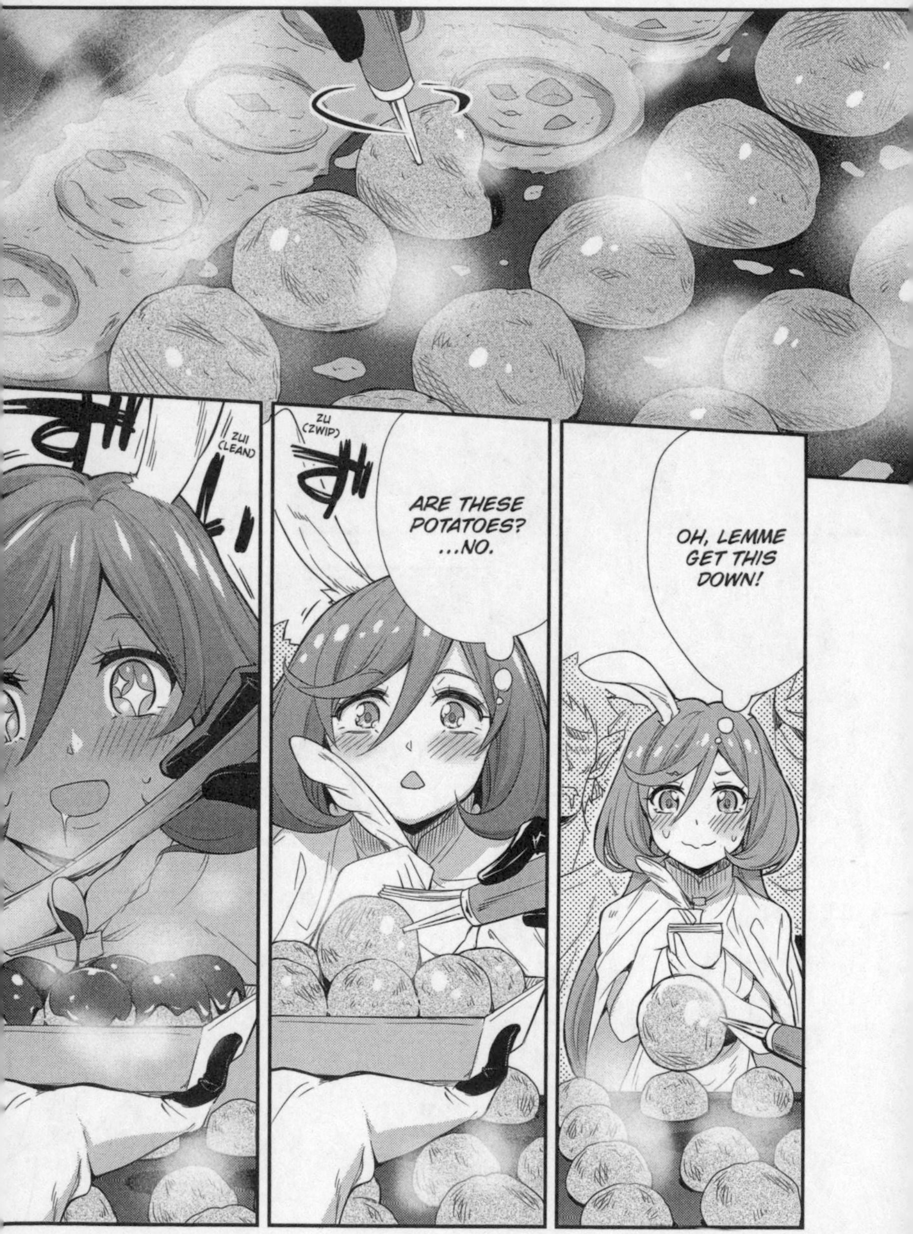
OH, LEMME GET THIS DOWN!
ARE THESE POTATOES? ...NO.
ZU (ZWIP)
ZUI (CLEAN)

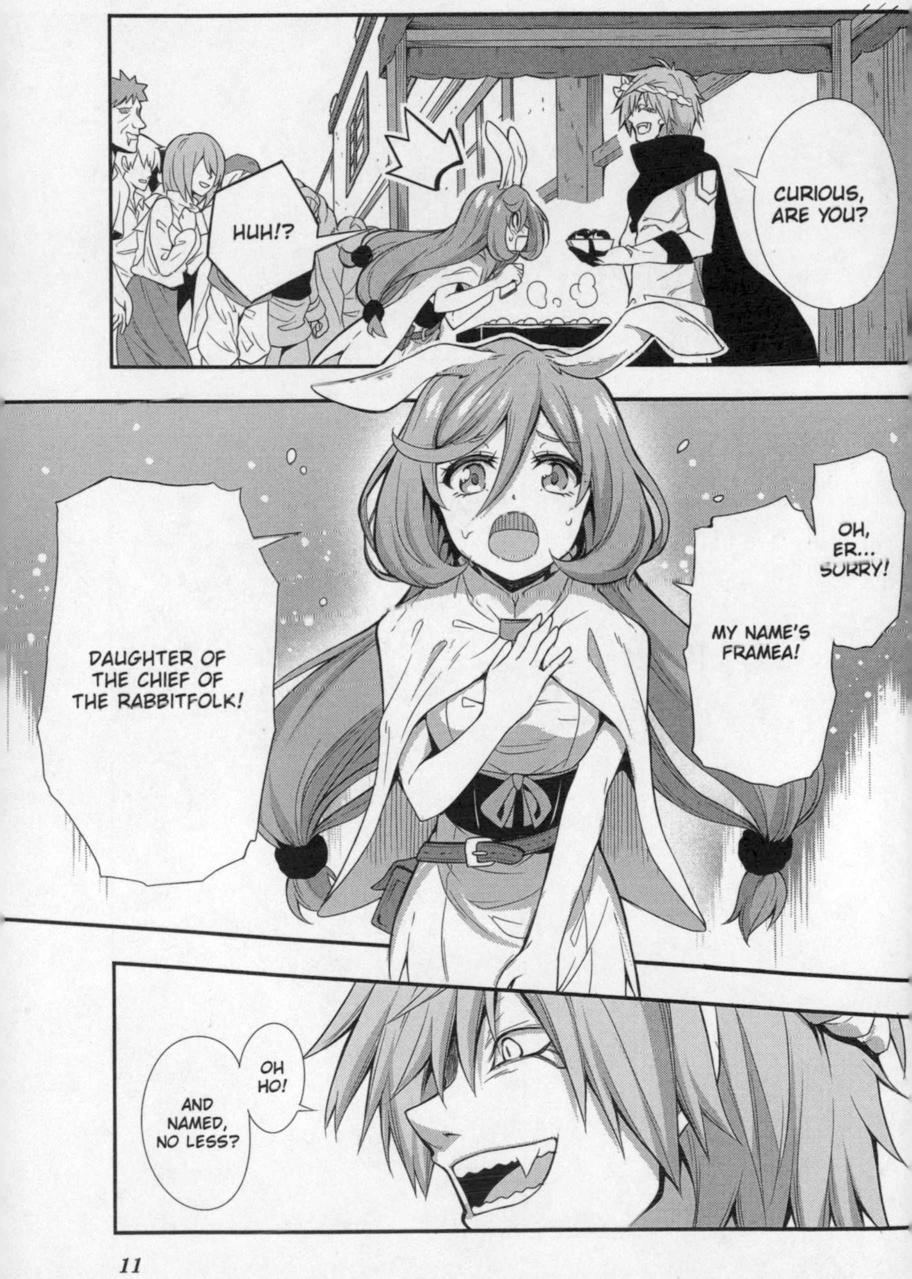
CURIOUS, ARE YOU?
HUH!?
OH, ER... SORRY!
MY NAME'S FRAMEA!
DAUGHTER OF THE CHIEF OF THE RABBITFOLK!
OH HO!
AND NAMED, NO LESS?

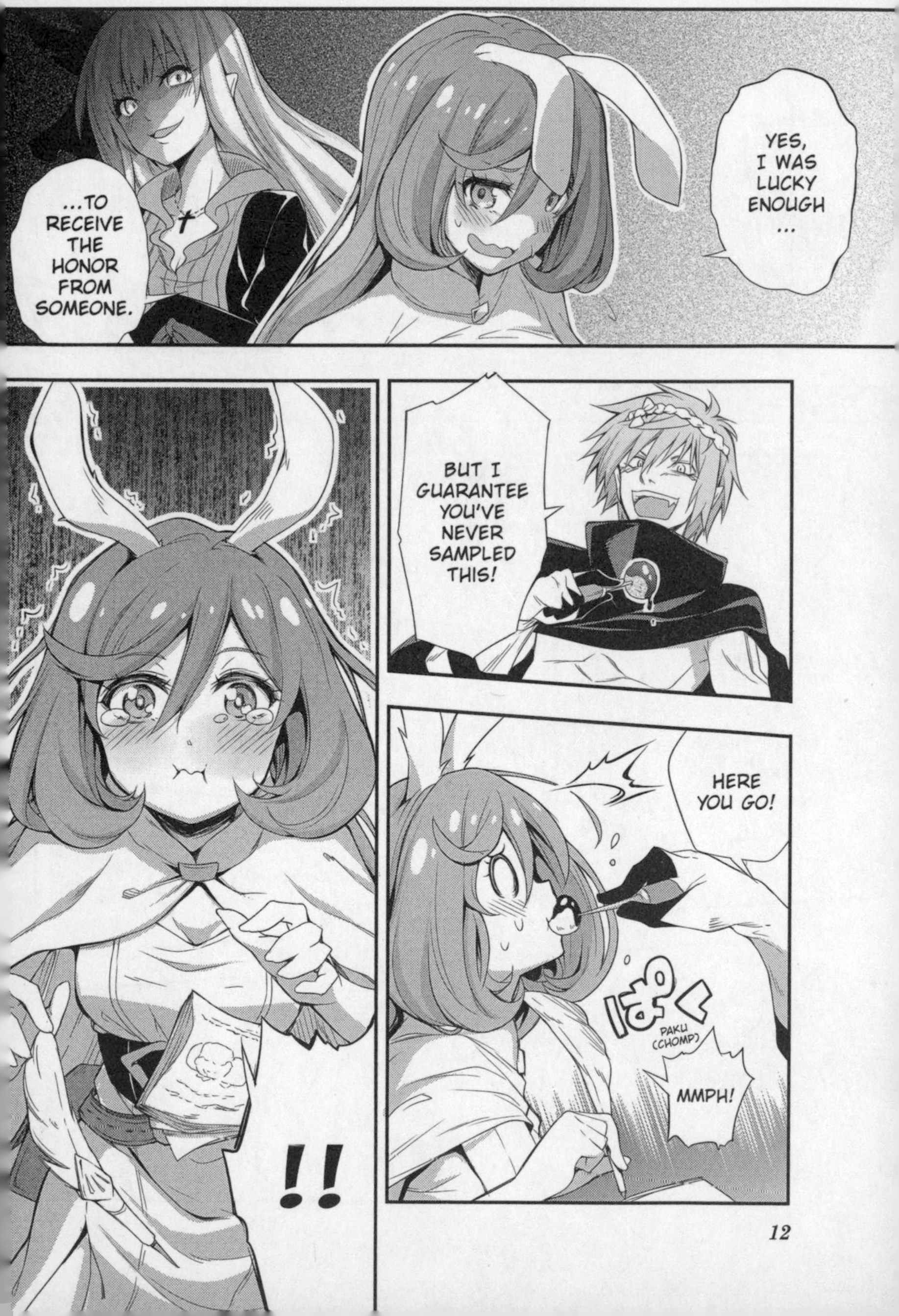
YES, I WAS LUCKY ENOUGH ...
...TO RECEIVE THE HONOR FROM SOMEONE.
BUT I GUARANTEE YOU'VE NEVER SAMPLED THIS!
HERE YOU GO!
ぱく
PAKU (CHOMP)
MMPH!
!!

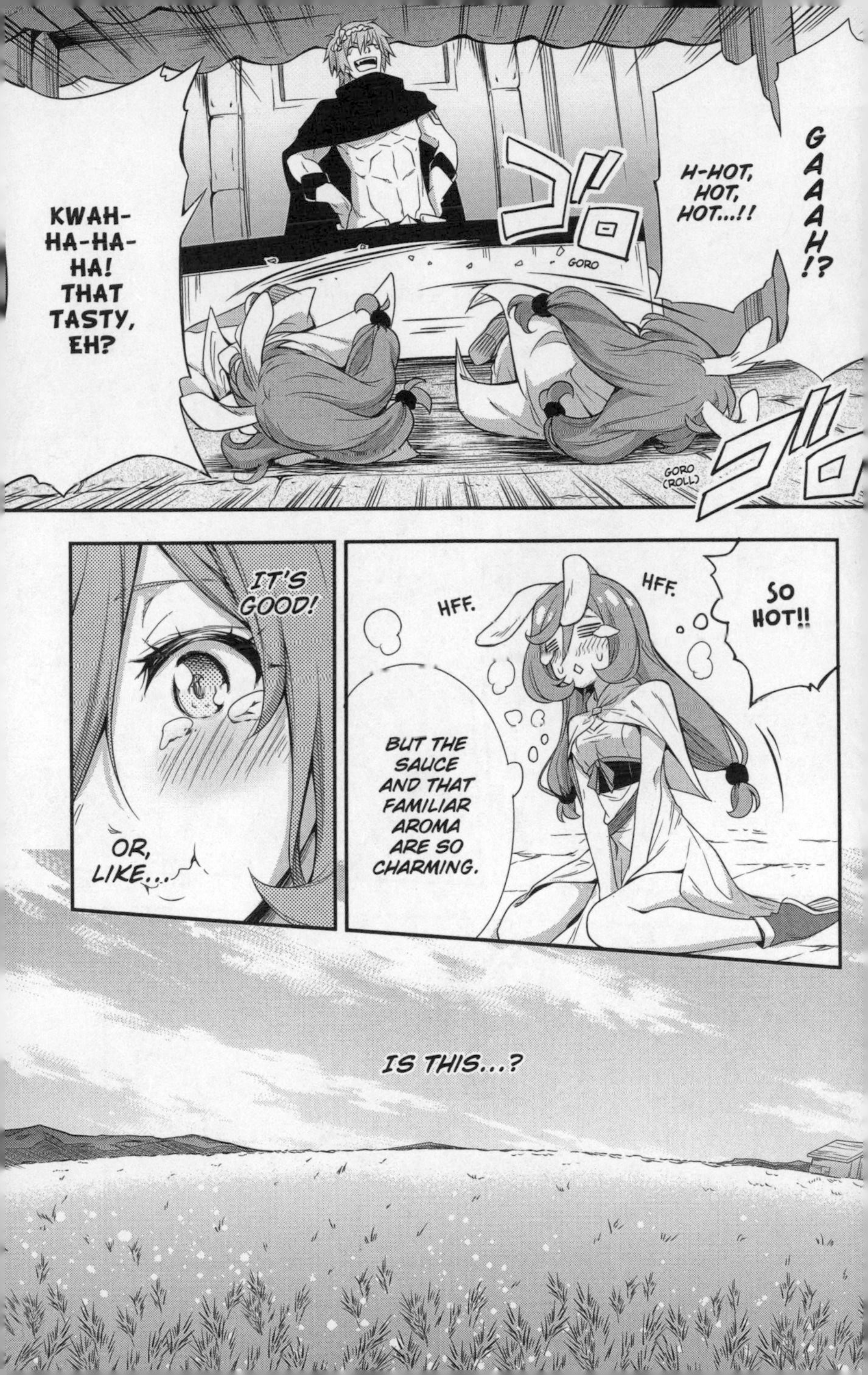
GAAAAH!?
H-HOT, HOT, HOT...!!
GORO
GORO (ROLL)
KWAH-HA-HA-HA! THAT TASTY, EH?
SO HOT!!
HFF.
HFF.
BUT THE SAUCE AND THAT FAMILIAR AROMA ARE SO CHARMING.
IT'S GOOD!
OR, LIKE...
IS THIS...?

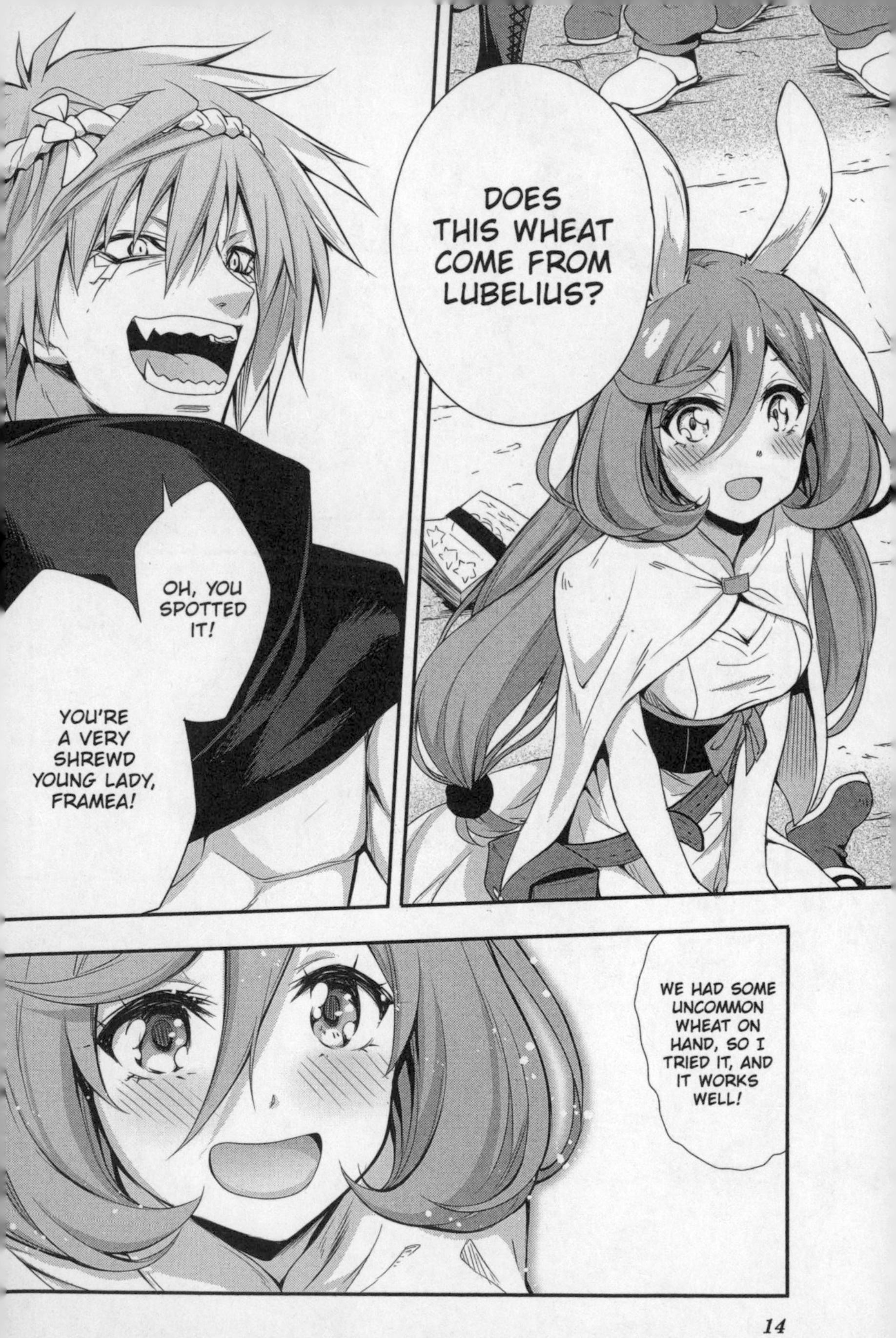
DOES THIS WHEAT COME FROM LUBELIUS?
OH, YOU SPOTTED IT!
YOU'RE A VERY SHREWD YOUNG LADY, FRAMEA!
WE HAD SOME UNCOMMON WHEAT ON HAND, SO I TRIED IT, AND IT WORKS WELL!

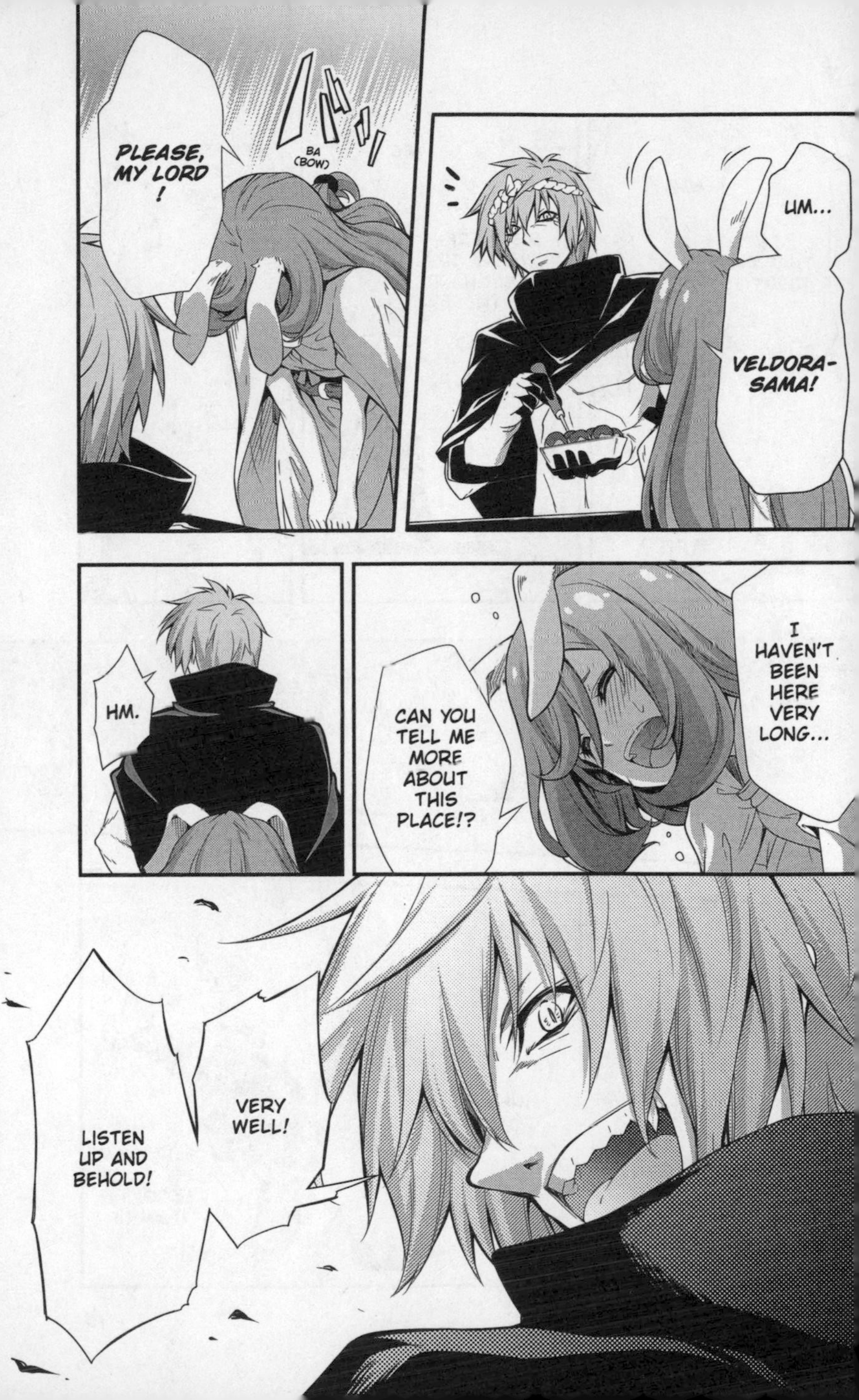
UM...
VELDORA-SAMA!
BA (BOW)
PLEASE, MY LORD!
I HAVEN'T BEEN HERE VERY LONG...
CAN YOU TELL ME MORE ABOUT THIS PLACE!?
HM.
VERY WELL!
LISTEN UP AND BEHOLD!

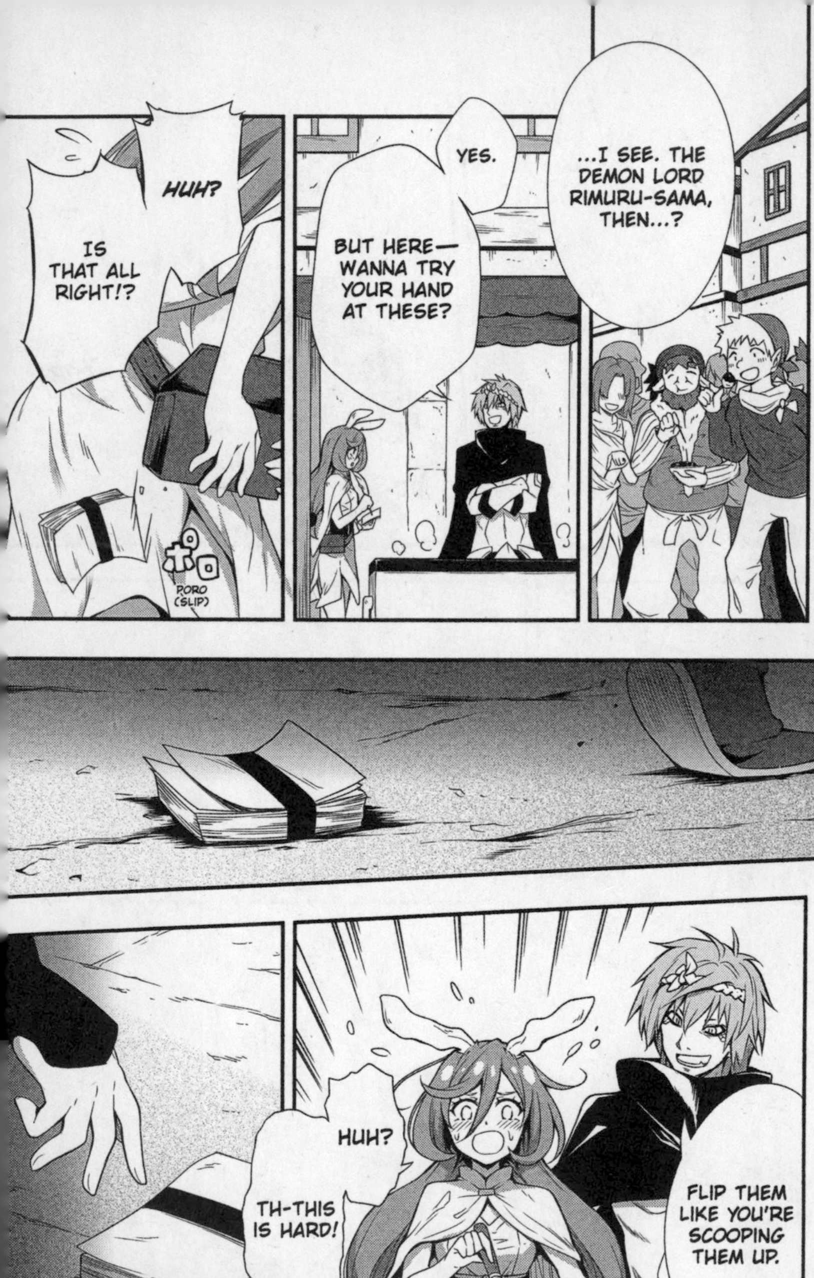
...I SEE. THE DEMON LORD RIMURU-SAMA, THEN...?
YES.
BUT HERE—WANNA TRY YOUR HAND AT THESE?
HUH?
IS THAT ALL RIGHT!?
ポロ
PORO (SLIP)
FLIP THEM LIKE YOU'RE SCOOPING THEM UP.
HUH?
TH-THIS IS HARD!

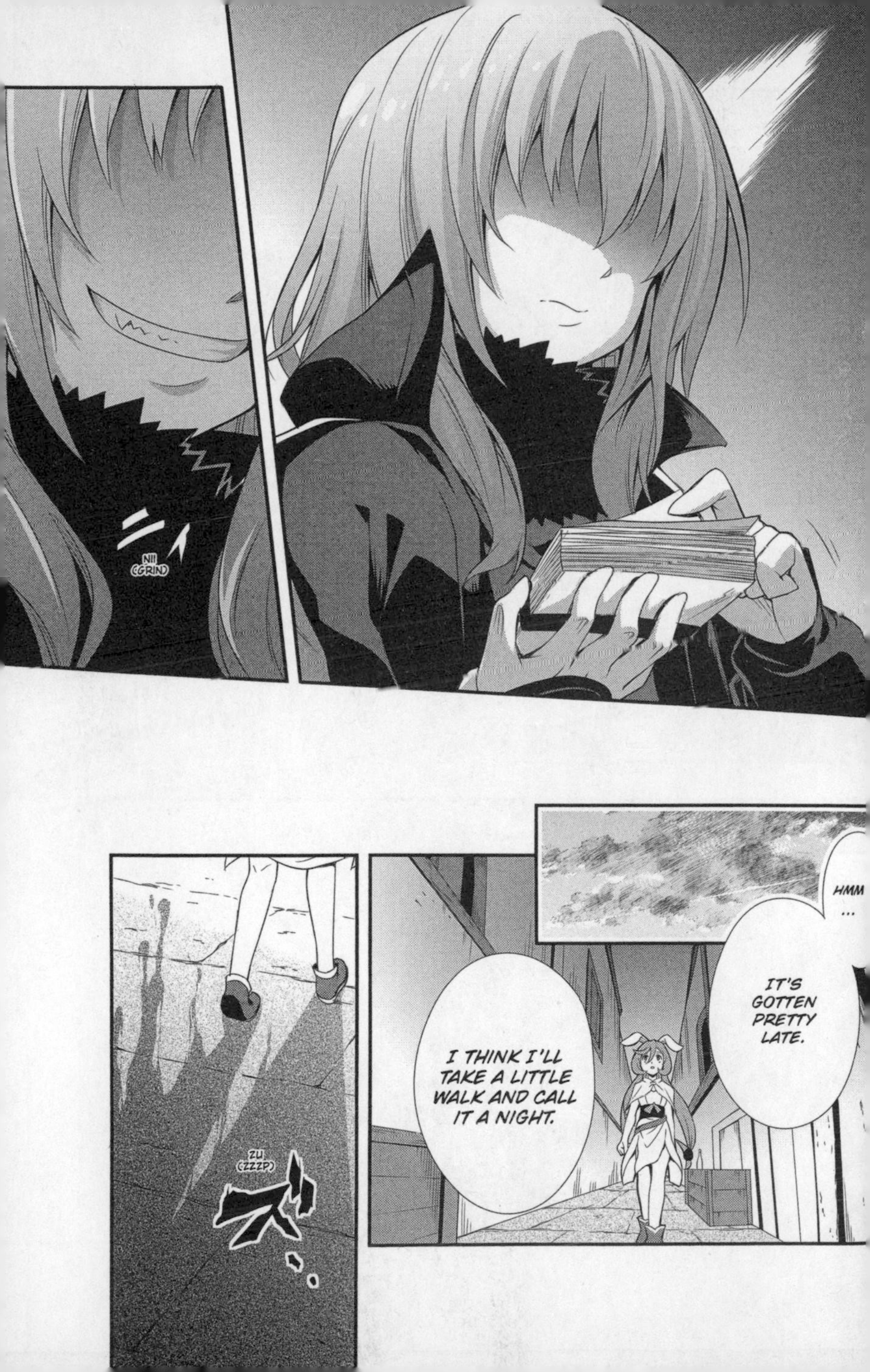
NII (GRIN)
HMM...
IT'S GOTTEN PRETTY LATE.
I THINK I'LL TAKE A LITTLE WALK AND CALL IT A NIGHT.
ZU (ZZZP)

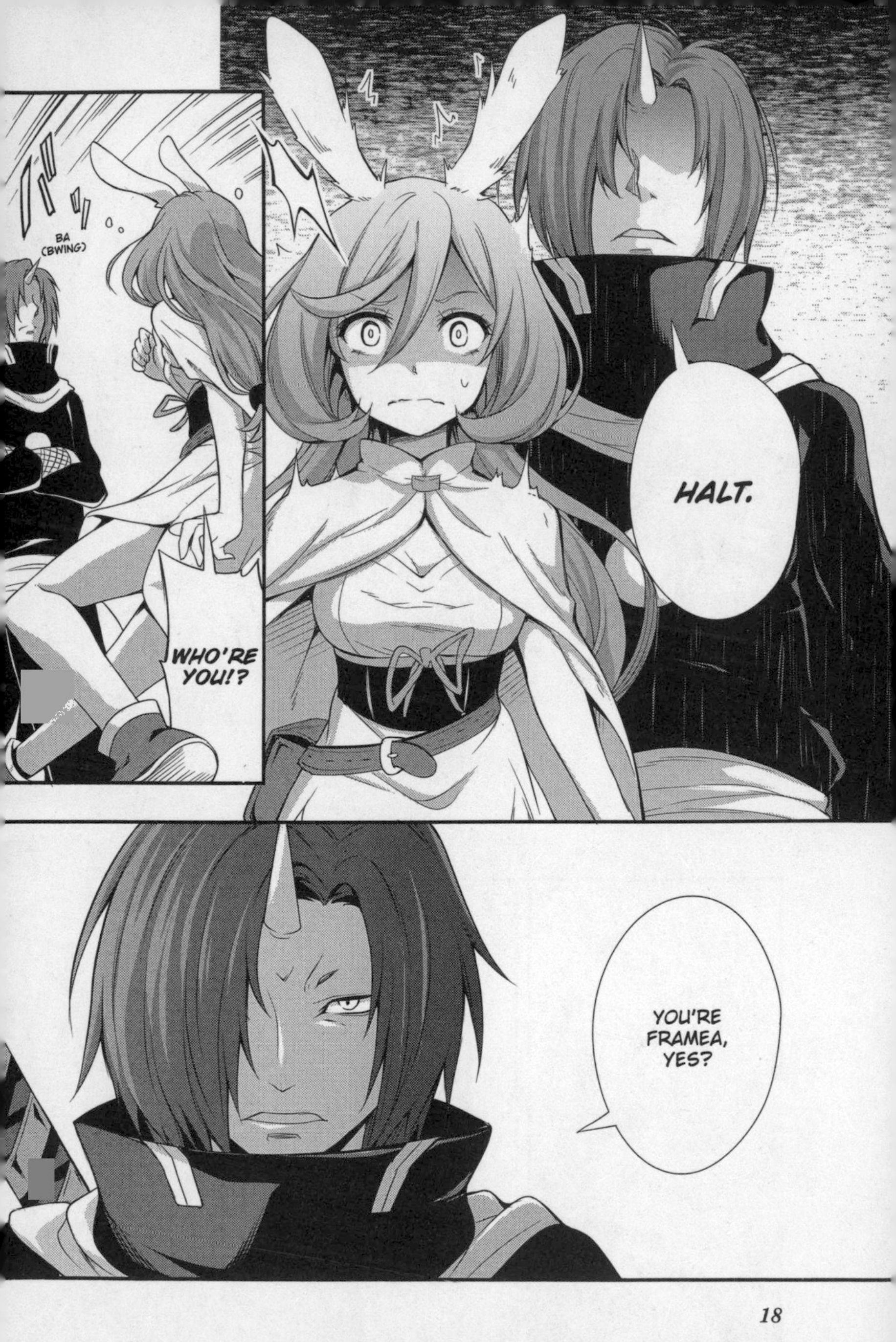
HALT.
BA
(BWING)
WHO'RE YOU!?
YOU'RE FRAMEA, YES?

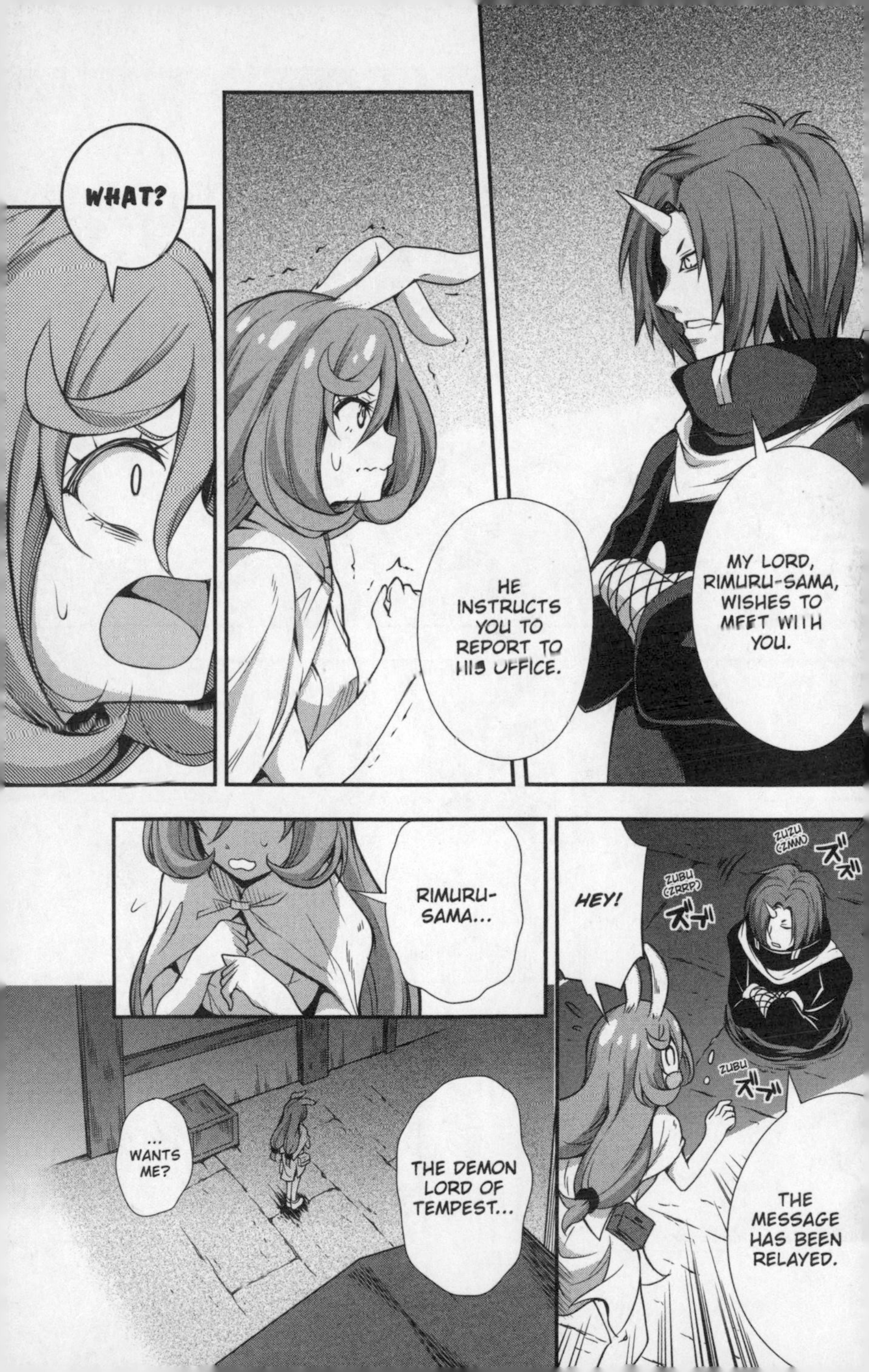
MY LORD, RIMURU-SAMA, WISHES TO MEET WITH YOU.
HE INSTRUCTS YOU TO REPORT TO HIS OFFICE.
WHAT?
ZUZU (ZMM)
ズズ
ZUBU (ZRRP)
ズブ
HEY!
ZUBU
ズブ
THE MESSAGE HAS BEEN RELAYED.
RIMURU-SAMA...
THE DEMON LORD OF TEMPEST...
...WANTS ME?

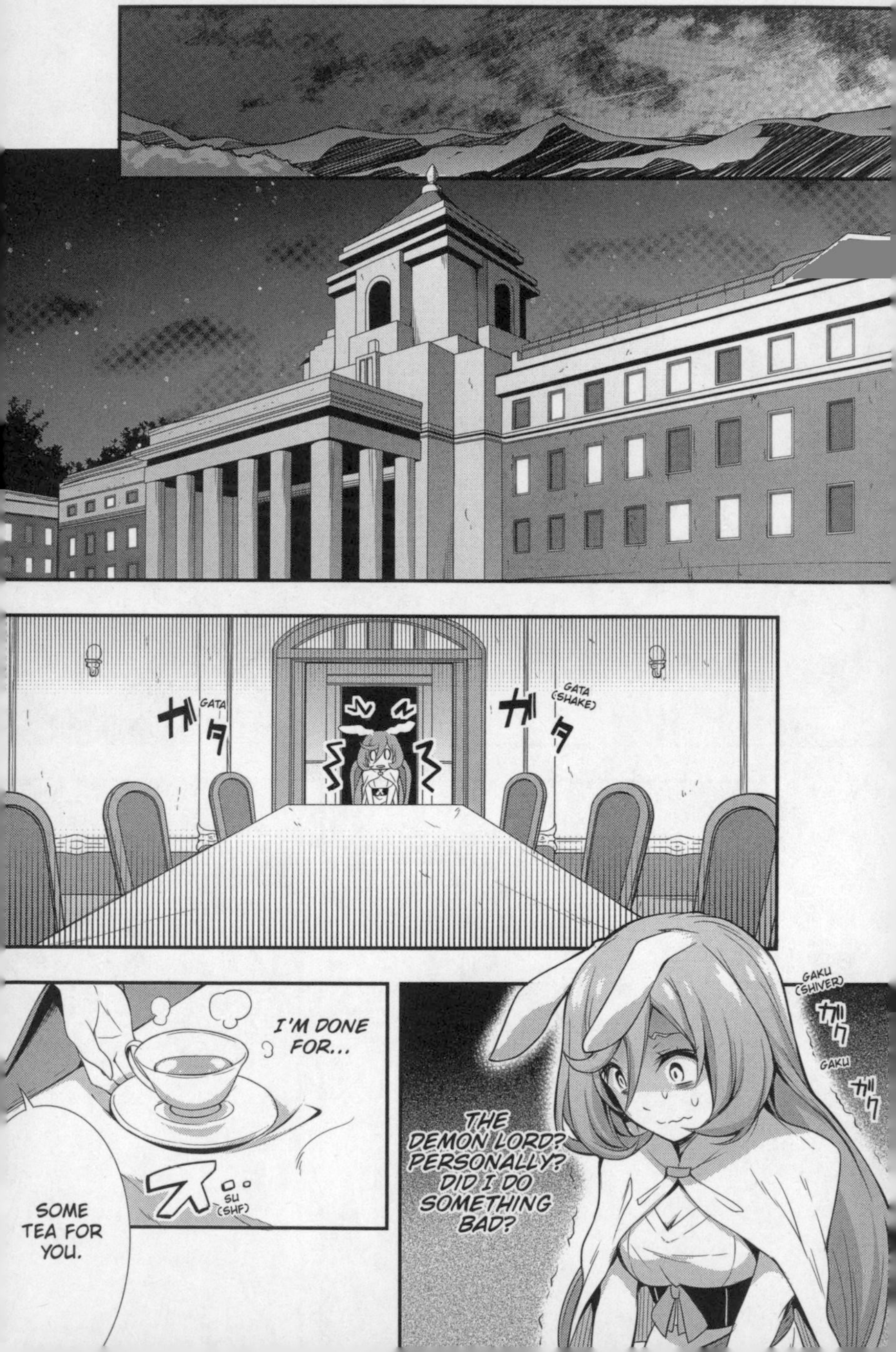
GATA (SHAKE)
ガタ
GATA
ガタ
GAKU (SHIVER)
ガク
GAKU
ガク
THE DEMON LORD? PERSONALLY? DID I DO SOMETHING BAD?
I'M DONE FOR...
ス
SU (SHF)
SOME TEA FOR YOU.

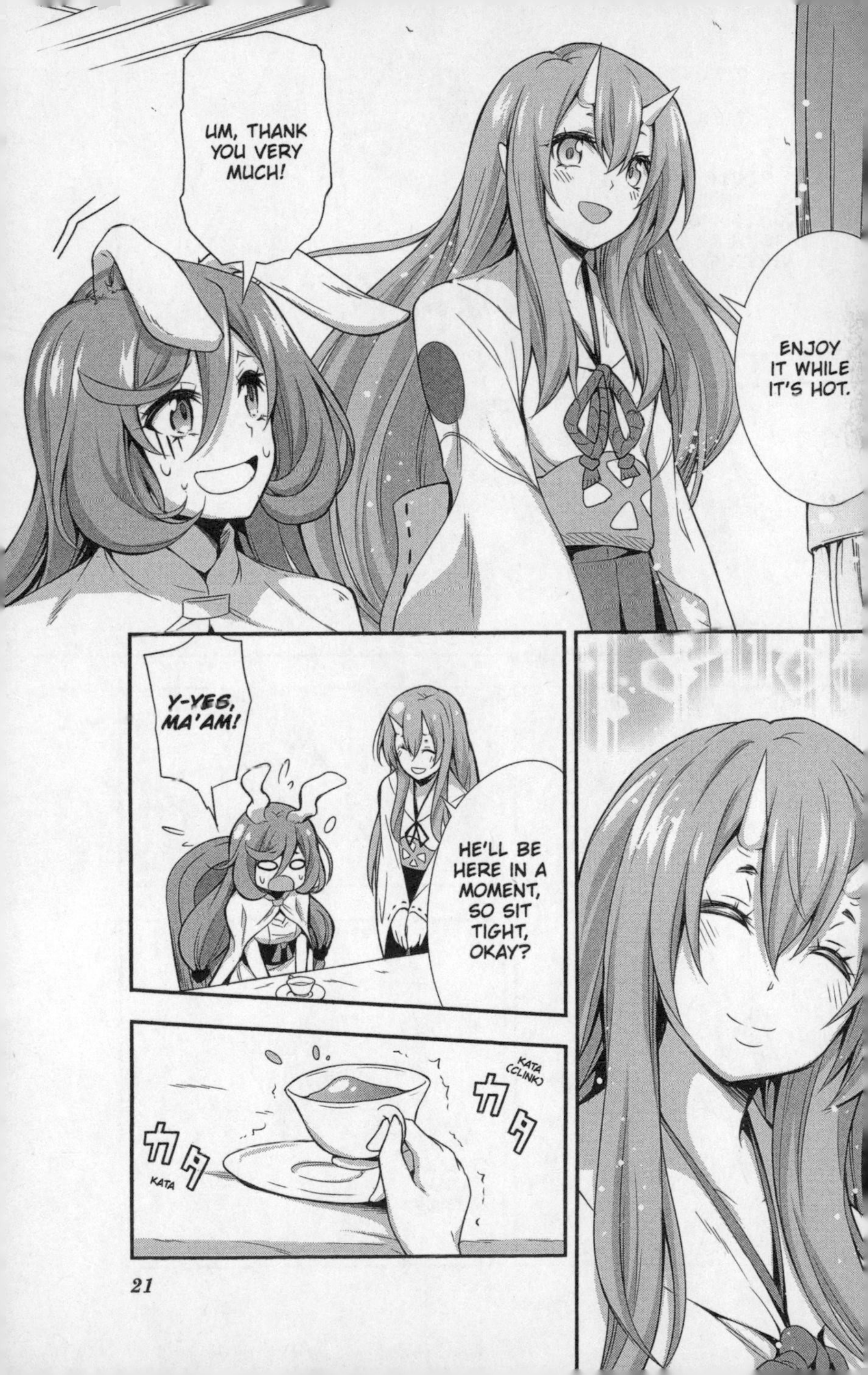
ENJOY IT WHILE IT'S HOT.
UM, THANK YOU VERY MUCH!
HE'LL BE HERE IN A MOMENT, SO SIT TIGHT, OKAY?
Y-YES, MA'AM!
カタ
KATA (CLINK)
カタ
KATA

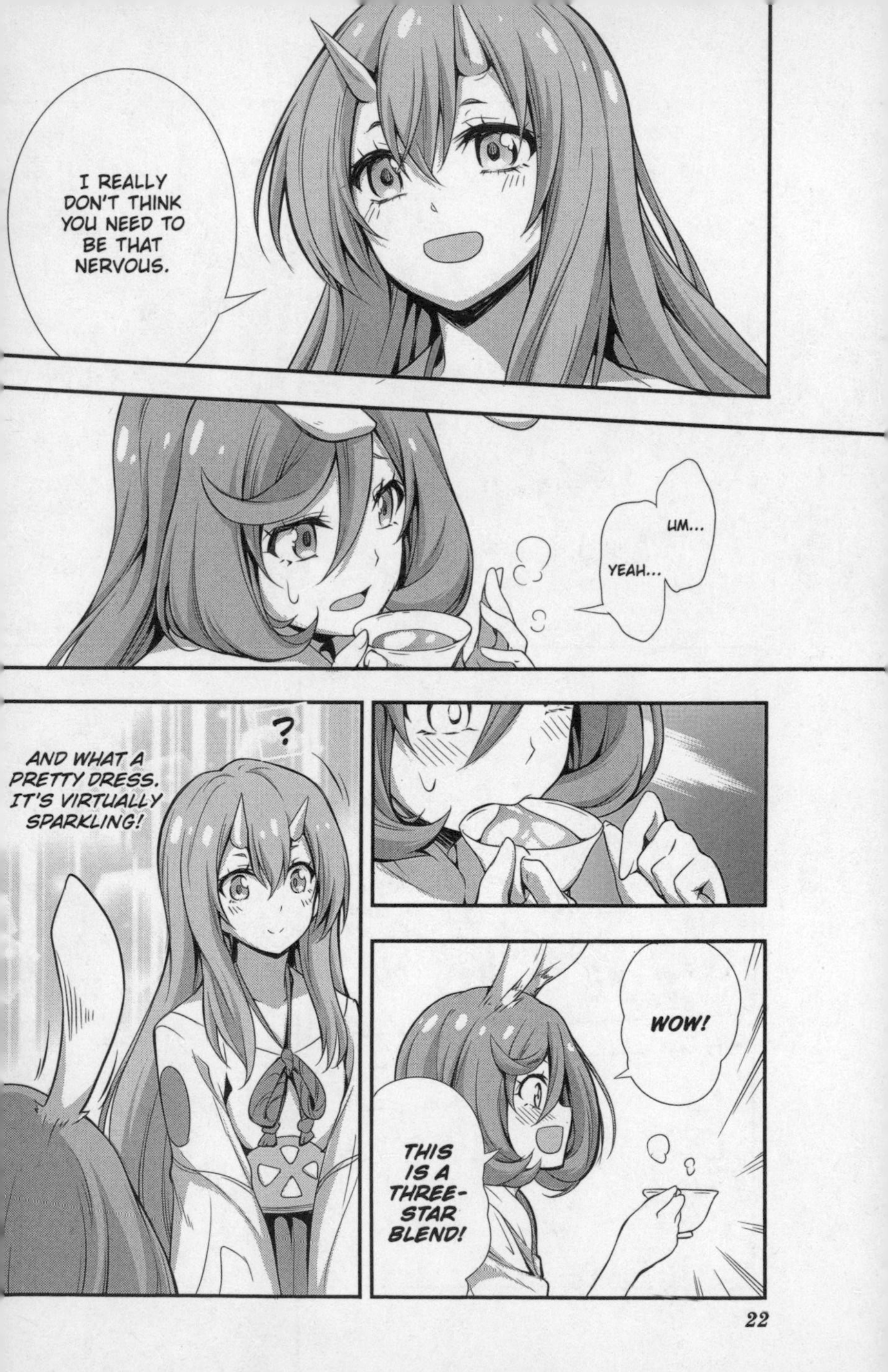
I REALLY DON'T THINK YOU NEED TO BE THAT NERVOUS.
UM...
YEAH...
WOW!
THIS IS A THREE-STAR BLEND!
?
AND WHAT A PRETTY DRESS. IT'S VIRTUALLY SPARKLING!

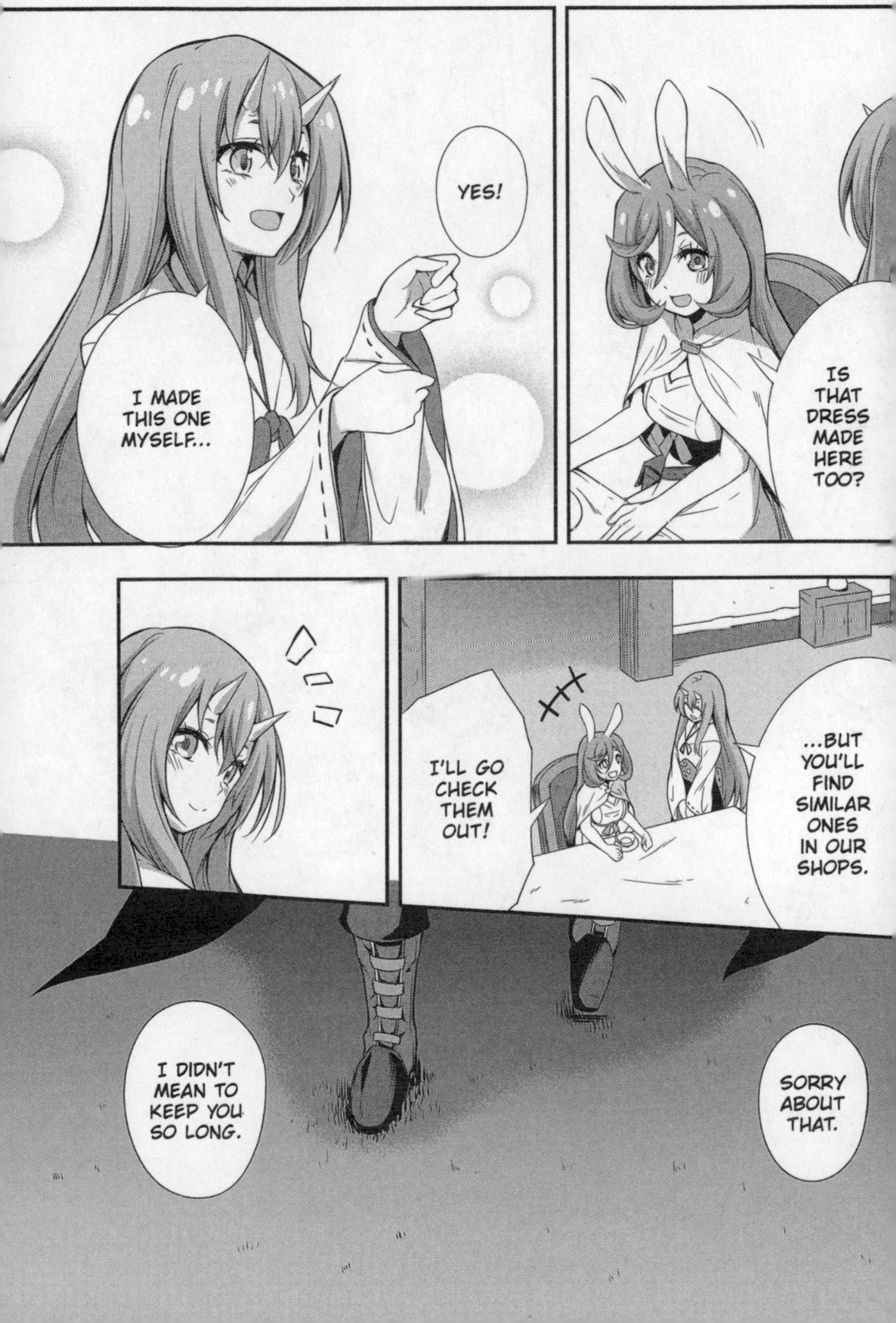
IS THAT DRESS MADE HERE TOO?
YES!
I MADE THIS ONE MYSELF...
...BUT YOU'LL FIND SIMILAR ONES IN OUR SHOPS.
I'LL GO CHECK THEM OUT!
SORRY ABOUT THAT.
I DIDN'T MEAN TO KEEP YOU SO LONG.

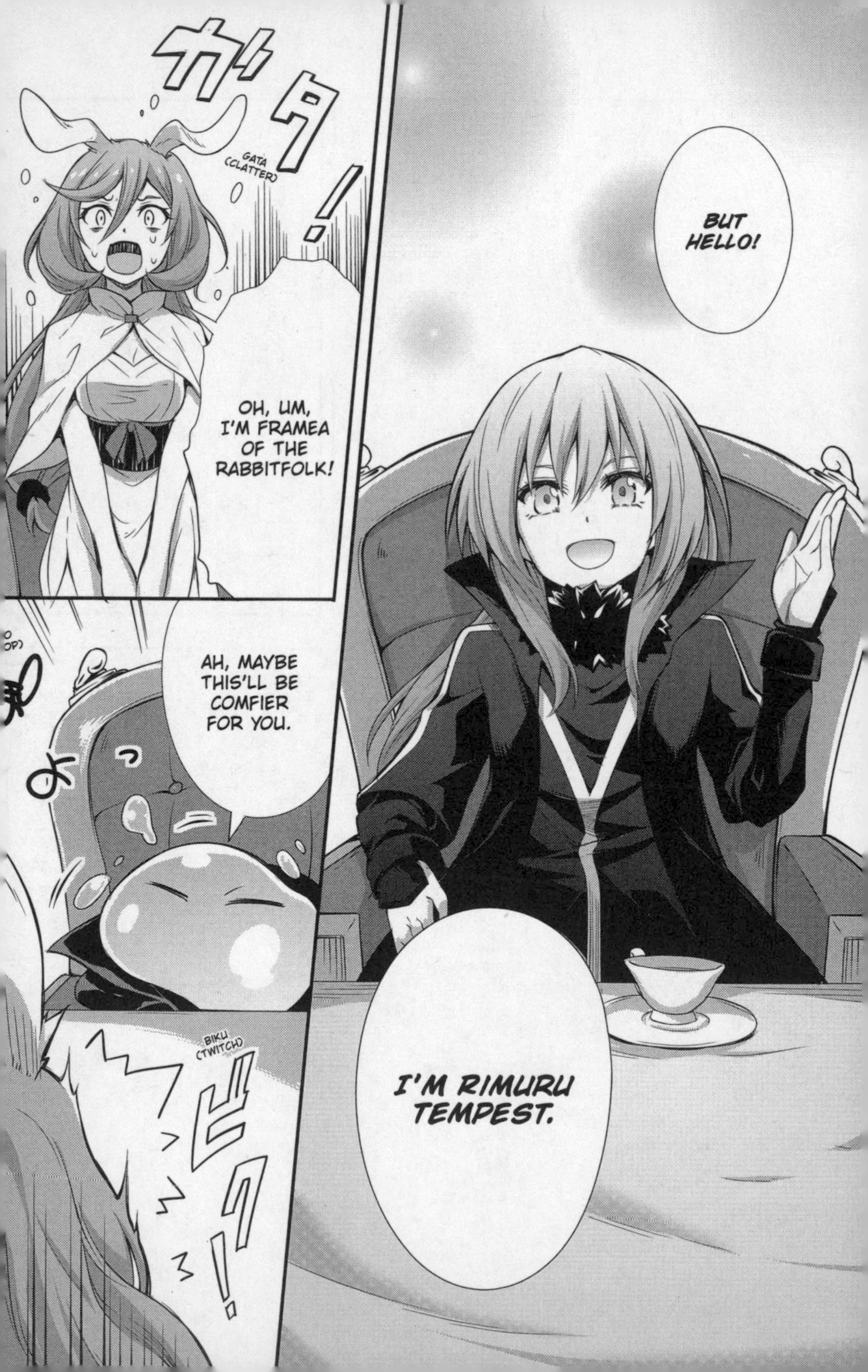
BUT HELLO!
I'M RIMURU TEMPEST.
GATA (CLATTER)
OH, UM, I'M FRAMEA OF THE RABBITFOLK!
AH, MAYBE THIS'LL BE COMFIER FOR YOU.
BIKU (TWITCH)

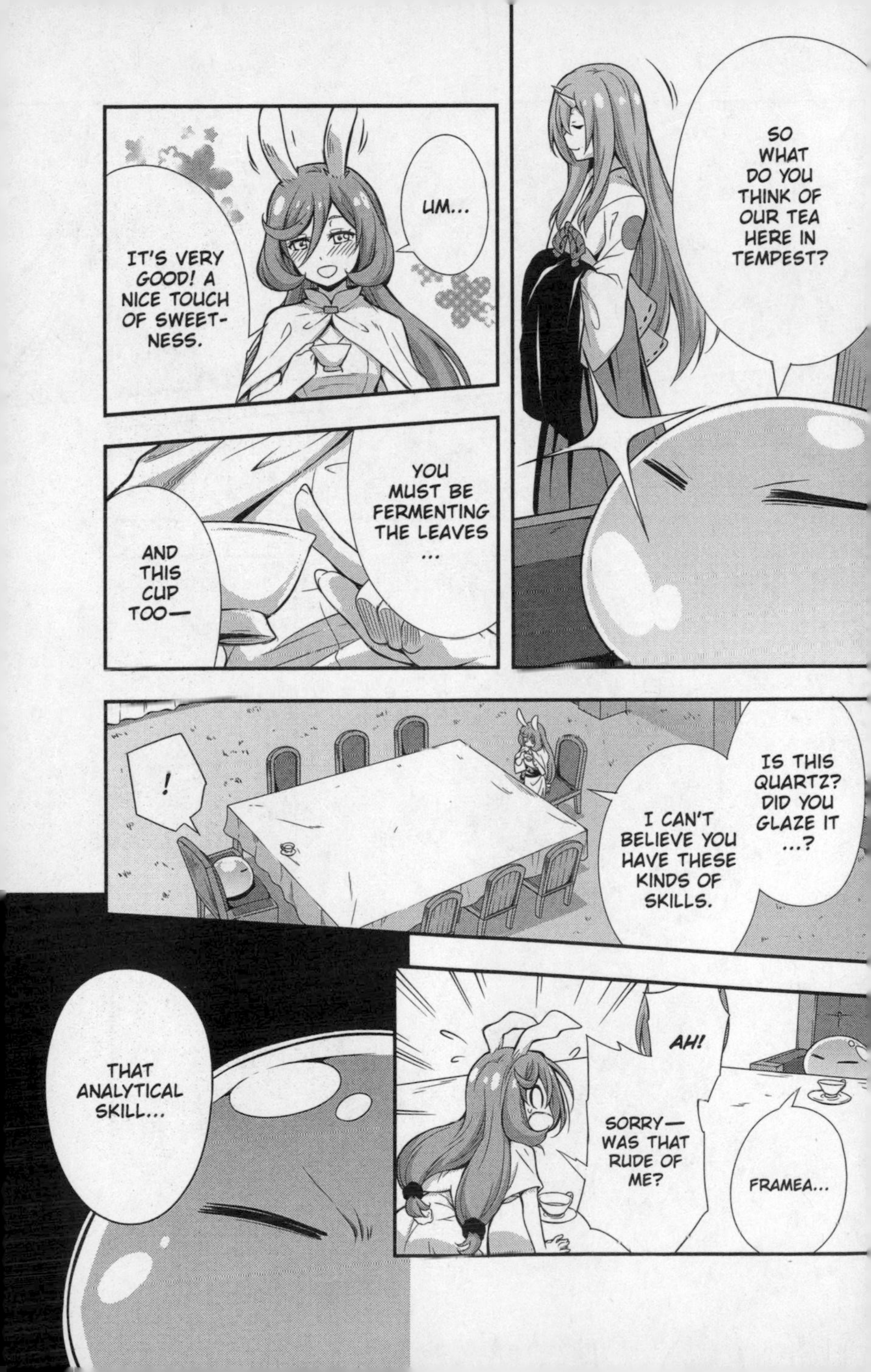
SO WHAT DO YOU THINK OF OUR TEA HERE IN TEMPEST?
UM...
IT'S VERY GOOD! A NICE TOUCH OF SWEET-NESS.
YOU MUST BE FERMENTING THE LEAVES...
AND THIS CUP TOO—
IS THIS QUARTZ? DID YOU GLAZE IT...?
I CAN'T BELIEVE YOU HAVE THESE KINDS OF SKILLS.
!
AH!
FRAMEA...
SORRY—WAS THAT RUDE OF ME?
THAT ANALYTICAL SKILL...

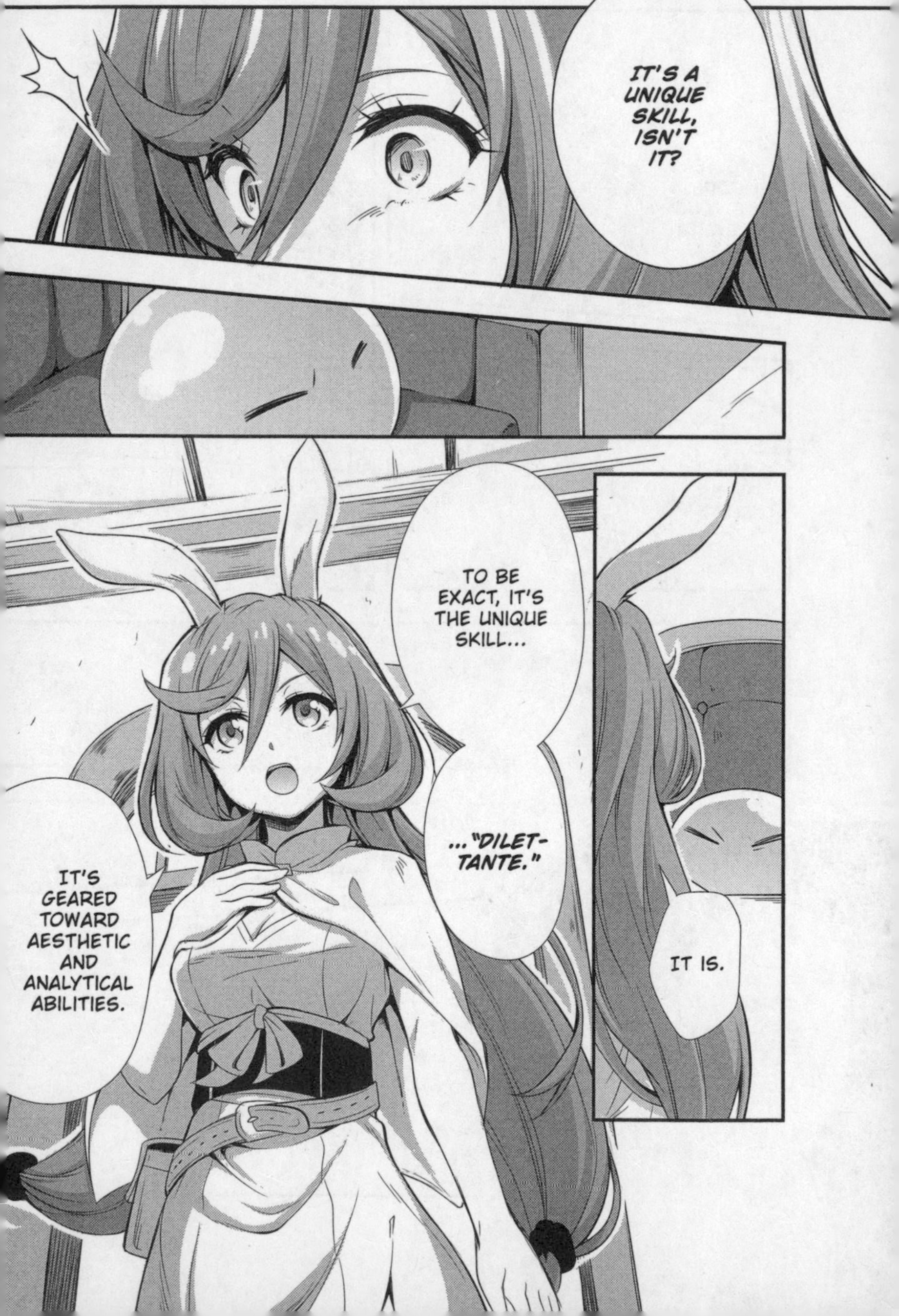
IT'S A UNIQUE SKILL, ISN'T IT?
IT IS.
TO BE EXACT, IT'S THE UNIQUE SKILL...
..."DILETTANTE."
IT'S GEARED TOWARD AESTHETIC AND ANALYTICAL ABILITIES.

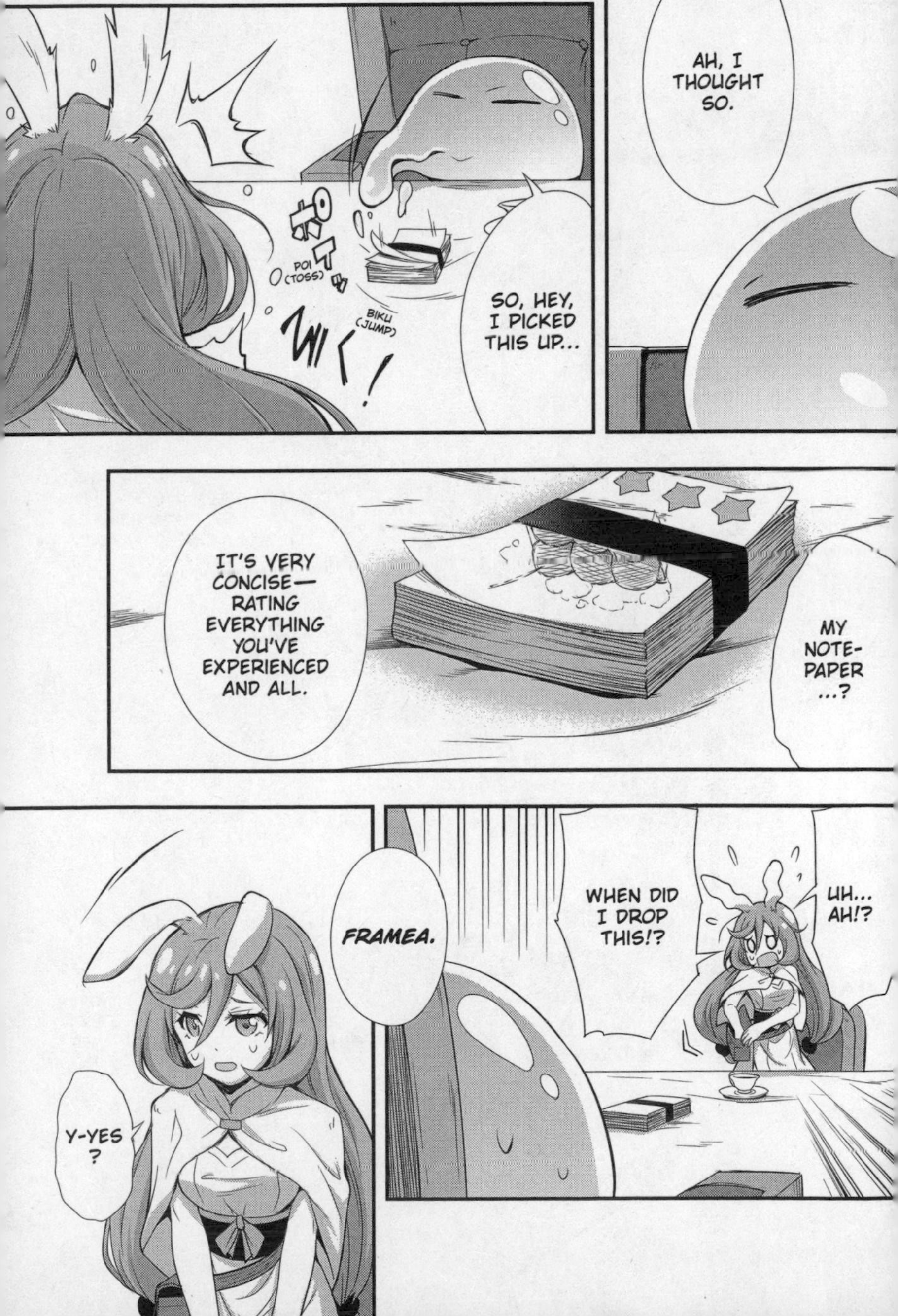
AH, I THOUGHT SO.
SO, HEY, I PICKED THIS UP...
POI (TOSS)
BIKU (JUMP)
MY NOTE-PAPER ...?
IT'S VERY CONCISE—RATING EVERYTHING YOU'VE EXPERIENCED AND ALL.
UH... AH!?
WHEN DID I DROP THIS!?
FRAMEA.
Y-YES ?

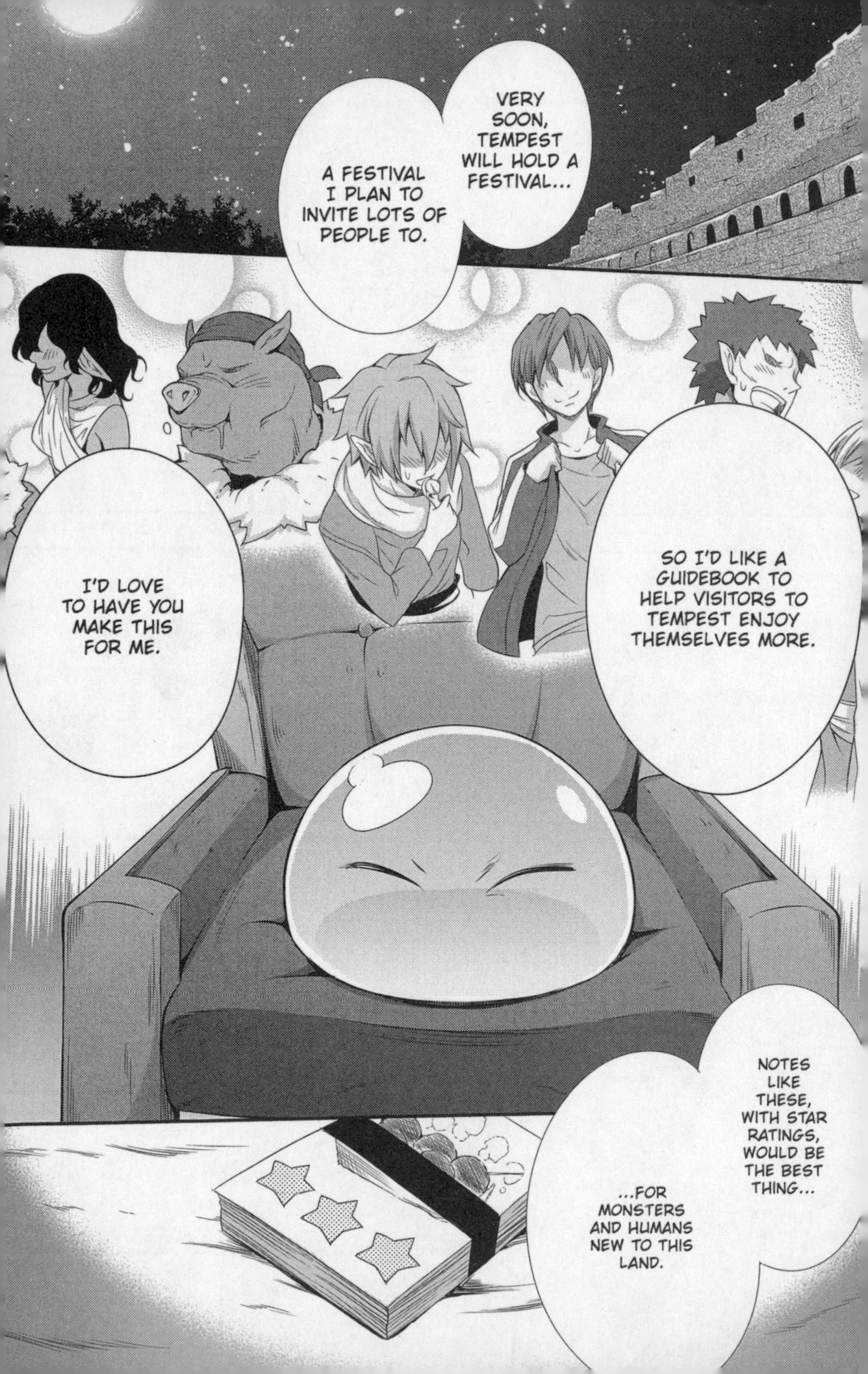
VERY SOON, TEMPEST WILL HOLD A FESTIVAL...
A FESTIVAL I PLAN TO INVITE LOTS OF PEOPLE TO.
SO I'D LIKE A GUIDEBOOK TO HELP VISITORS TO TEMPEST ENJOY THEMSELVES MORE.
I'D LOVE TO HAVE YOU MAKE THIS FOR ME.
NOTES LIKE THESE, WITH STAR RATINGS, WOULD BE THE BEST THING...
...FOR MONSTERS AND HUMANS NEW TO THIS LAND.

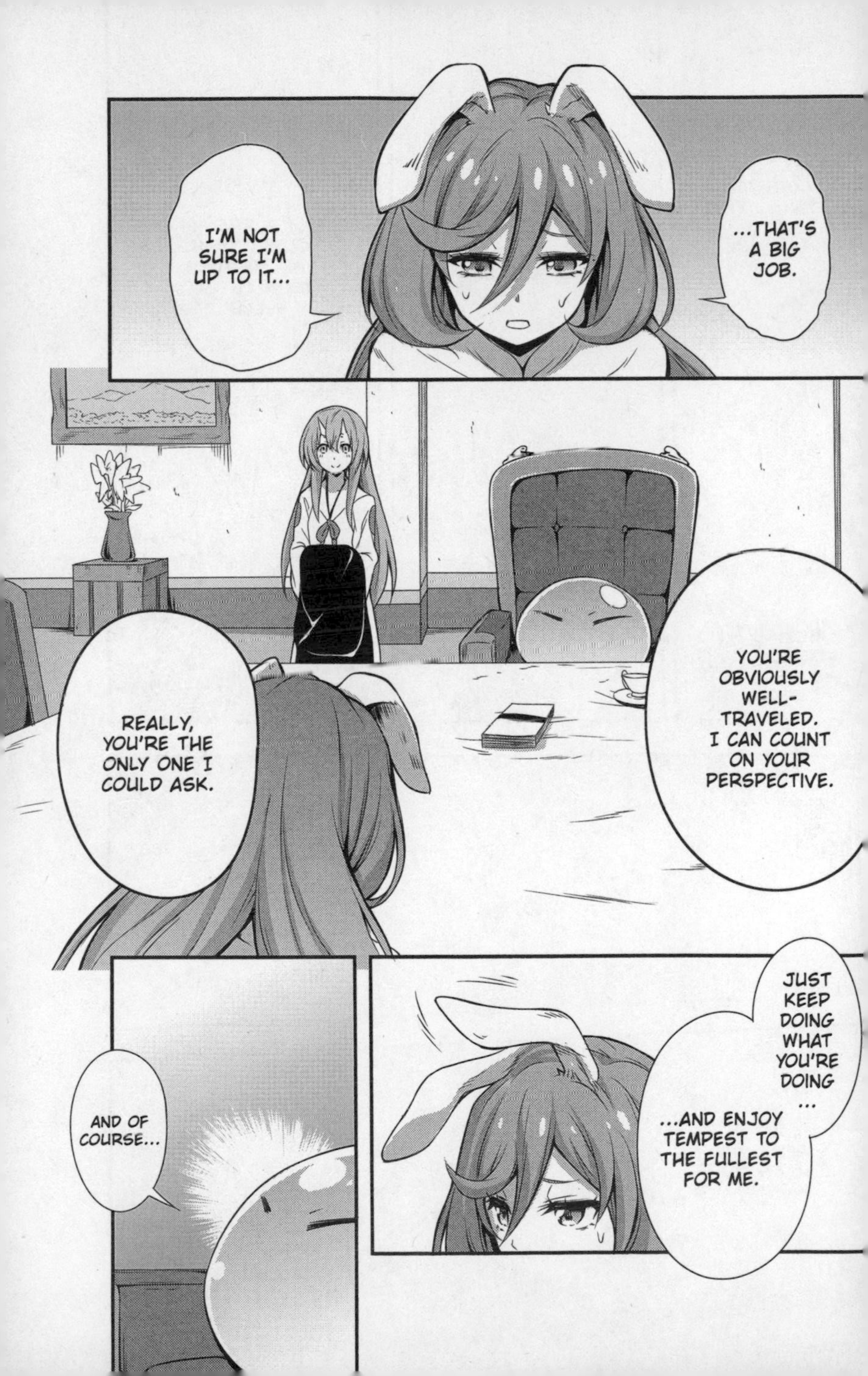
...THAT'S A BIG JOB.
I'M NOT SURE I'M UP TO IT...
YOU'RE OBVIOUSLY WELL-TRAVELED. I CAN COUNT ON YOUR PERSPECTIVE.
REALLY, YOU'RE THE ONLY ONE I COULD ASK.
JUST KEEP DOING WHAT YOU'RE DOING...
...AND ENJOY TEMPEST TO THE FULLEST FOR ME.
AND OF COURSE...

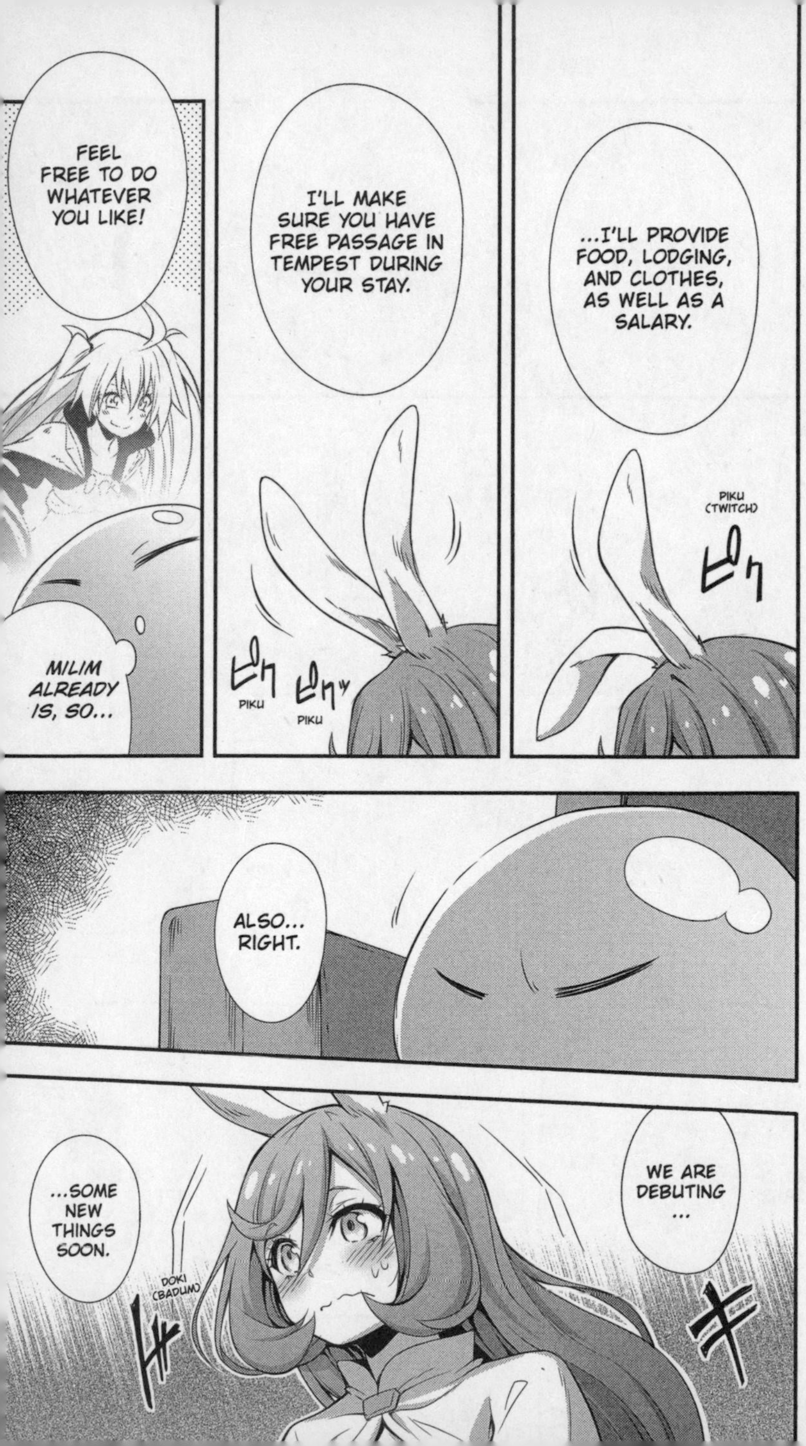
...I'LL PROVIDE FOOD, LODGING, AND CLOTHES, AS WELL AS A SALARY.
PIKU (TWITCH)
I'LL MAKE SURE YOU HAVE FREE PASSAGE IN TEMPEST DURING YOUR STAY.
PIKU
PIKU
FEEL FREE TO DO WHATEVER YOU LIKE!
MILIM ALREADY IS, SO...
ALSO... RIGHT.
WE ARE DEBUTING ...
...SOME NEW THINGS SOON.
DOKI (BADUM)

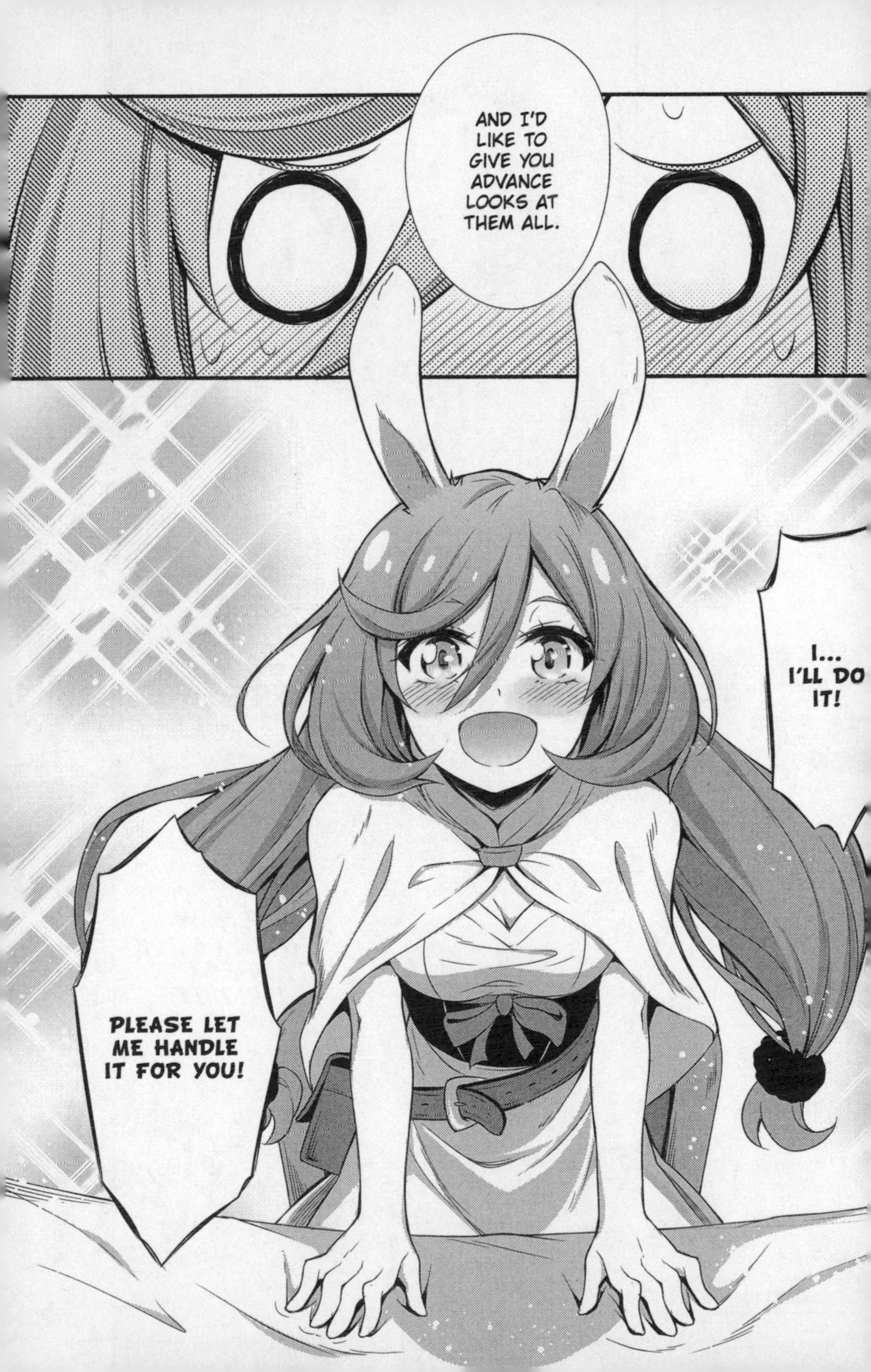
AND I'D LIKE TO GIVE YOU ADVANCE LOOKS AT THEM ALL.
I... I'LL DO IT!
PLEASE LET ME HANDLE IT FOR YOU!

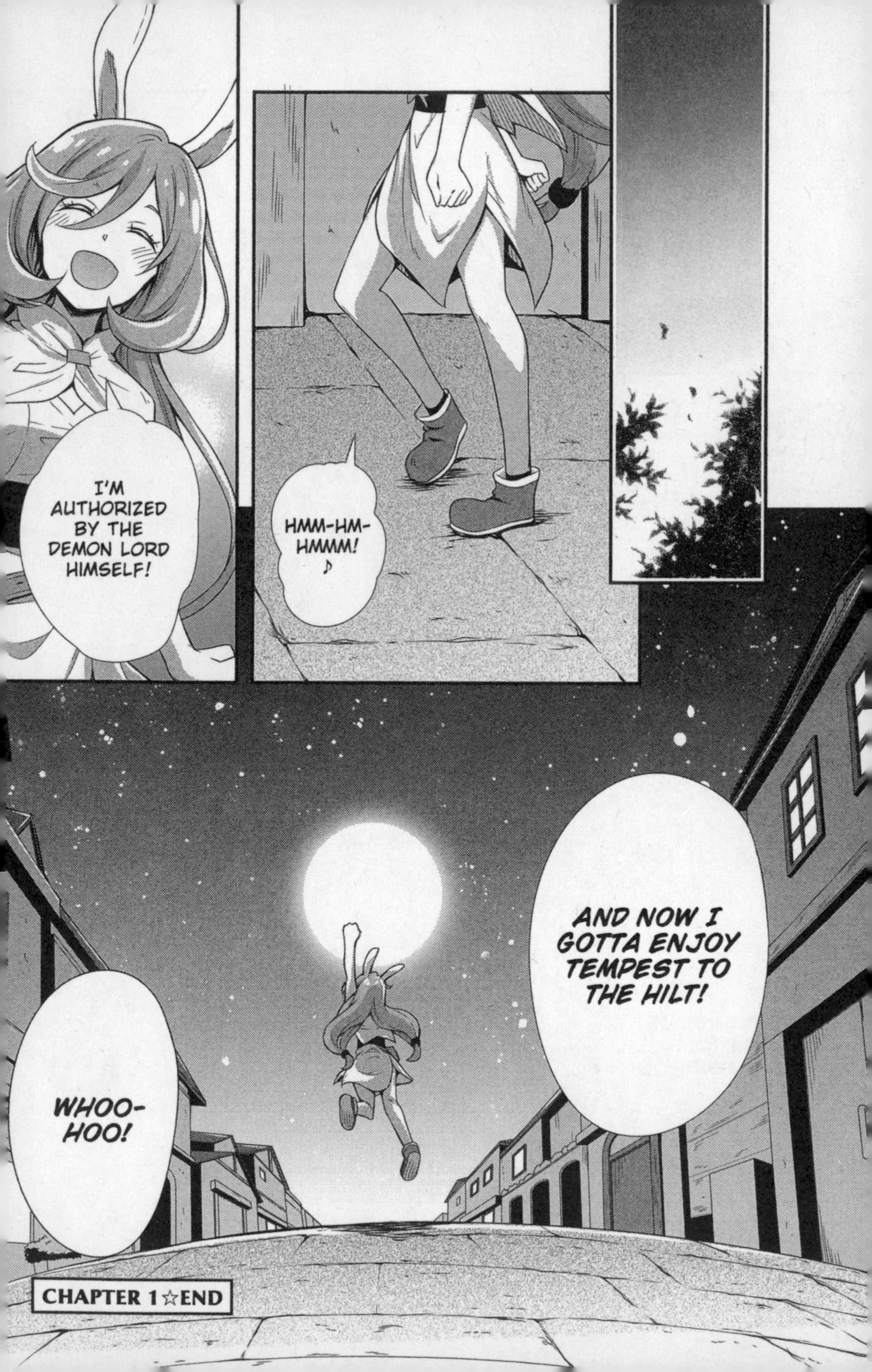
HMM-HM-HMMM! ♪
I'M AUTHORIZED BY THE DEMON LORD HIMSELF!
AND NOW I GOTTA ENJOY TEMPEST TO THE HILT!
WHOO-HOO!
CHAPTER 1☆END

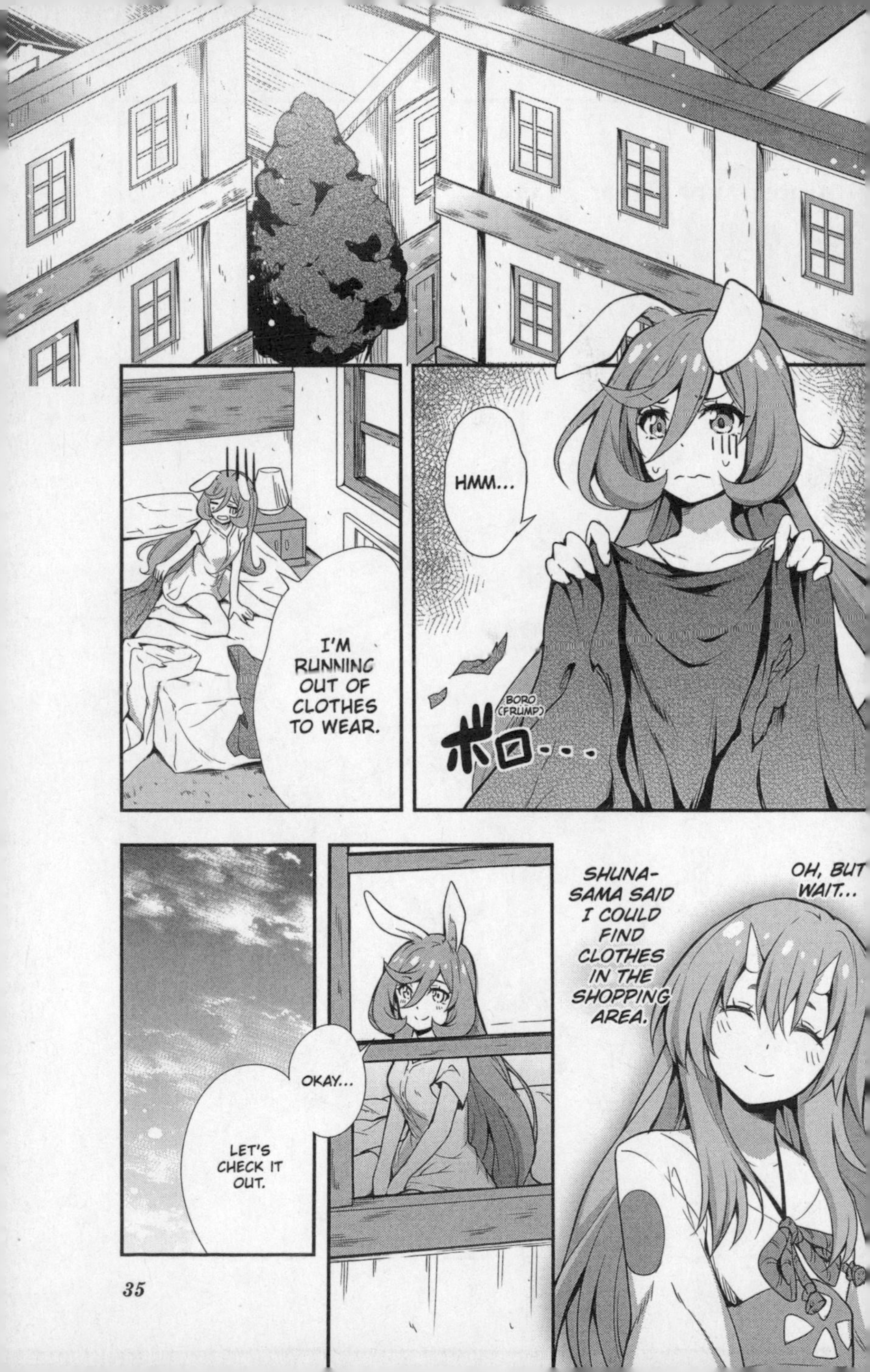
HMM...
BORO (FRUMP)
ボロ...
I'M RUNNING OUT OF CLOTHES TO WEAR.
OH, BUT WAIT...
SHUNA-SAMA SAID I COULD FIND CLOTHES IN THE SHOPPING AREA.
OKAY...
LET'S CHECK IT OUT.

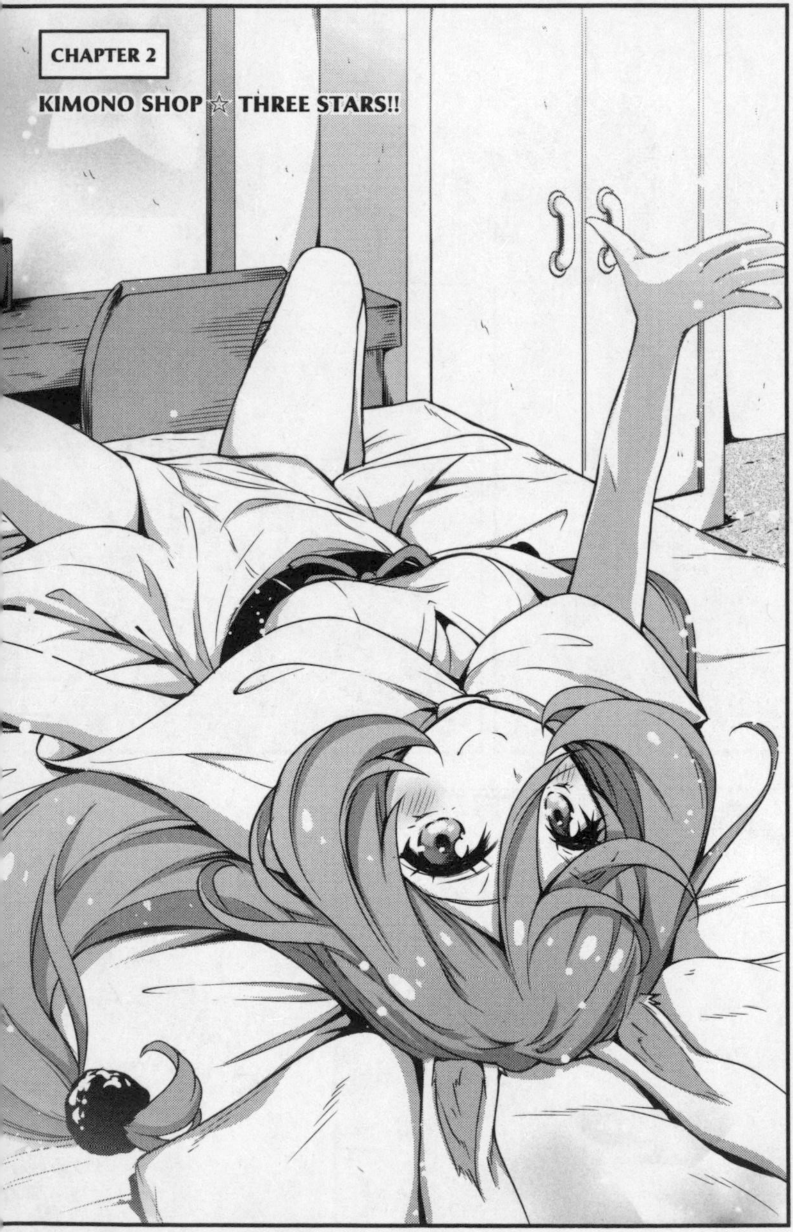
CHAPTER 2
KIMONO SHOP ☆ THREE STARS!!

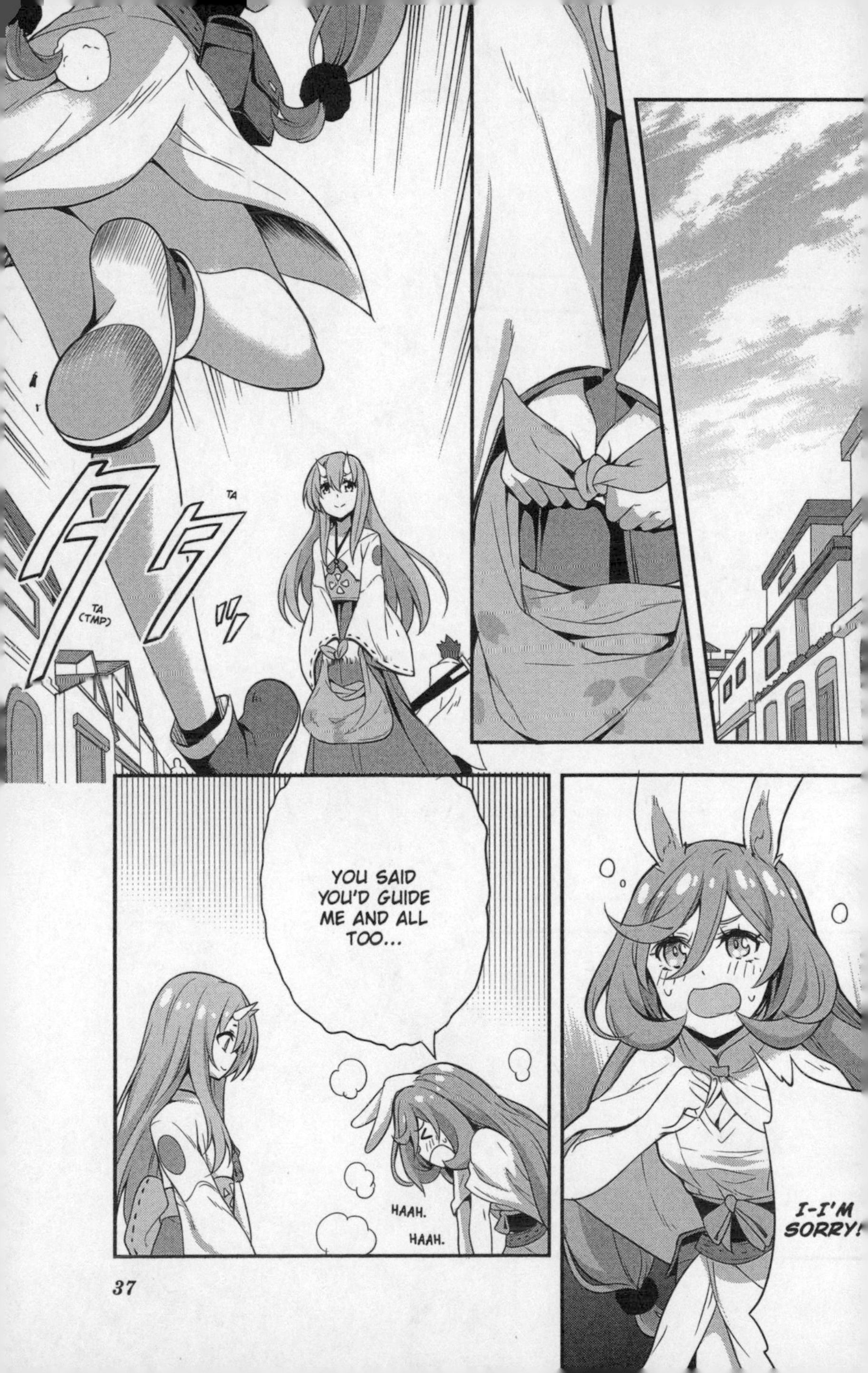
TA
TA (TMP)
I-I'M SORRY!
YOU SAID YOU'D GUIDE ME AND ALL TOO...
HAAH.
HAAH.

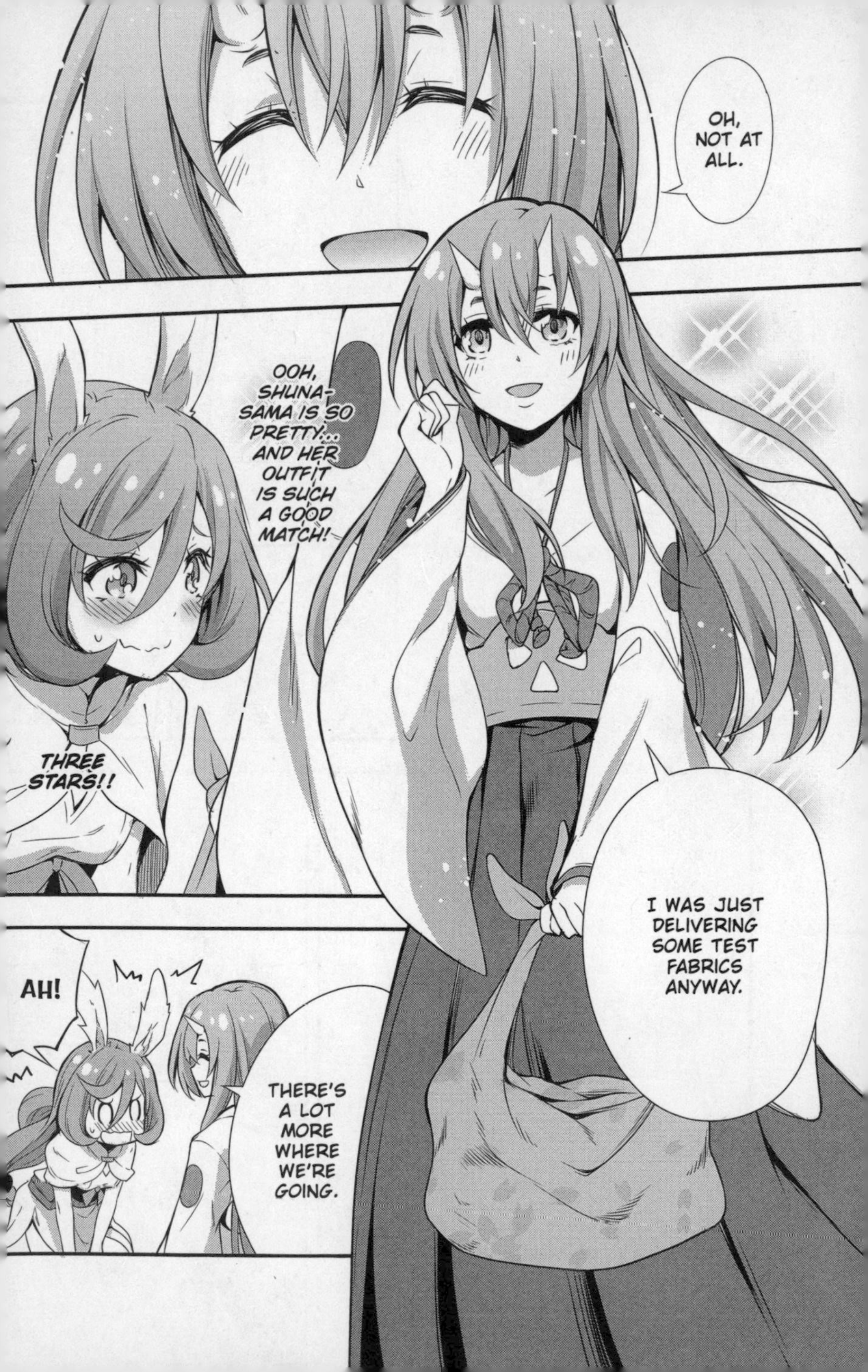
OH, NOT AT ALL.
I WAS JUST DELIVERING SOME TEST FABRICS ANYWAY.
OOH, SHUNA-SAMA IS SO PRETTY... AND HER OUTFIT IS SUCH A GOOD MATCH!
THREE STARS!!
THERE'S A LOT MORE WHERE WE'RE GOING.
AH!

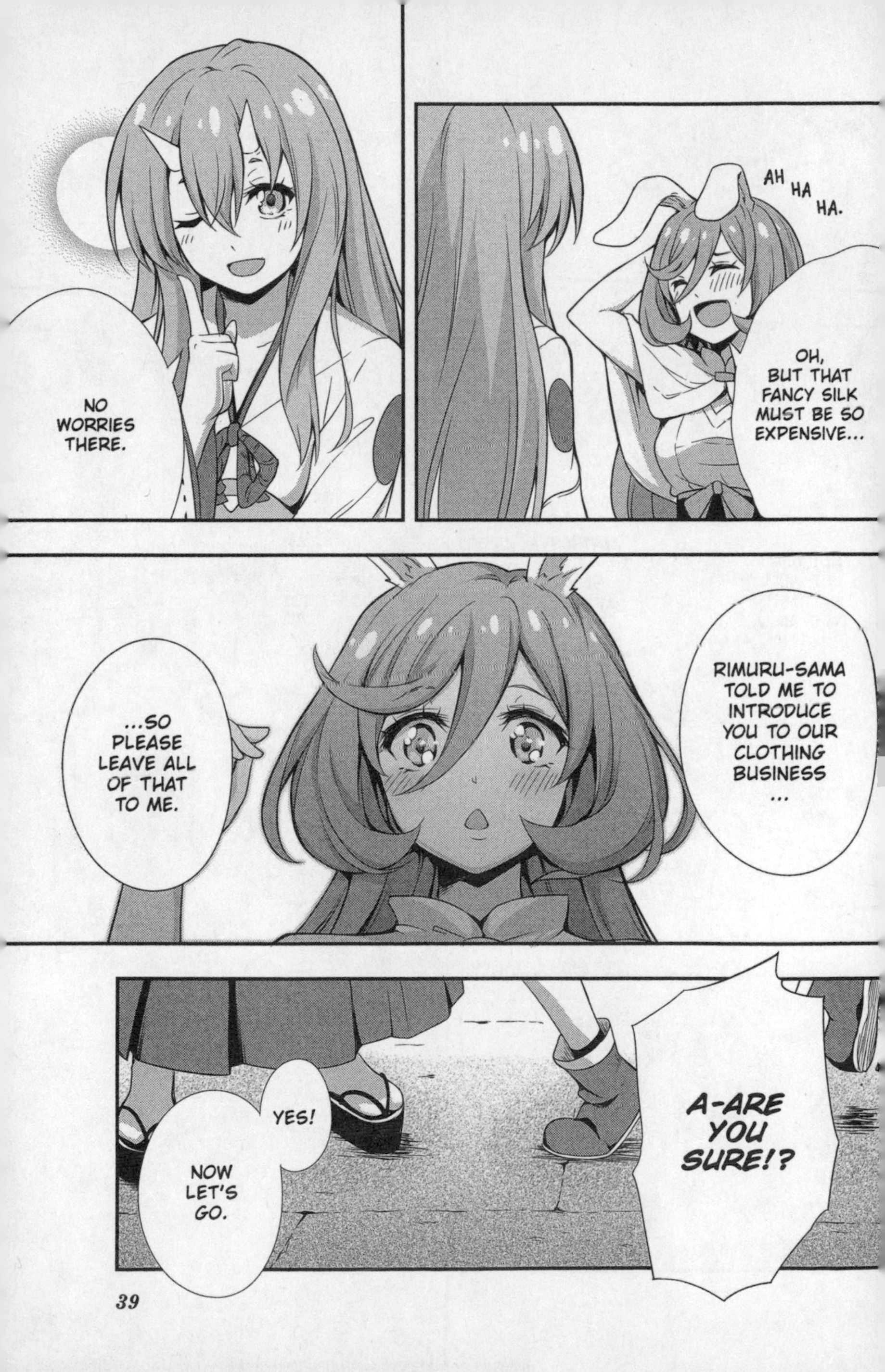
AH HA HA.
OH, BUT THAT FANCY SILK MUST BE SO EXPENSIVE...
NO WORRIES THERE.
RIMURU-SAMA TOLD ME TO INTRODUCE YOU TO OUR CLOTHING BUSINESS ...
...SO PLEASE LEAVE ALL OF THAT TO ME.
A-ARE YOU SURE!?
YES!
NOW LET'S GO.

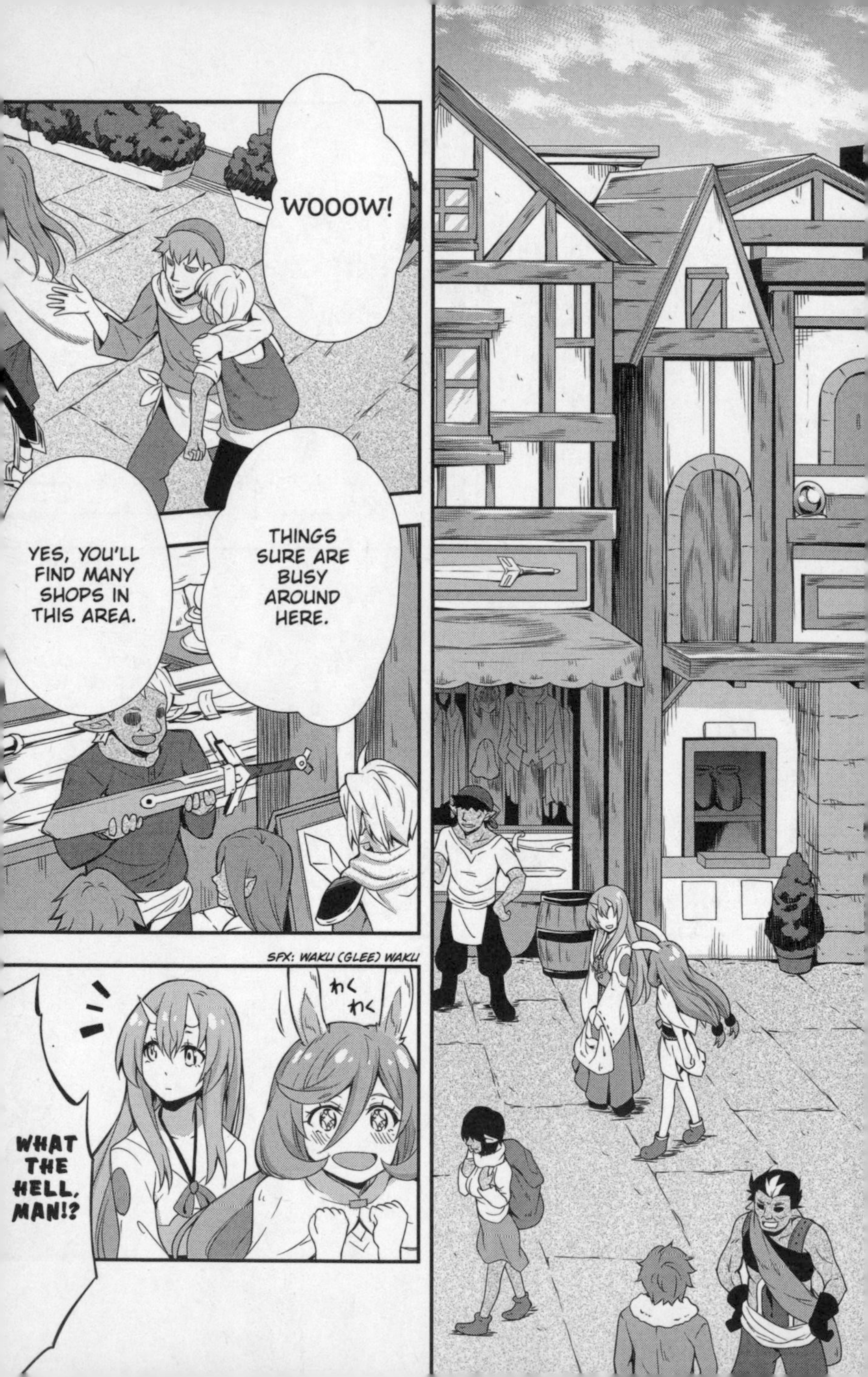
WOOOW!
THINGS SURE ARE BUSY AROUND HERE.
YES, YOU'LL FIND MANY SHOPS IN THIS AREA.
SFX: WAKU (GLEE) WAKU
わく わく
WHAT THE HELL, MAN!?

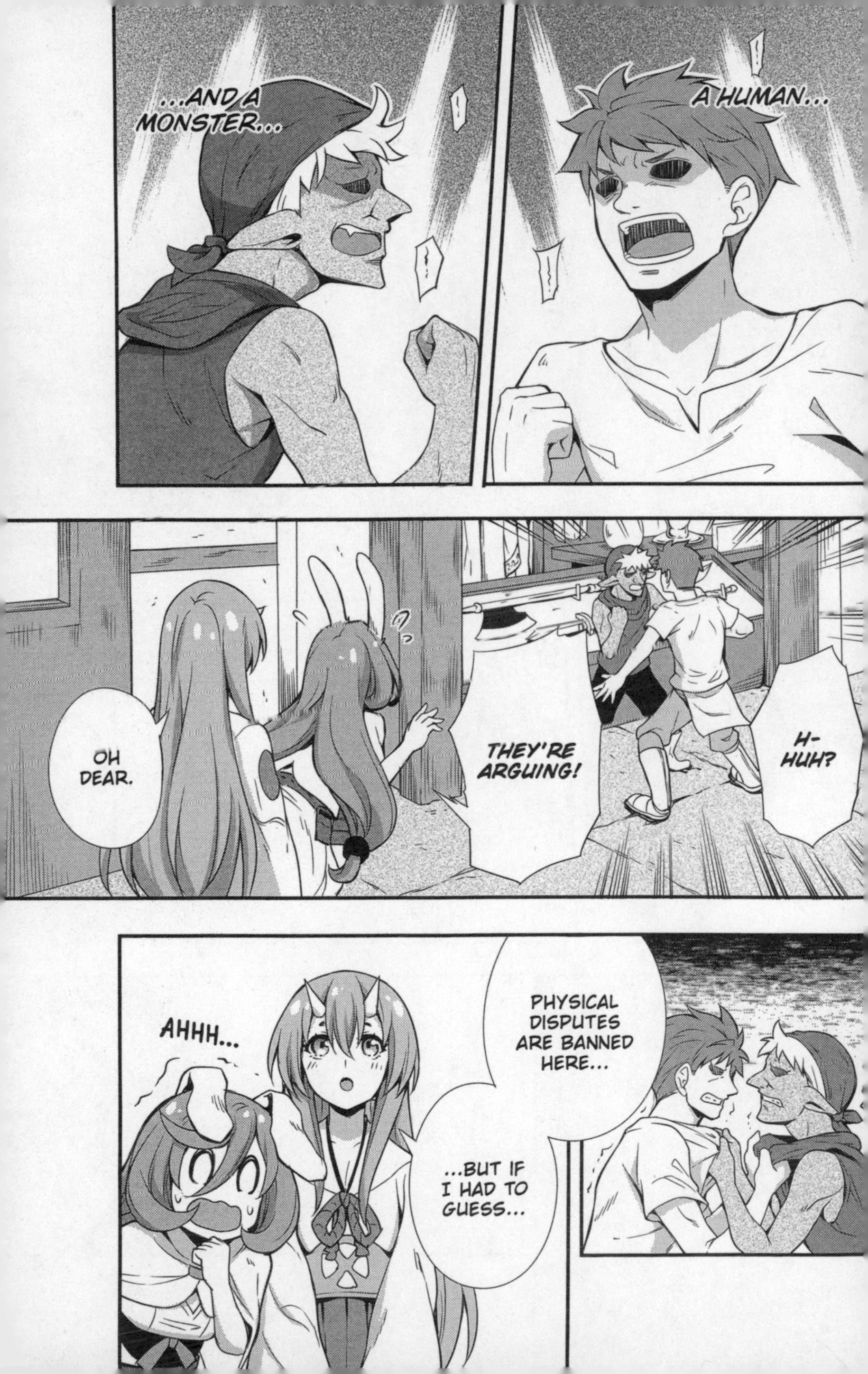
A HUMAN...
...AND A MONSTER...
H-HUH?
THEY'RE ARGUING!
OH DEAR.
PHYSICAL DISPUTES ARE BANNED HERE...
AHHH...
...BUT IF I HAD TO GUESS...

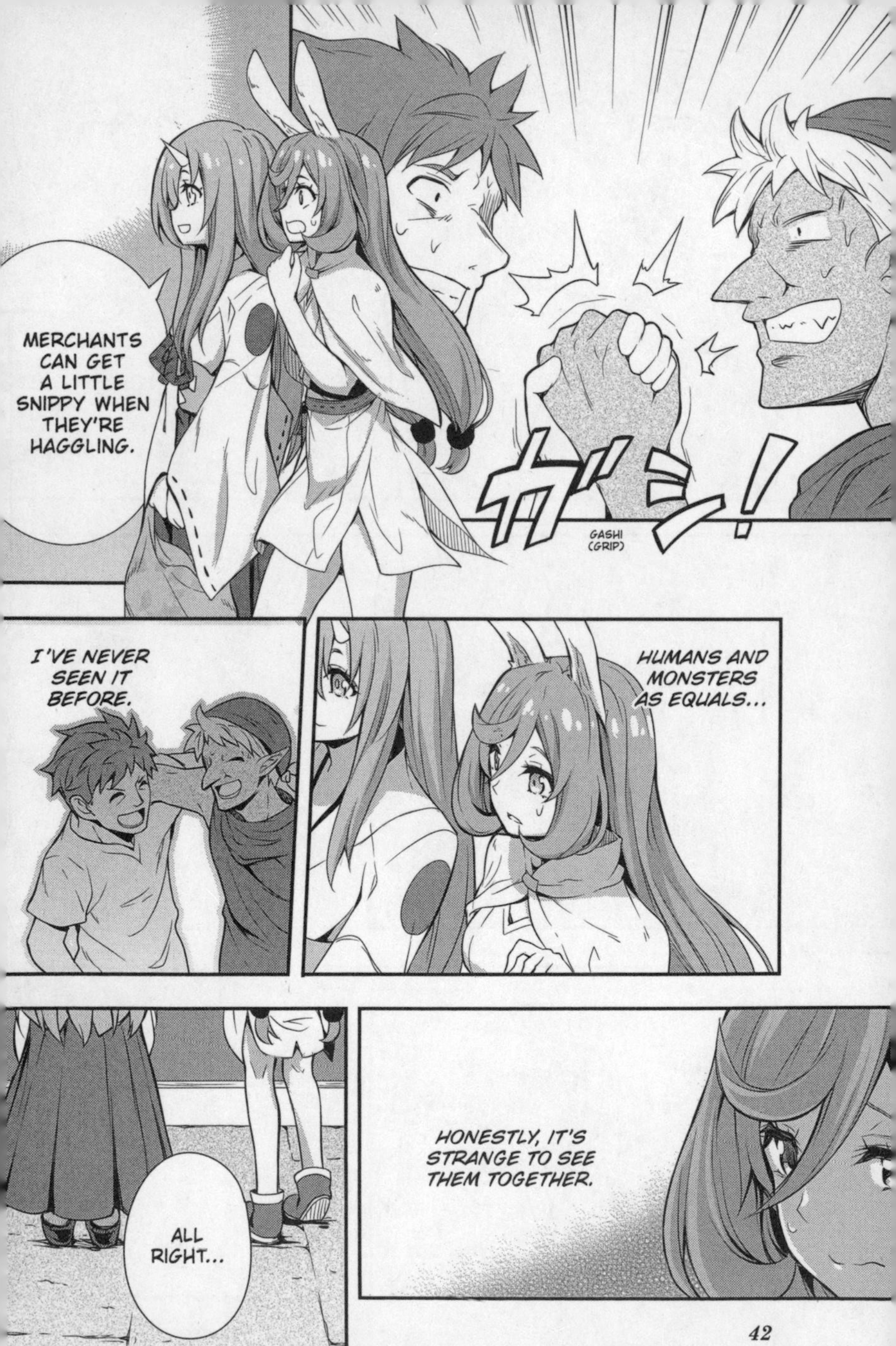
ガシッ!
GASHI (GRIP)
MERCHANTS CAN GET A LITTLE SNIPPY WHEN THEY'RE HAGGLING.
HUMANS AND MONSTERS AS EQUALS...
I'VE NEVER SEEN IT BEFORE.
HONESTLY, IT'S STRANGE TO SEE THEM TOGETHER.
ALL RIGHT...

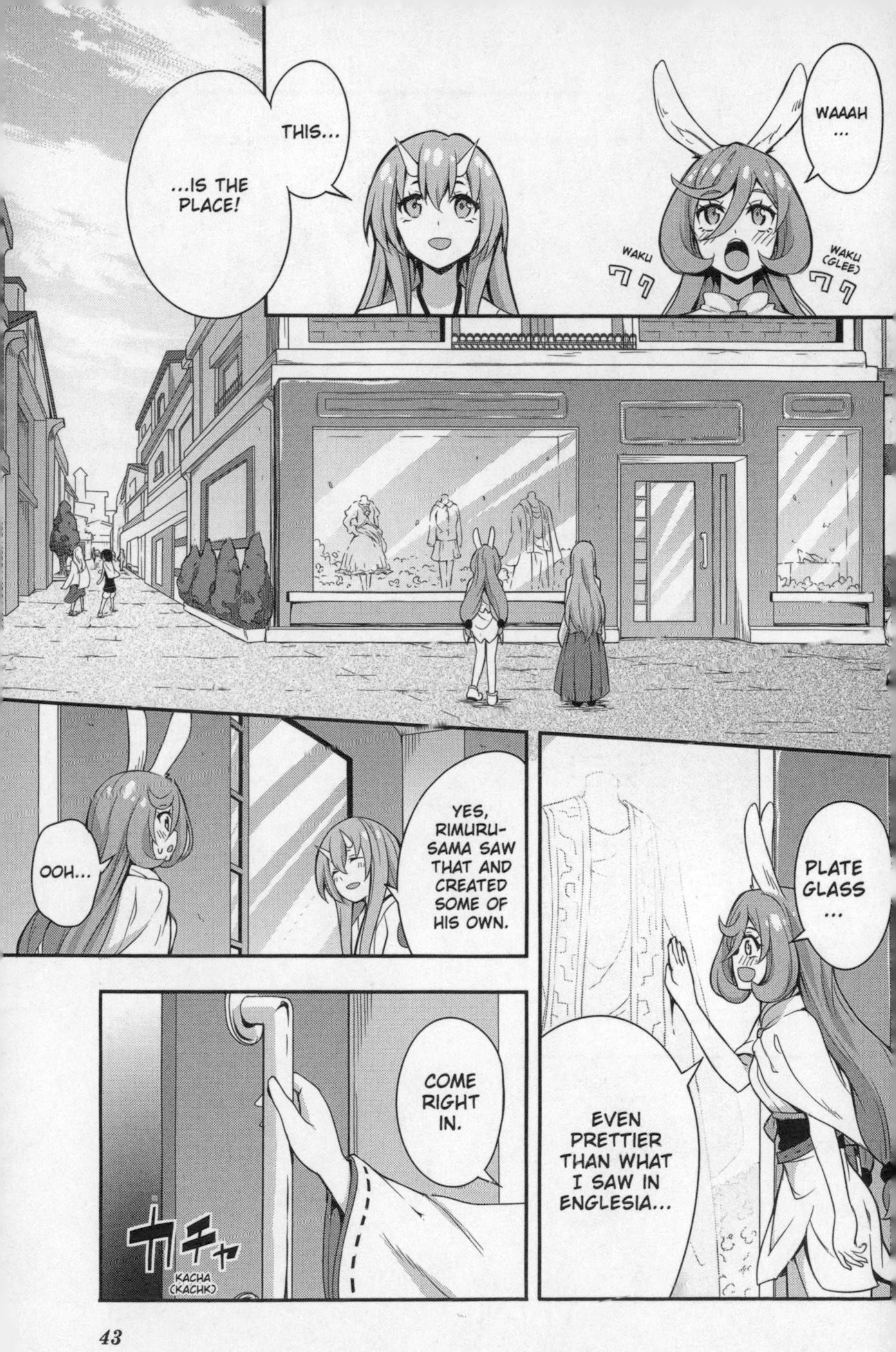
WAAAH...
WAKU WAKU (GLEE)
ワク ワク
THIS...
...IS THE PLACE!
PLATE GLASS...
EVEN PRETTIER THAN WHAT I SAW IN ENGLESIA...
YES, RIMURU-SAMA SAW THAT AND CREATED SOME OF HIS OWN.
OOH...
COME RIGHT IN.
カチャ
KACHA (KACHK)

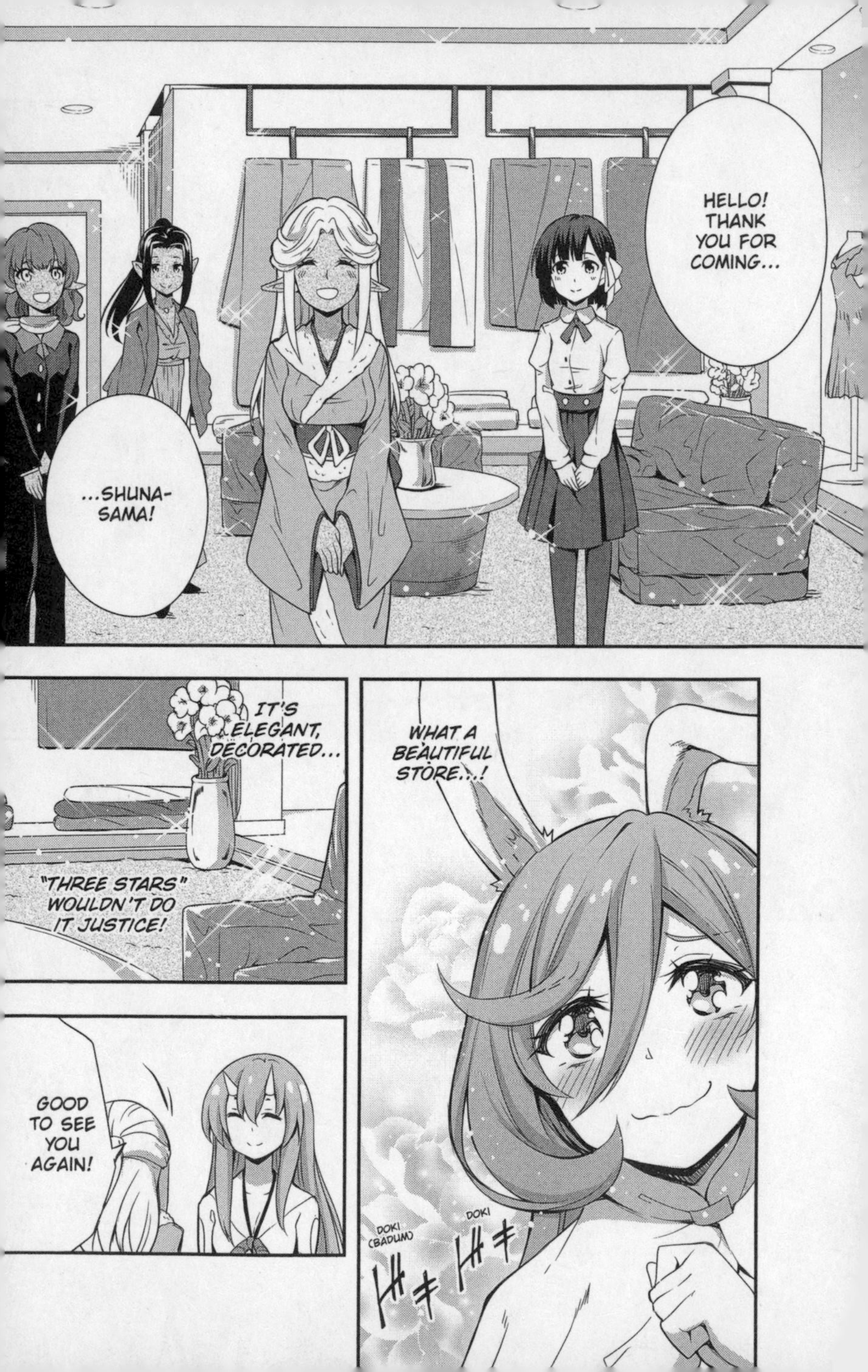
HELLO! THANK YOU FOR COMING...
...SHUNA-SAMA!
WHAT A BEAUTIFUL STORE...!
DOKI
DOKI (BADUM)
IT'S ELEGANT, DECORATED...
"THREE STARS" WOULDN'T DO IT JUSTICE!
GOOD TO SEE YOU AGAIN!

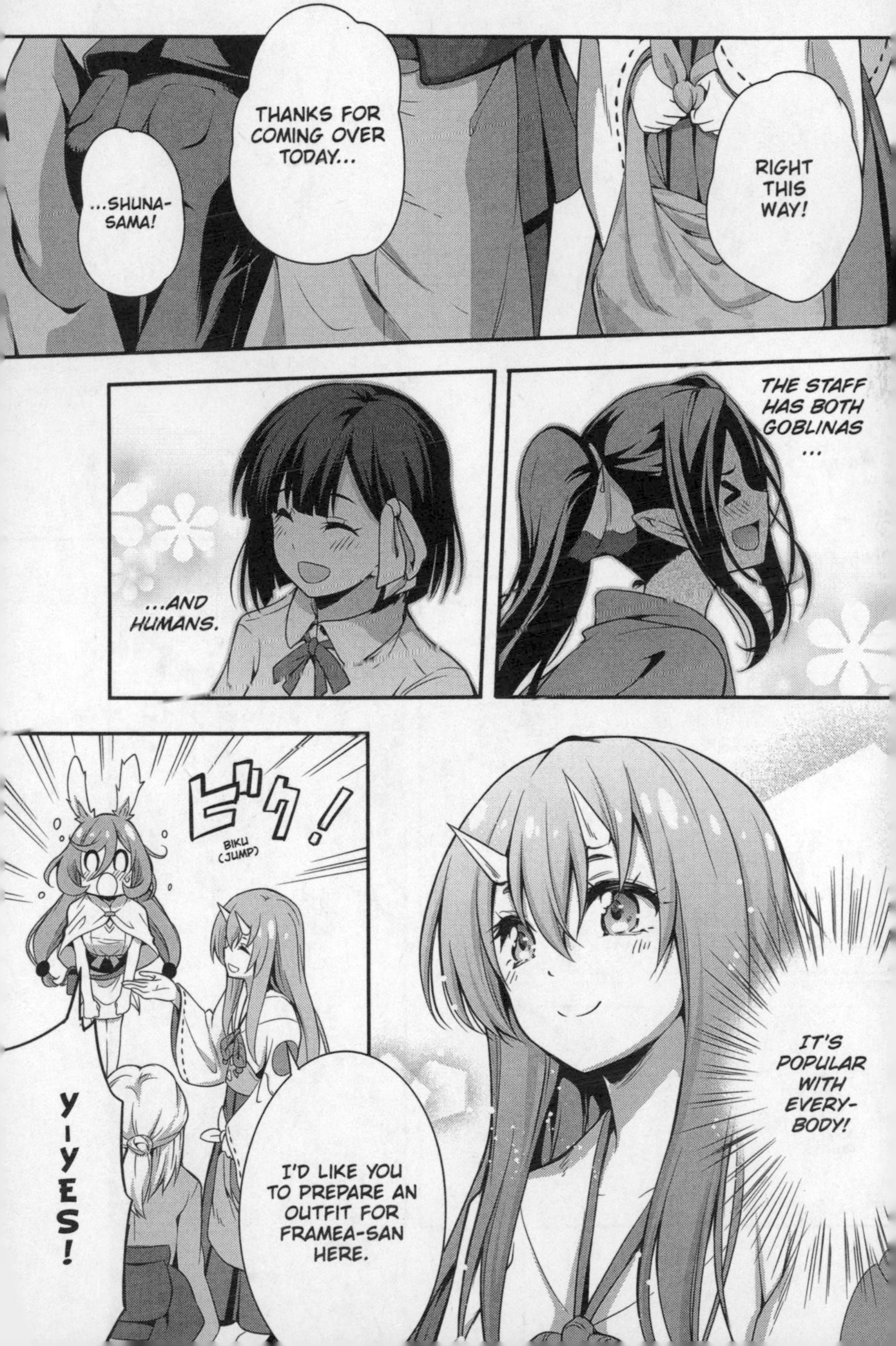
RIGHT THIS WAY!
THANKS FOR COMING OVER TODAY...
...SHUNA-SAMA!
THE STAFF HAS BOTH GOBLINAS ...
...AND HUMANS.
IT'S POPULAR WITH EVERY-BODY!
I'D LIKE YOU TO PREPARE AN OUTFIT FOR FRAMEA-SAN HERE.
ビク!
BIKU (JUMP)
Y-YES!

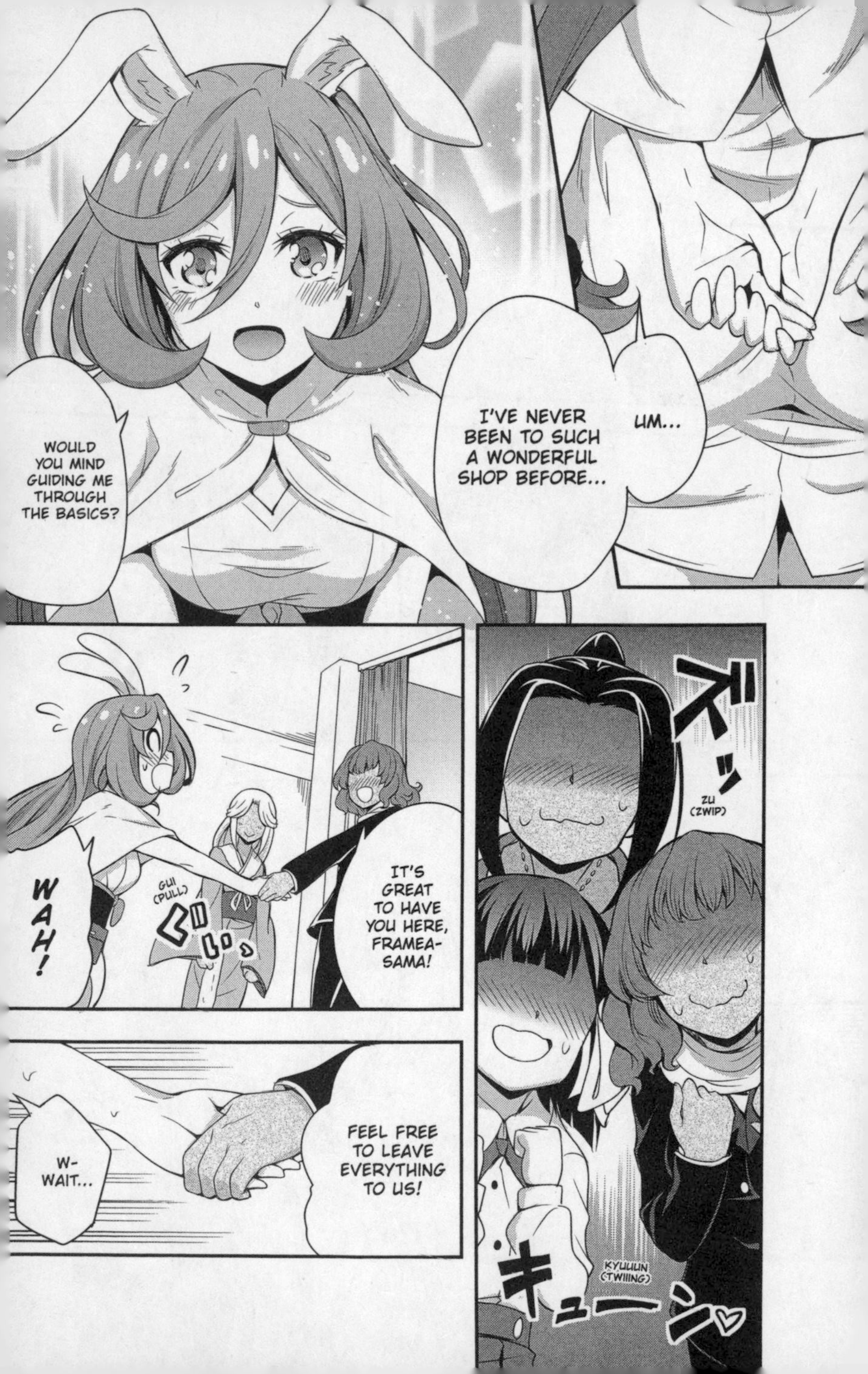
UM...
I'VE NEVER BEEN TO SUCH A WONDERFUL SHOP BEFORE...
WOULD YOU MIND GUIDING ME THROUGH THE BASICS?
ズッ
ZU (ZWIP)
キューン♡
KYUUUN (TWIIING)
IT'S GREAT TO HAVE YOU HERE, FRAMEA-SAMA!
GUI (PULL)
WAH!
FEEL FREE TO LEAVE EVERYTHING TO US!
W-WAIT...

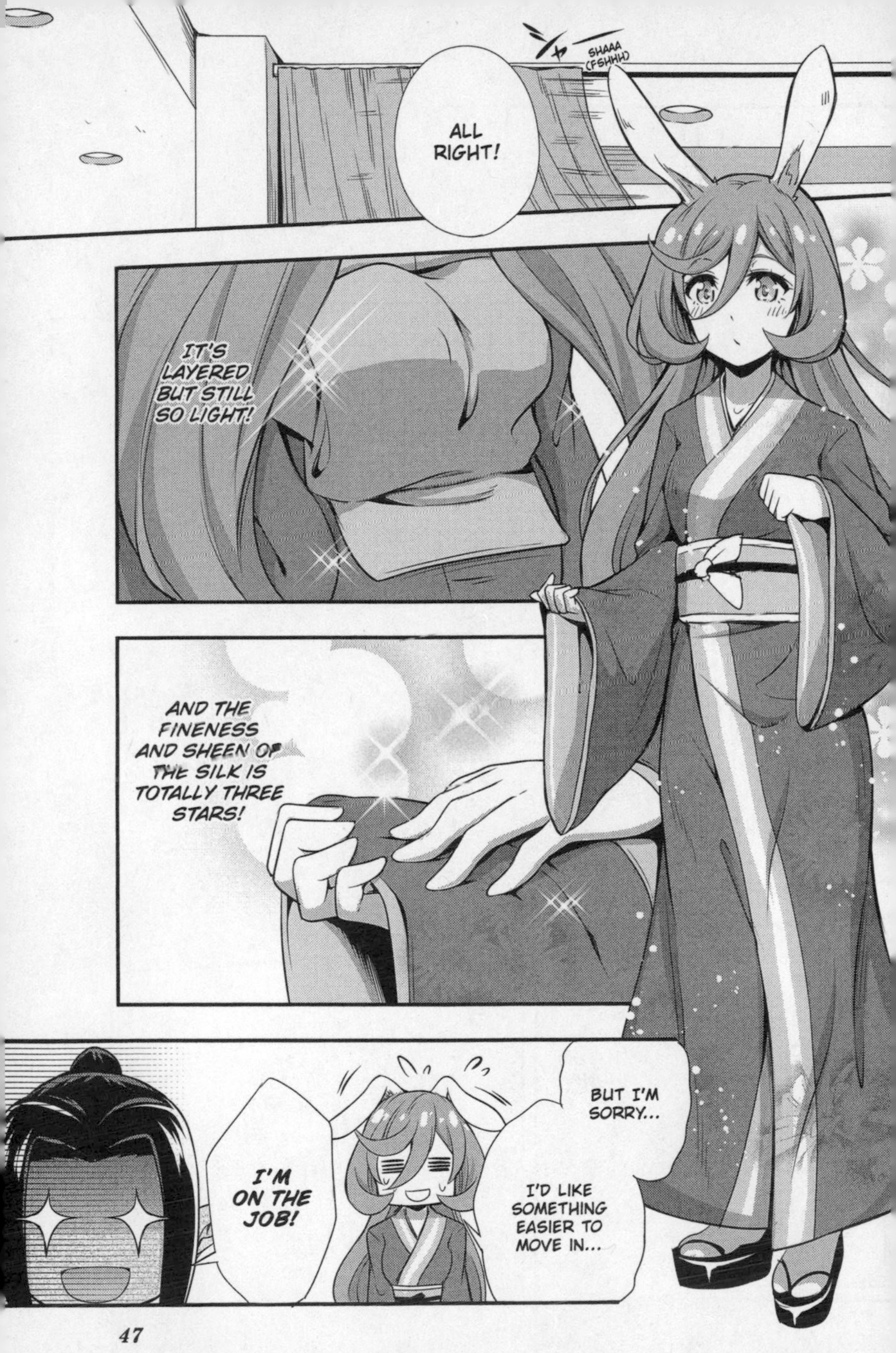
SHAAA (FSHHH)
ALL RIGHT!
IT'S LAYERED BUT STILL SO LIGHT!
AND THE FINENESS AND SHEEN OF THE SILK IS TOTALLY THREE STARS!
BUT I'M SORRY...
I'D LIKE SOMETHING EASIER TO MOVE IN...
I'M ON THE JOB!

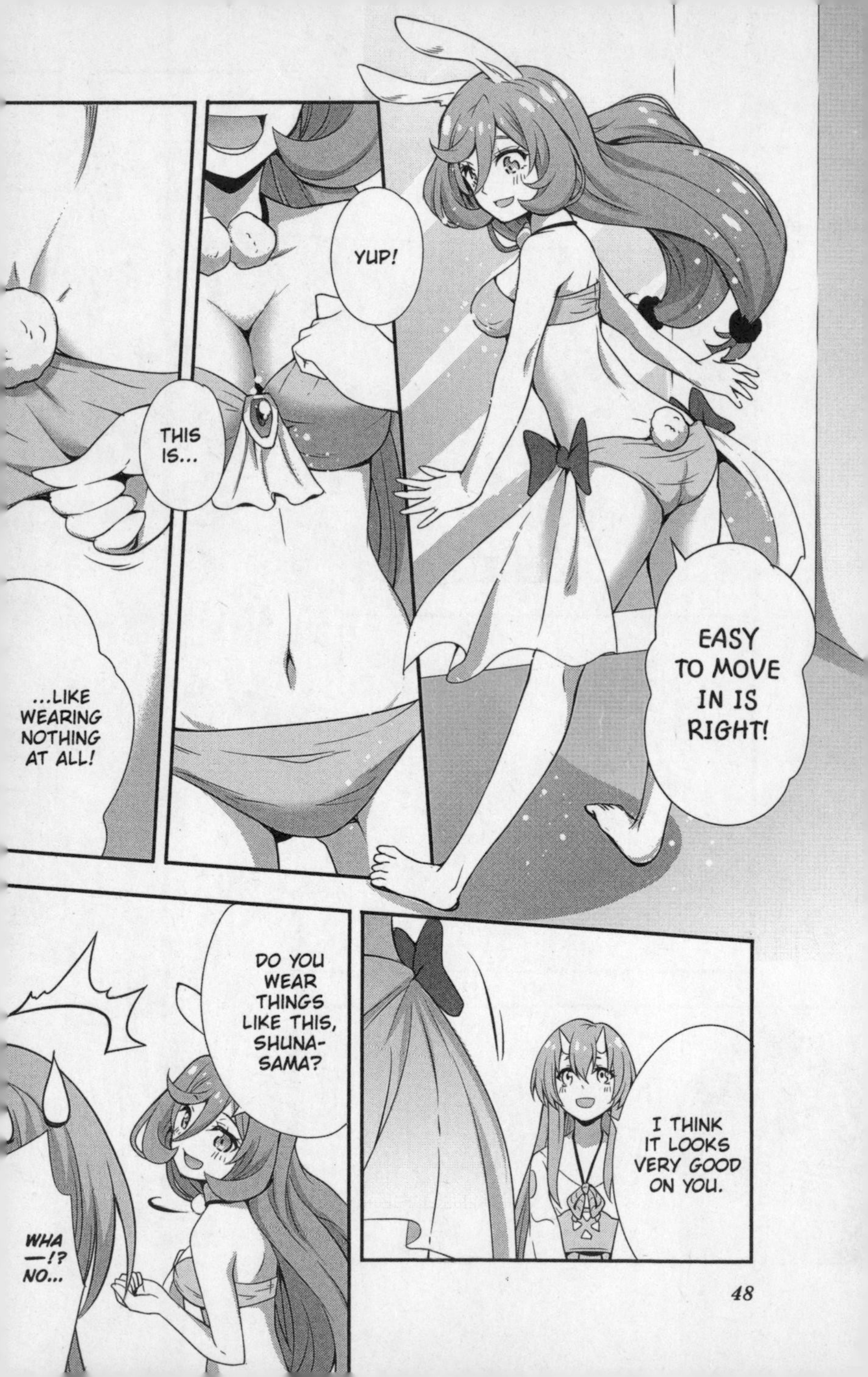
YUP!
EASY TO MOVE IN IS RIGHT!
THIS IS...
...LIKE WEARING NOTHING AT ALL!
I THINK IT LOOKS VERY GOOD ON YOU.
DO YOU WEAR THINGS LIKE THIS, SHUNA-SAMA?
WHA—!? NO...

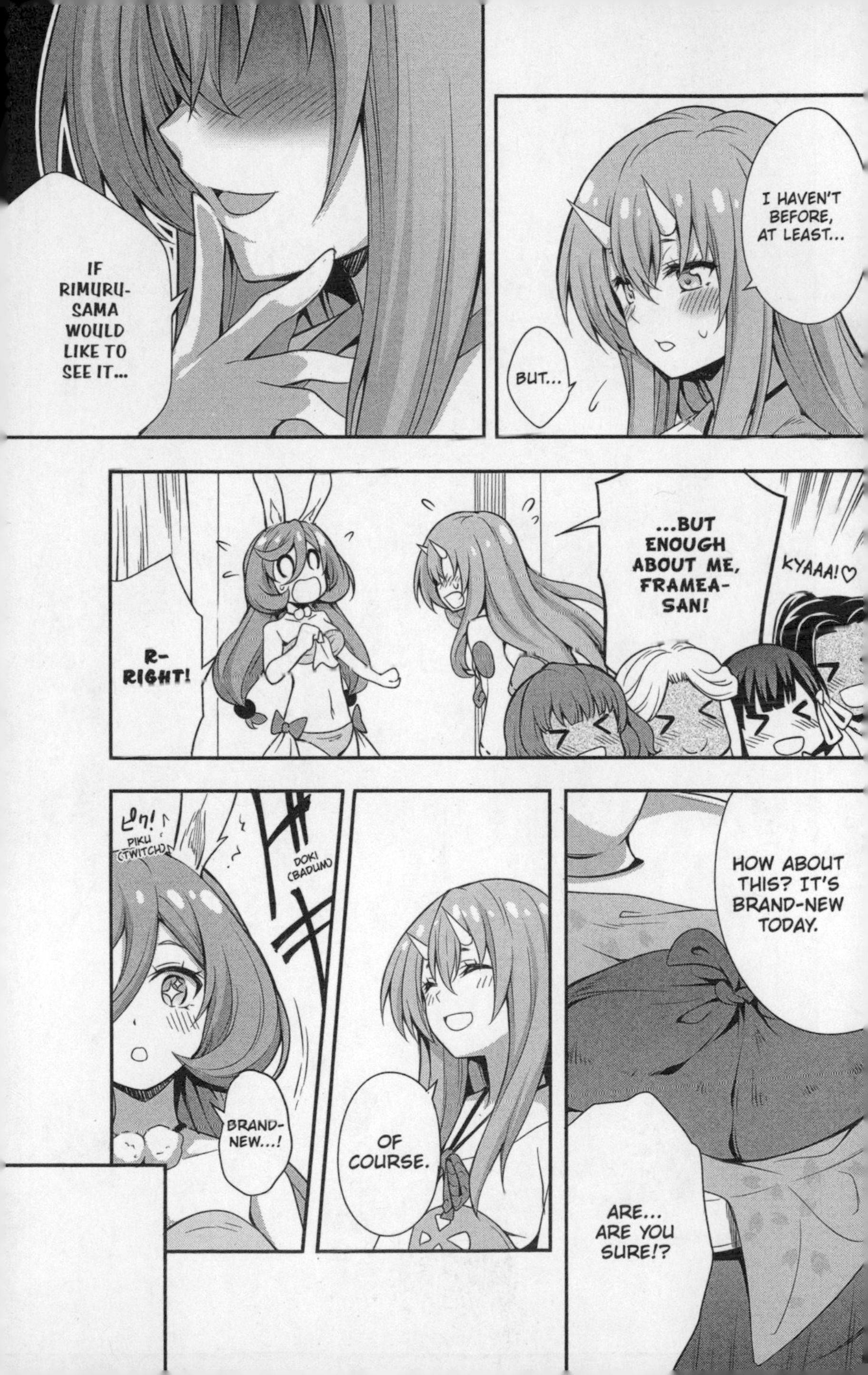
I HAVEN'T BEFORE, AT LEAST...
BUT...
IF RIMURU-SAMA WOULD LIKE TO SEE IT...
...BUT ENOUGH ABOUT ME, FRAMEA-SAN!
KYAAA!♡
R-RIGHT!
HOW ABOUT THIS? IT'S BRAND-NEW TODAY.
ARE... ARE YOU SURE!?
DOKI (BADUM)
OF COURSE.
ピク!♪
PIKU (TWITCH)
BRAND-NEW...!

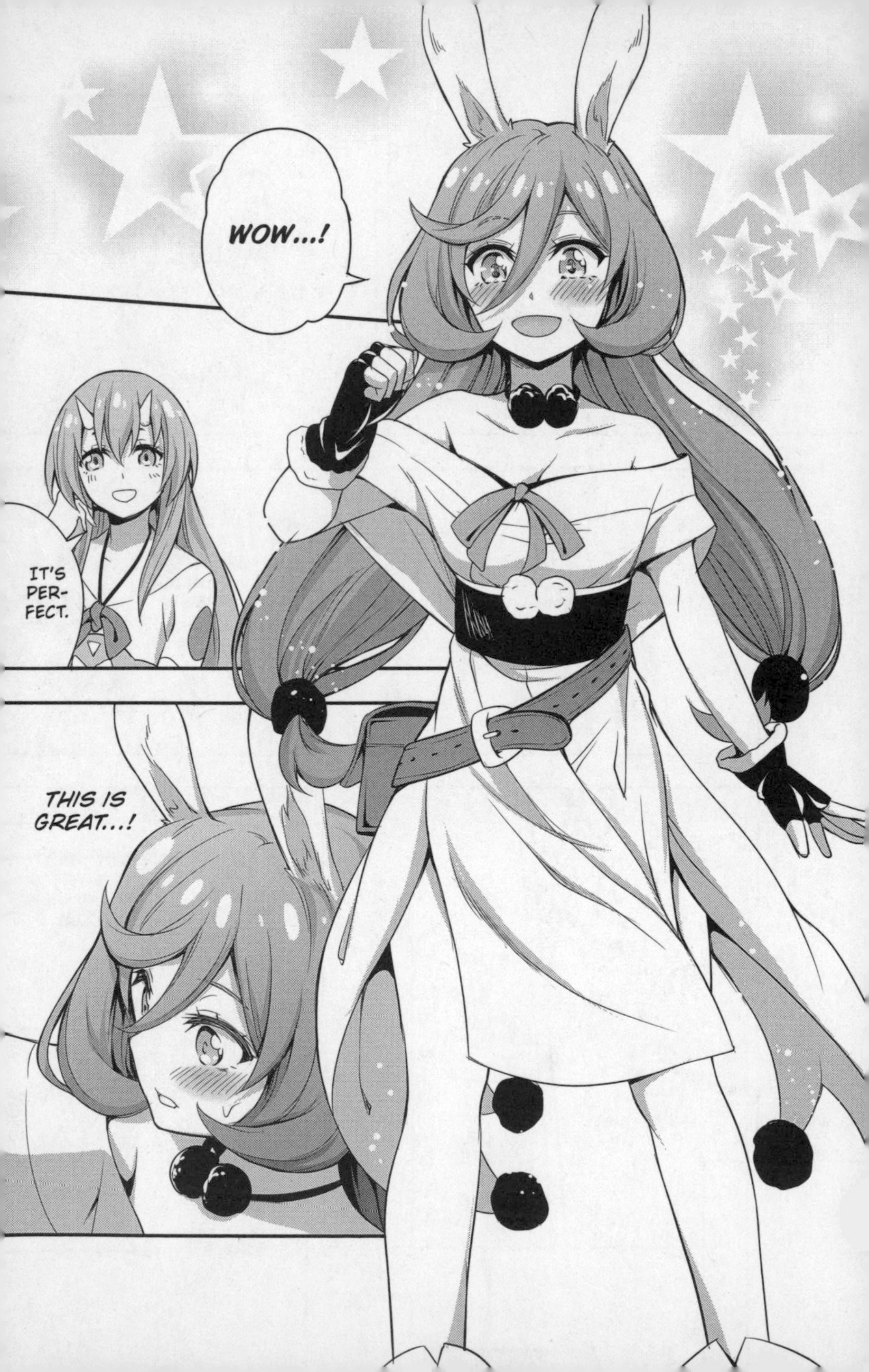
WOW...!
IT'S PERFECT.
THIS IS GREAT...!

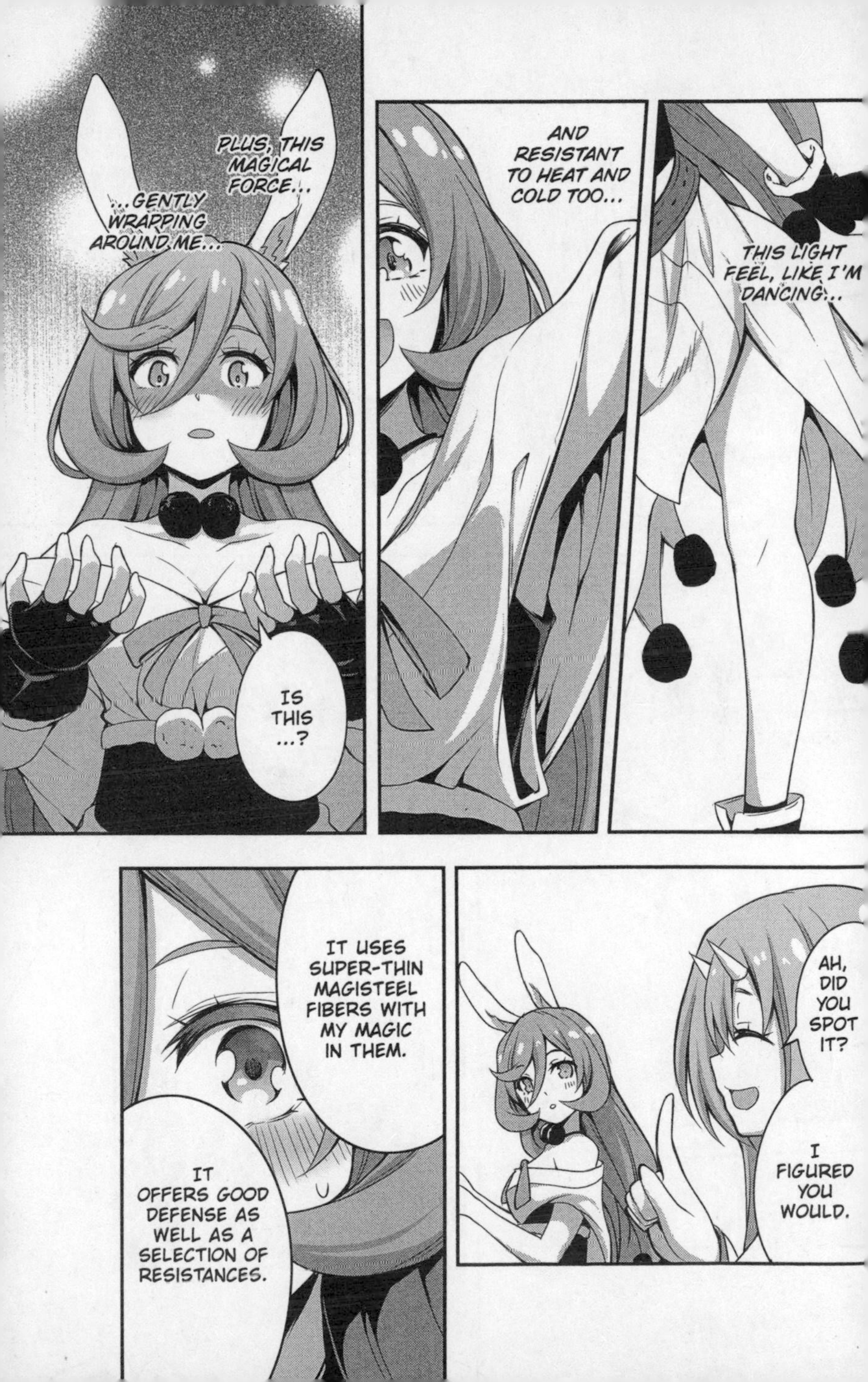
THIS LIGHT FEEL, LIKE I'M DANCING...
AND RESISTANT TO HEAT AND COLD TOO...
PLUS, THIS MAGICAL FORCE...
...GENTLY WRAPPING AROUND ME...
IS THIS ...?
AH, DID YOU SPOT IT?
I FIGURED YOU WOULD.
IT USES SUPER-THIN MAGISTEEL FIBERS WITH MY MAGIC IN THEM.
IT OFFERS GOOD DEFENSE AS WELL AS A SELECTION OF RESISTANCES.

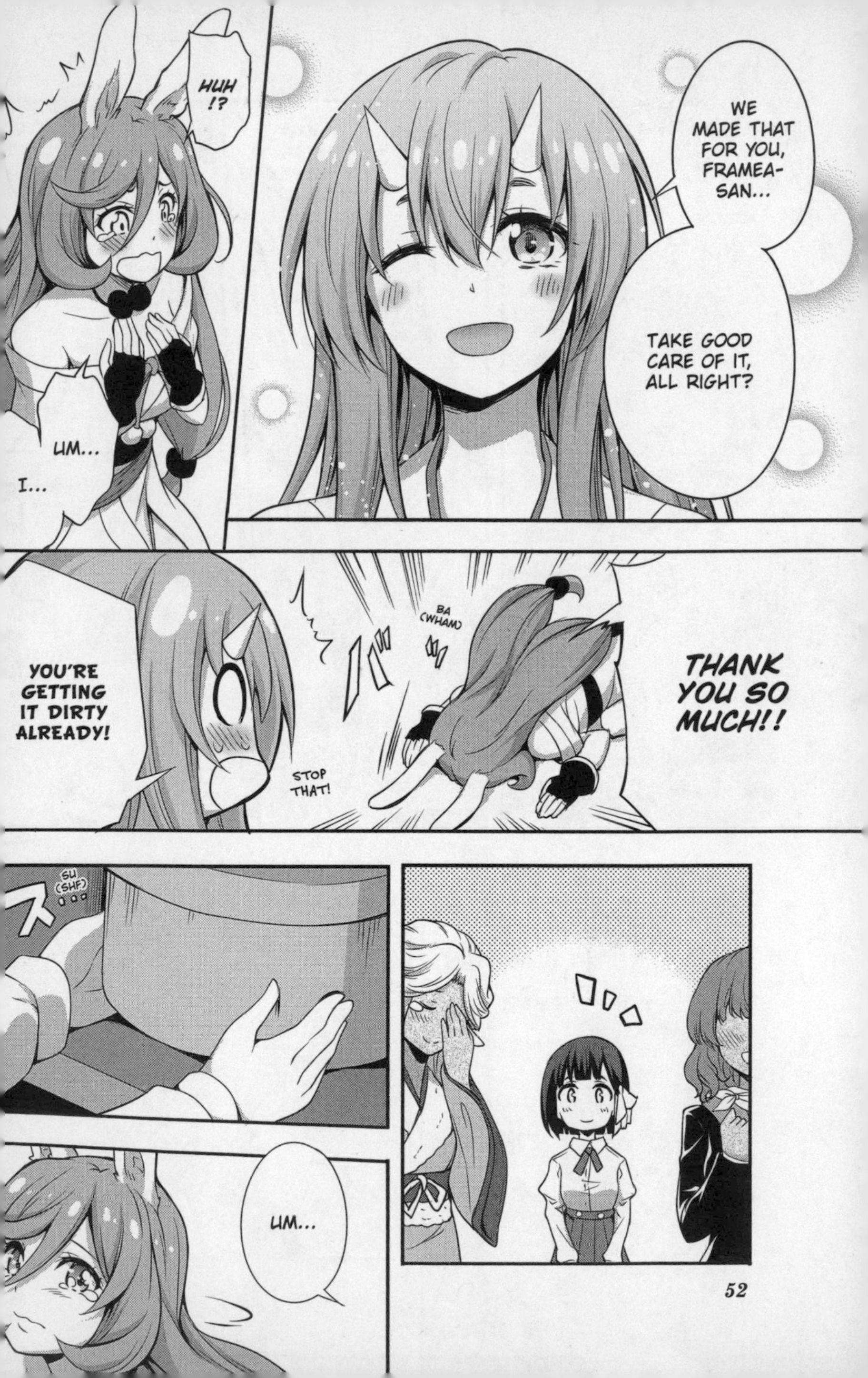
WE MADE THAT FOR YOU, FRAMEA-SAN...
TAKE GOOD CARE OF IT, ALL RIGHT?
HUH!?
UM...
I...
THANK YOU SO MUCH!!
BA (WHAM)
STOP THAT!
YOU'RE GETTING IT DIRTY ALREADY!
SU (SHF)
UM...

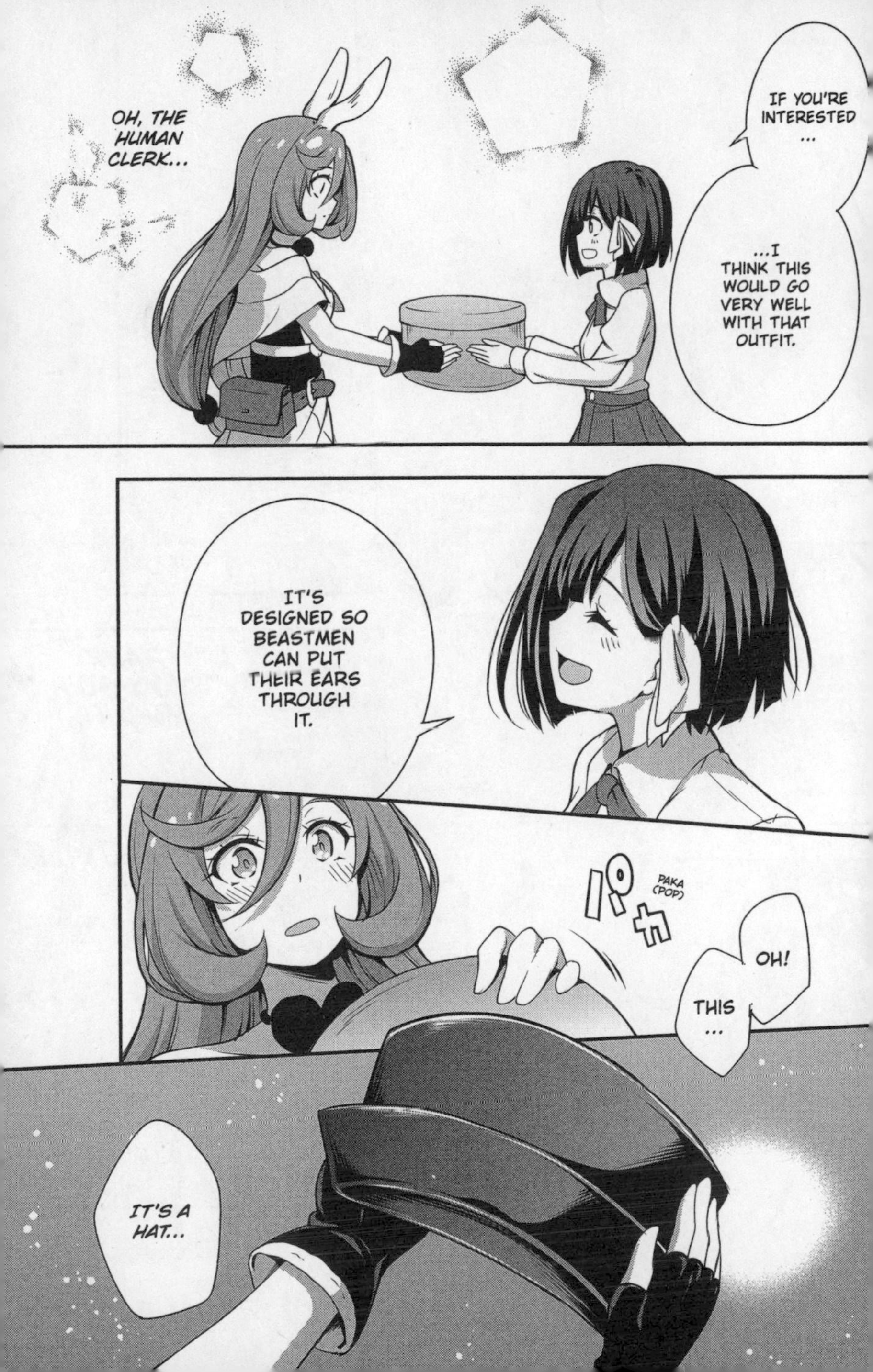
IF YOU'RE INTERESTED ...
...I THINK THIS WOULD GO VERY WELL WITH THAT OUTFIT.
OH, THE HUMAN CLERK...
IT'S DESIGNED SO BEASTMEN CAN PUT THEIR EARS THROUGH IT.
パカ
PAKA (POP)
OH!
THIS ...
IT'S A HAT...

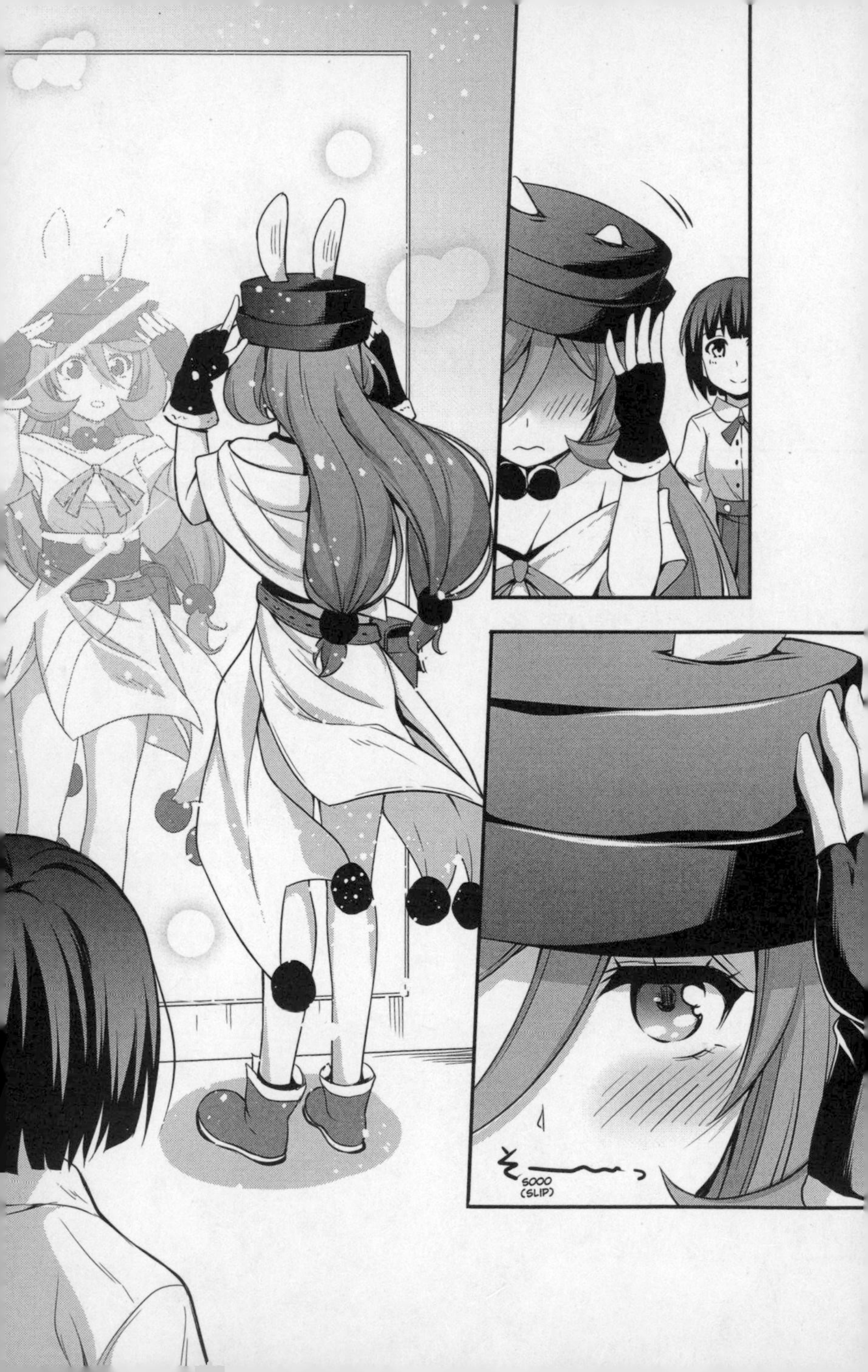
そ――っ
SOOO
(SLIP)

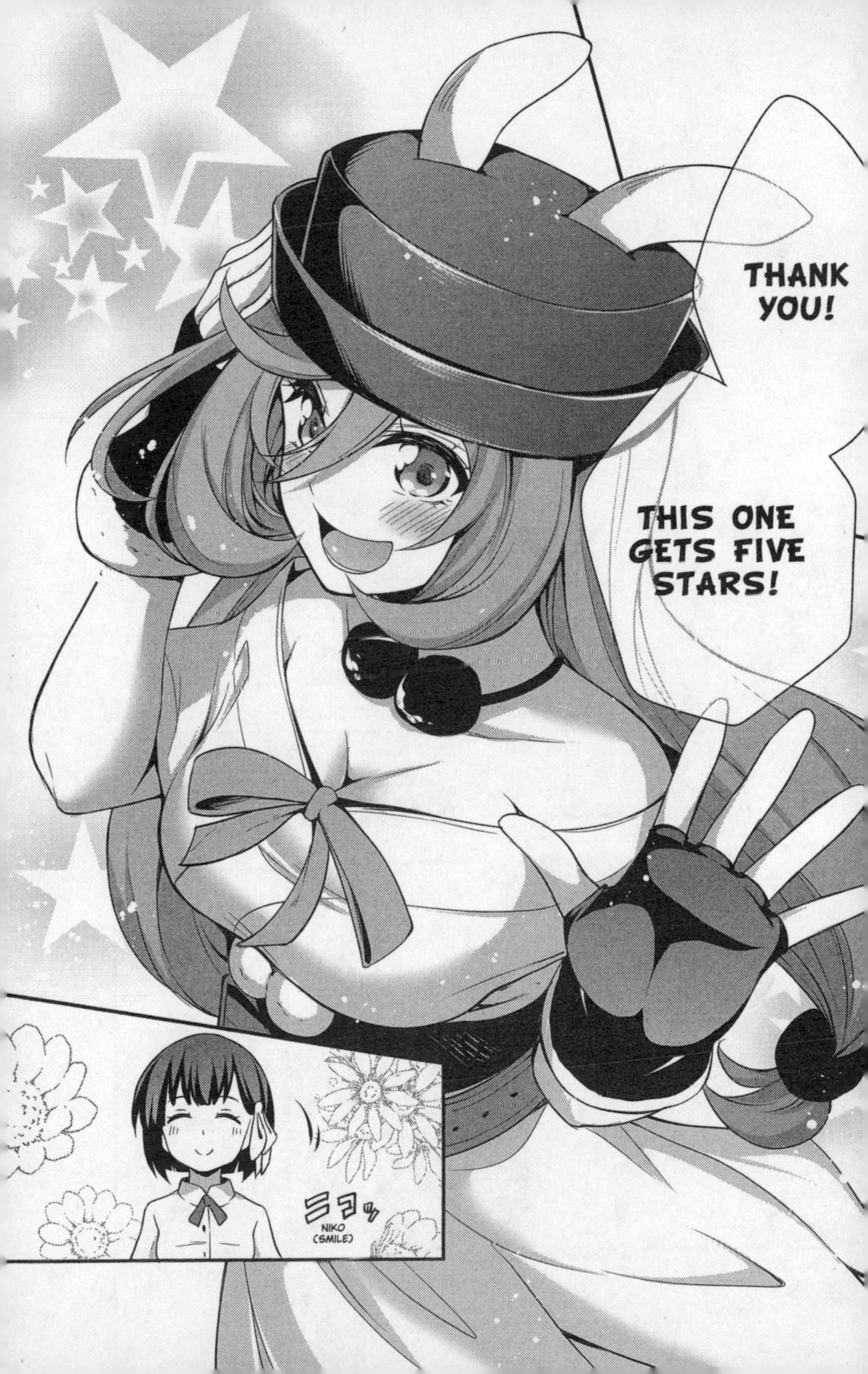
THANK YOU!
THIS ONE GETS FIVE STARS!
ニコッ
NIKO (SMILE)

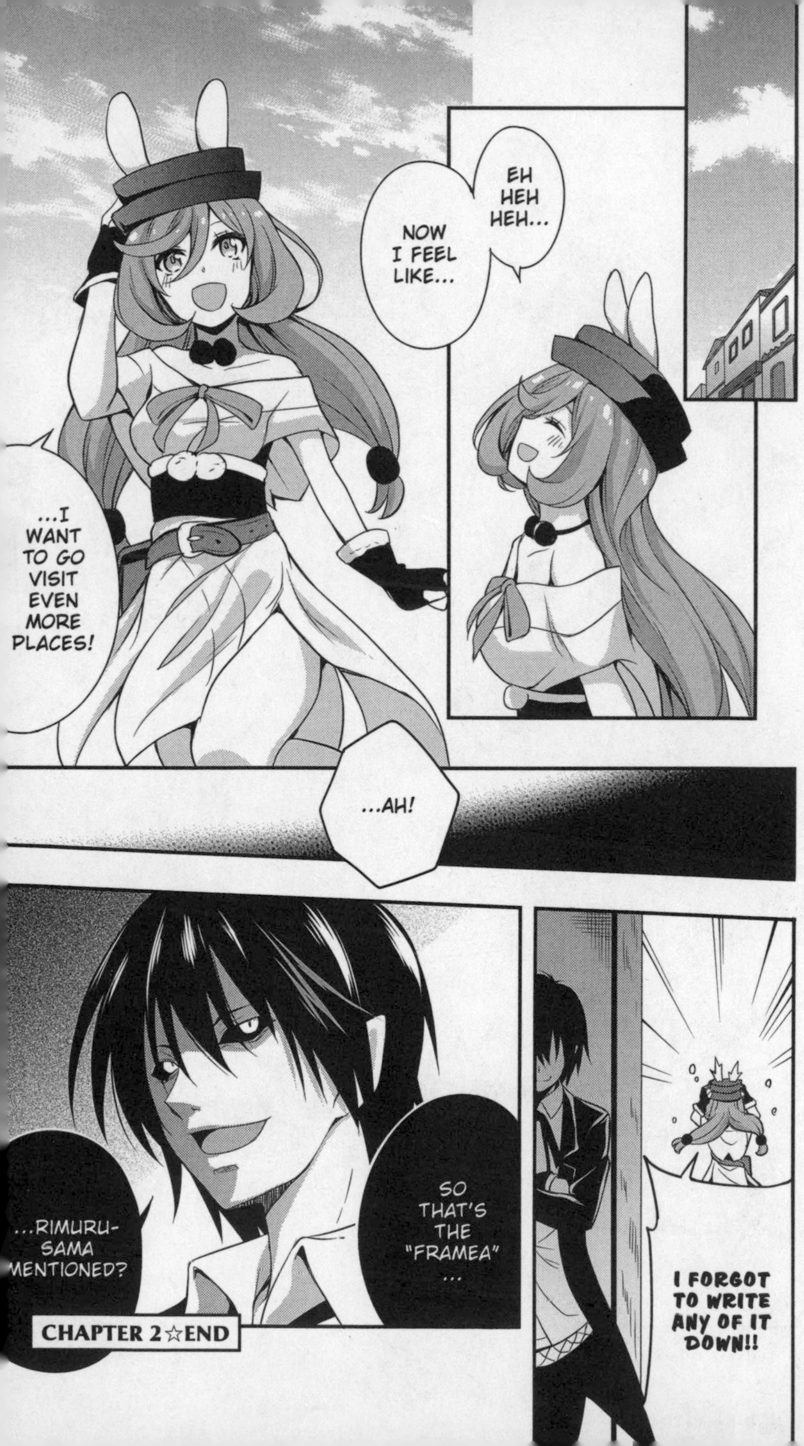
EH HEH HEH...
NOW I FEEL LIKE...
...I WANT TO GO VISIT EVEN MORE PLACES!
...AH!
I FORGOT TO WRITE ANY OF IT DOWN!!
SO THAT'S THE "FRAMEA"...
...RIMURU-SAMA MENTIONED?
CHAPTER 2☆END

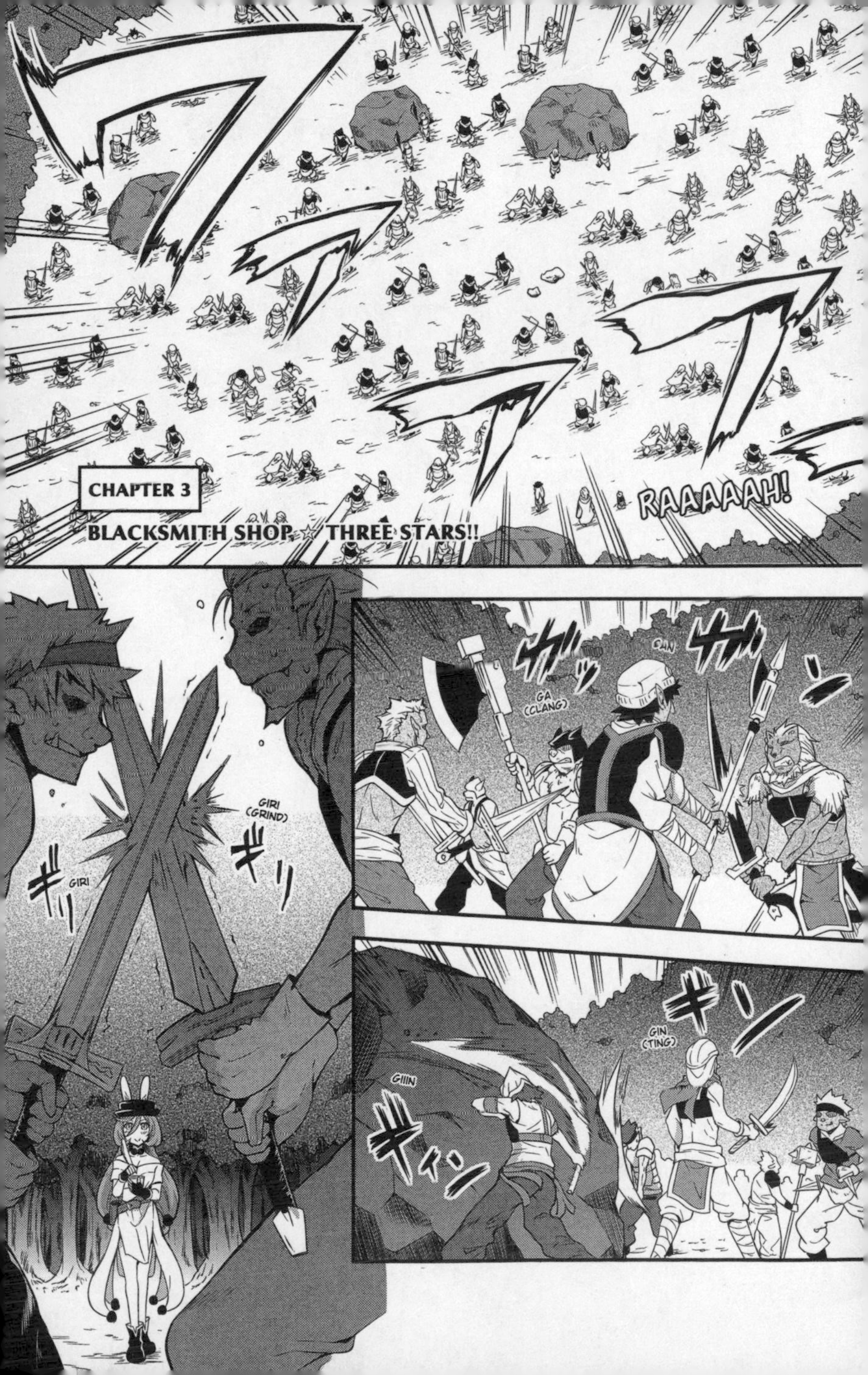
RAAAAAH!
CHAPTER 3
BLACKSMITH SHOP ☆ THREE STARS!!
GAN
GA (CLANG)
GIN (TING)
GIIN
GIRI (GRIND)
GIRI

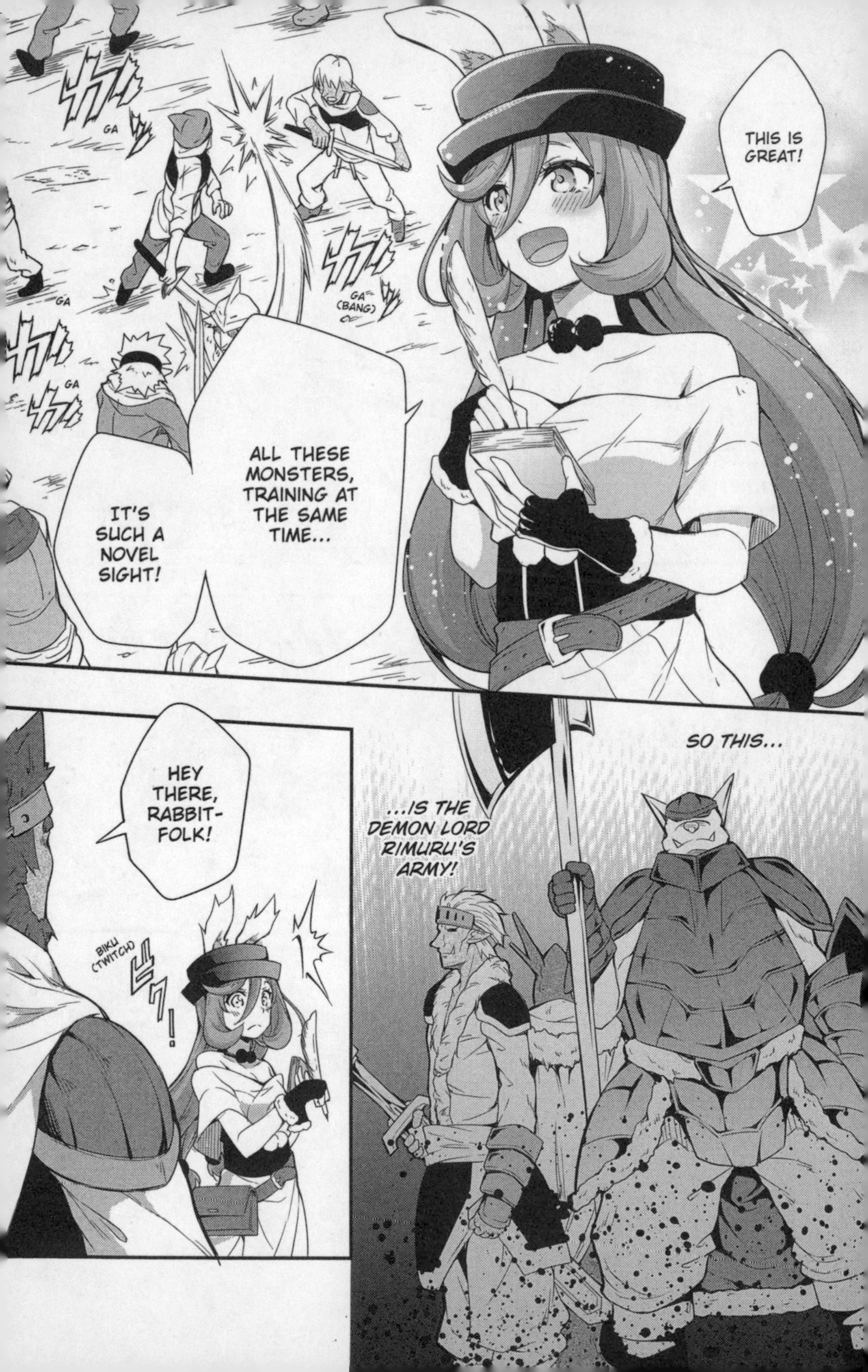
THIS IS GREAT!
ALL THESE MONSTERS, TRAINING AT THE SAME TIME...
IT'S SUCH A NOVEL SIGHT!
GA (BANG)
GA
GA
GA
SO THIS...
...IS THE DEMON LORD RIMURU'S ARMY!
HEY THERE, RABBIT-FOLK!
BIKU (TWITCH)

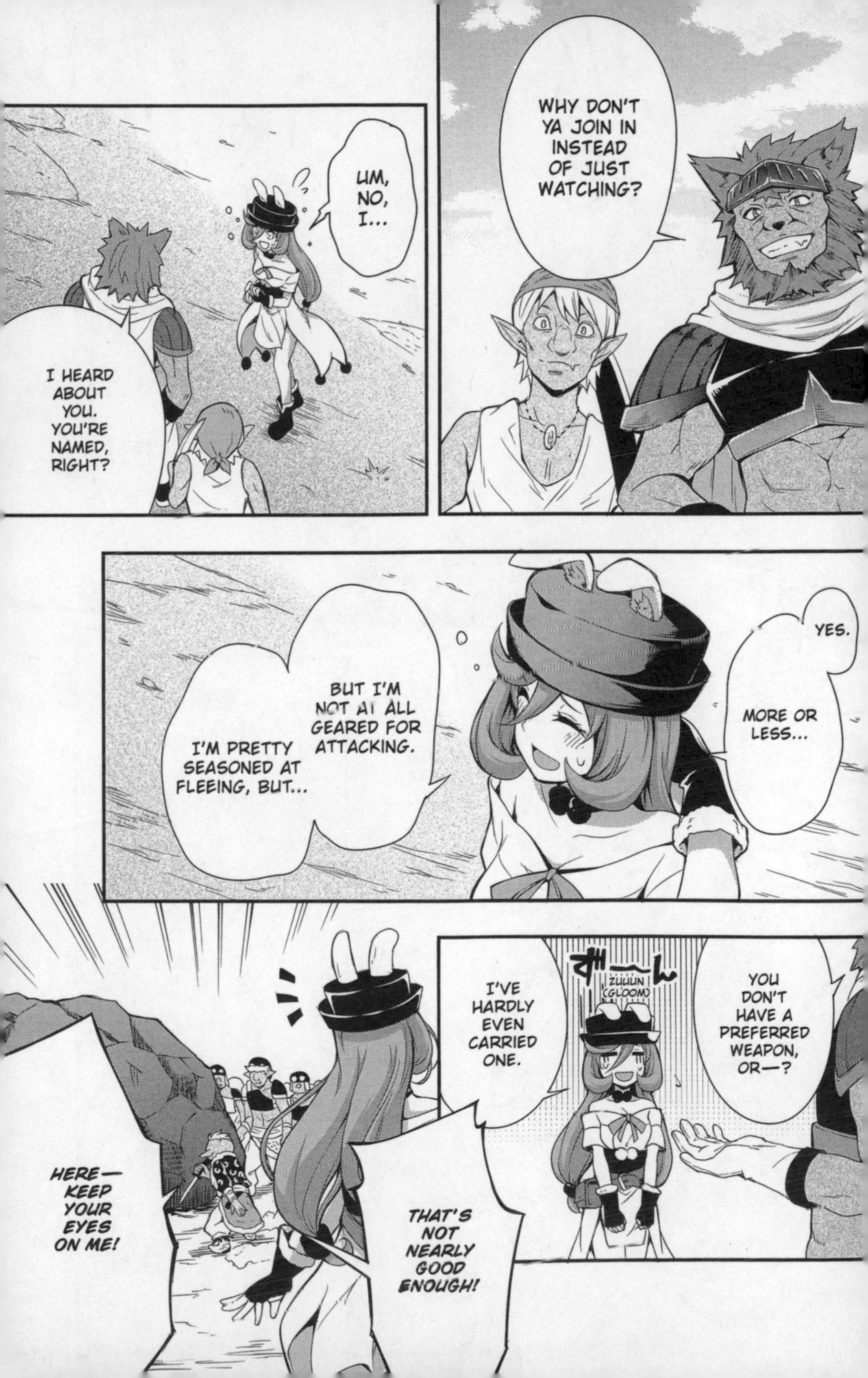
WHY DON'T YA JOIN IN INSTEAD OF JUST WATCHING?
UM, NO, I...
I HEARD ABOUT YOU. YOU'RE NAMED, RIGHT?
YES.
MORE OR LESS...
BUT I'M NOT AT ALL GEARED FOR ATTACKING.
I'M PRETTY SEASONED AT FLEEING, BUT...
YOU DON'T HAVE A PREFERRED WEAPON, OR—?
ずーん
ZUUUN (GLOOM)
I'VE HARDLY EVEN CARRIED ONE.
THAT'S NOT NEARLY GOOD ENOUGH!
HERE— KEEP YOUR EYES ON ME!

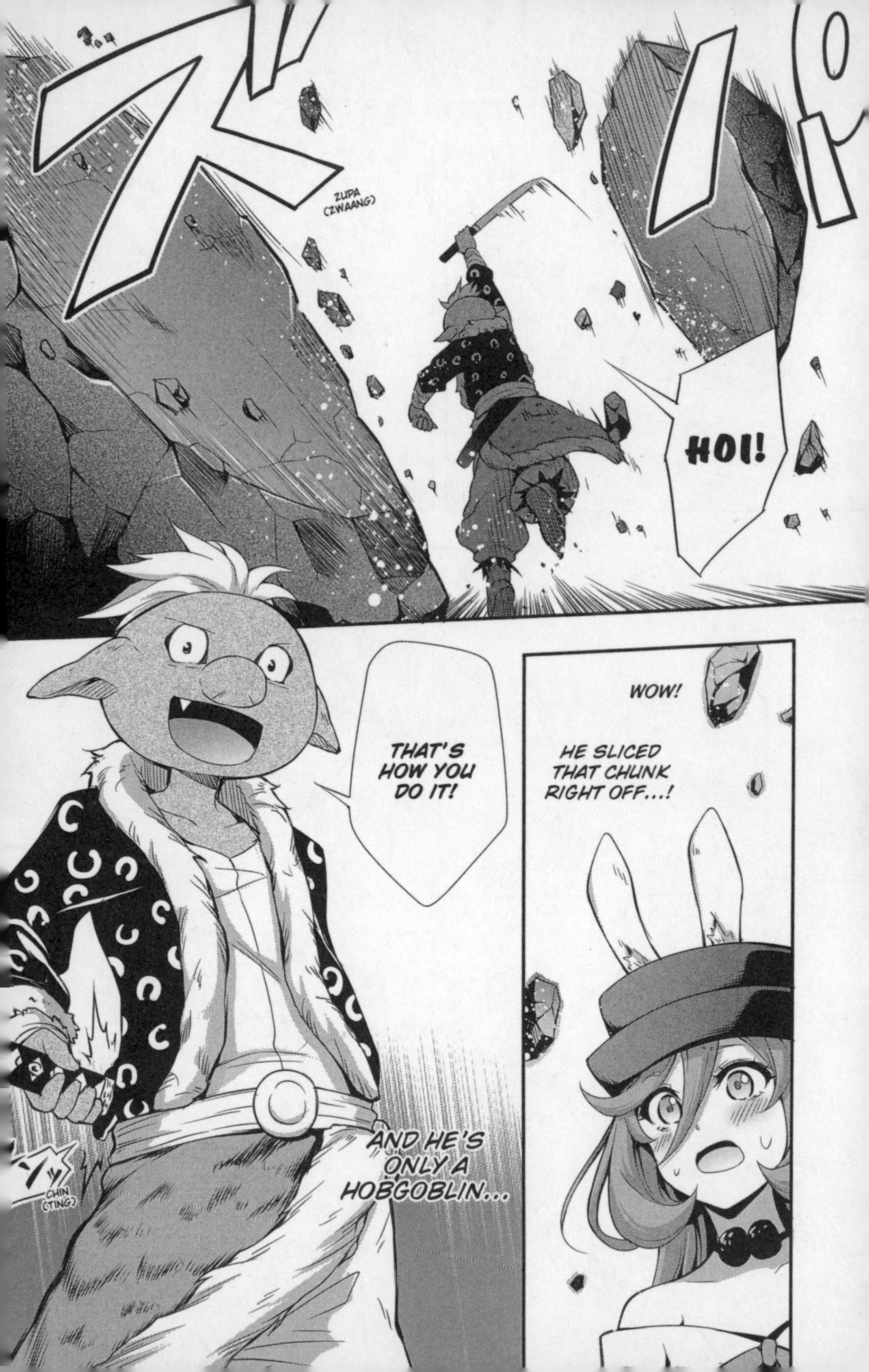
ZUPA
(ZWAANG)
HOI!
WOW!
HE SLICED THAT CHUNK RIGHT OFF...!
THAT'S HOW YOU DO IT!
AND HE'S ONLY A HOBGOBLIN...
CHIN
(TING)

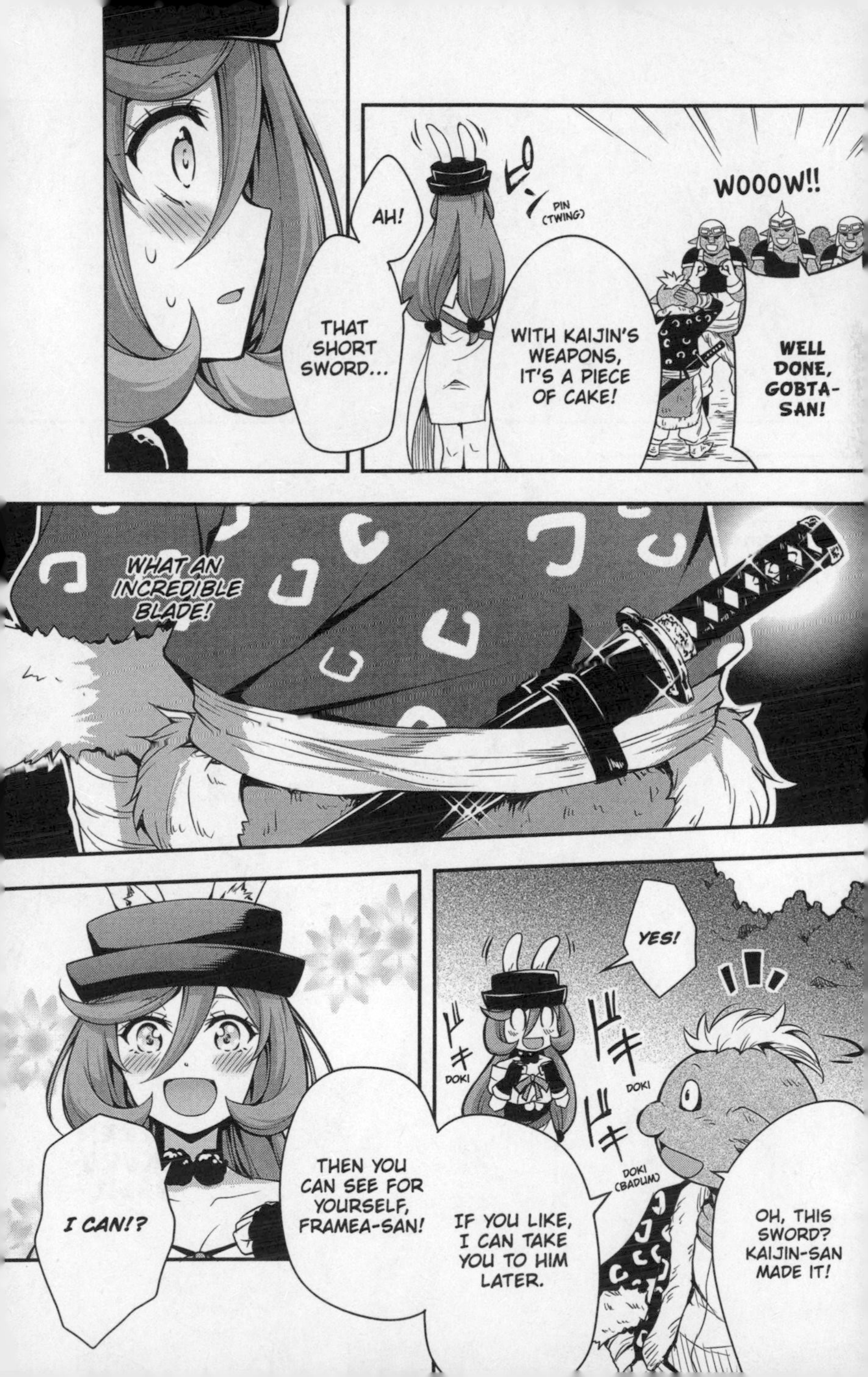
WOOOW!!
WELL DONE, GOBTA-SAN!
WITH KAIJIN'S WEAPONS, IT'S A PIECE OF CAKE!
PIN (TWING)
AH!
THAT SHORT SWORD...
WHAT AN INCREDIBLE BLADE!
YES!
DOKI
DOKI
DOKI (BADUM)
OH, THIS SWORD? KAIJIN-SAN MADE IT!
IF YOU LIKE, I CAN TAKE YOU TO HIM LATER.
THEN YOU CAN SEE FOR YOURSELF, FRAMEA-SAN!
I CAN!?

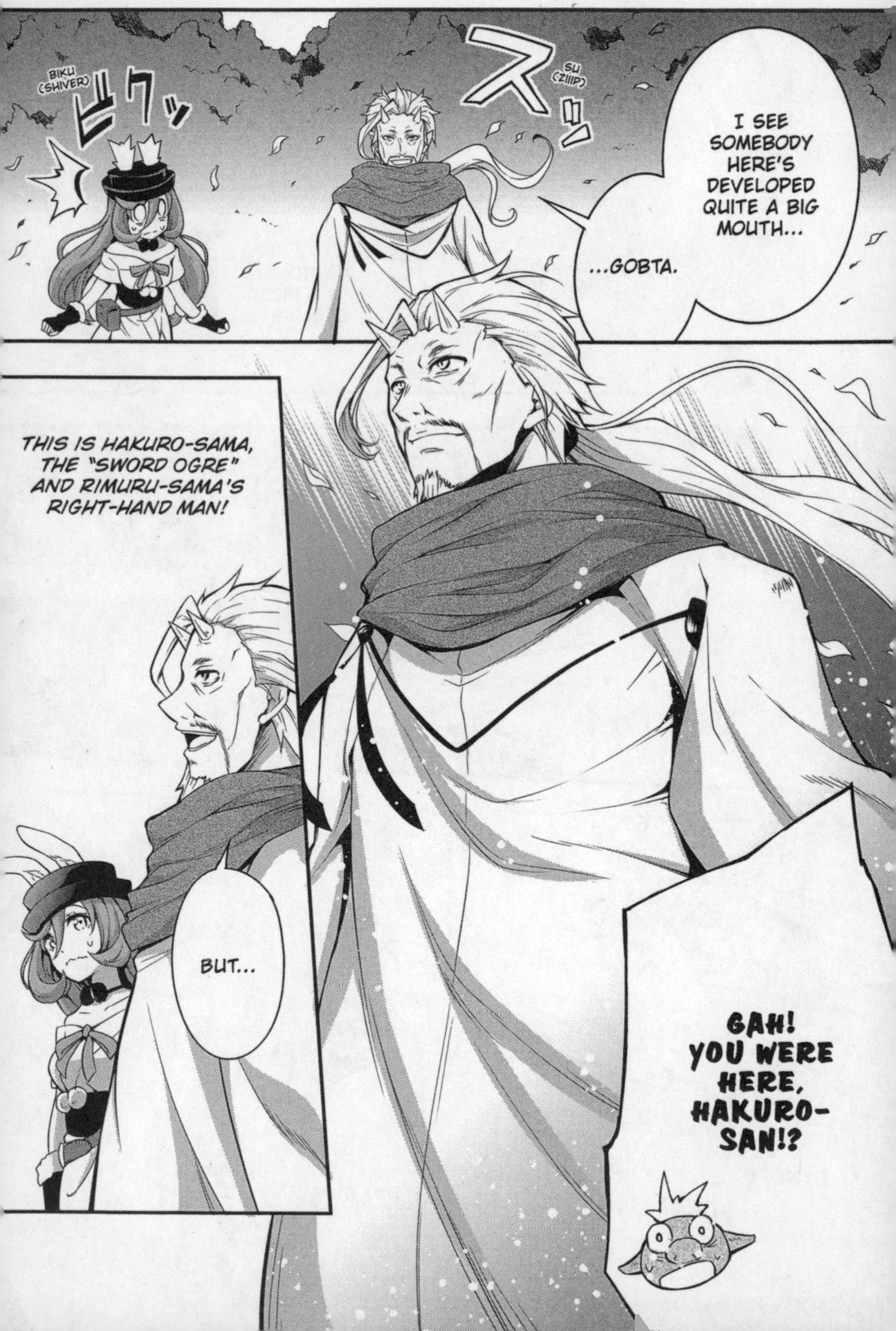
I SEE SOMEBODY HERE'S DEVELOPED QUITE A BIG MOUTH...
...GOBTA.
SU (ZIIIP)
BIKU (SHIVER)
GAH! YOU WERE HERE, HAKURO-SAN!?
THIS IS HAKURO-SAMA, THE "SWORD OGRE" AND RIMURU-SAMA'S RIGHT-HAND MAN!
BUT...

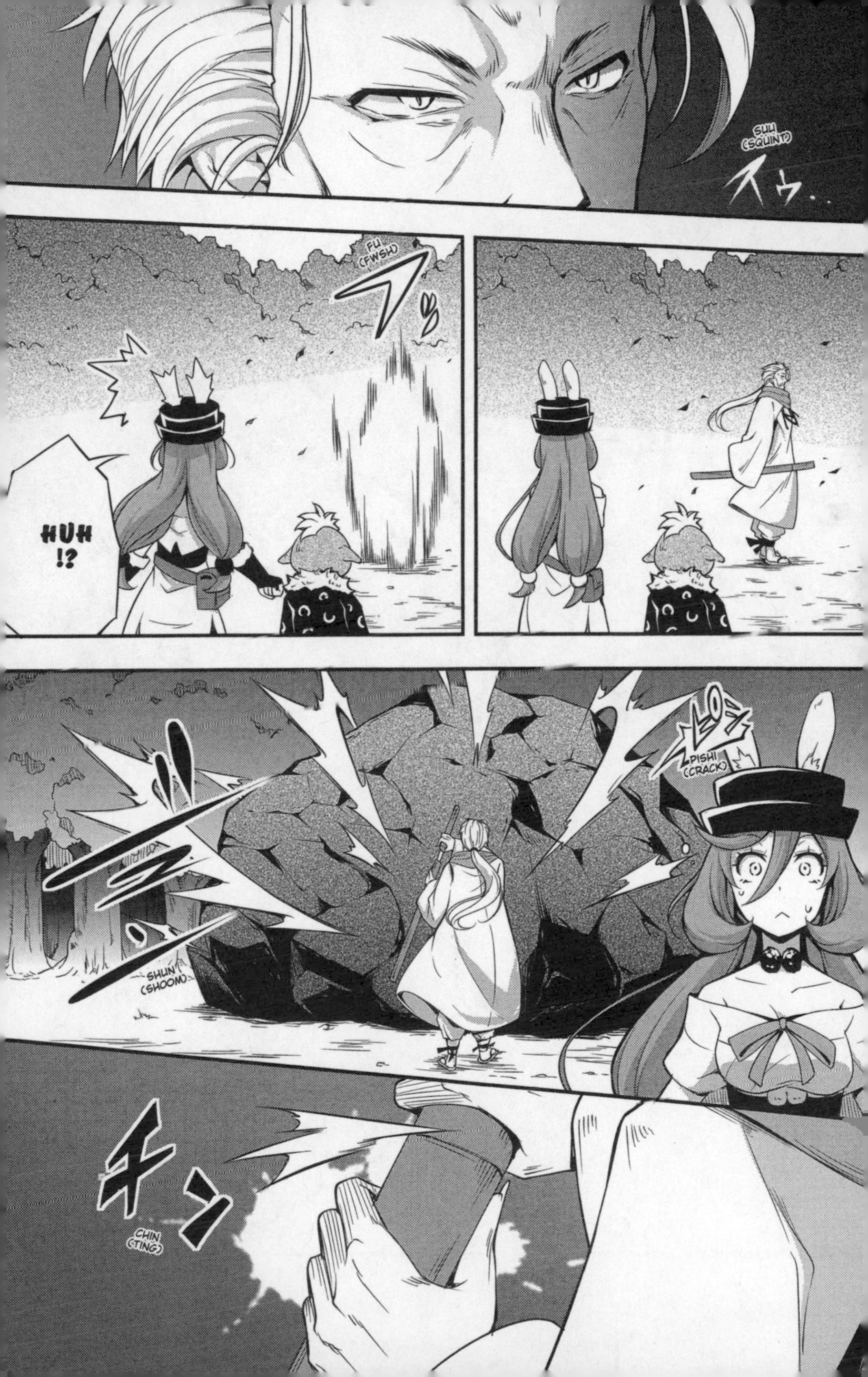
SUU (SQUINT)
FU (FWSH)
HUH !?
PISHI (CRACK)
SHUN (SHOOM)
CHIN (TING)

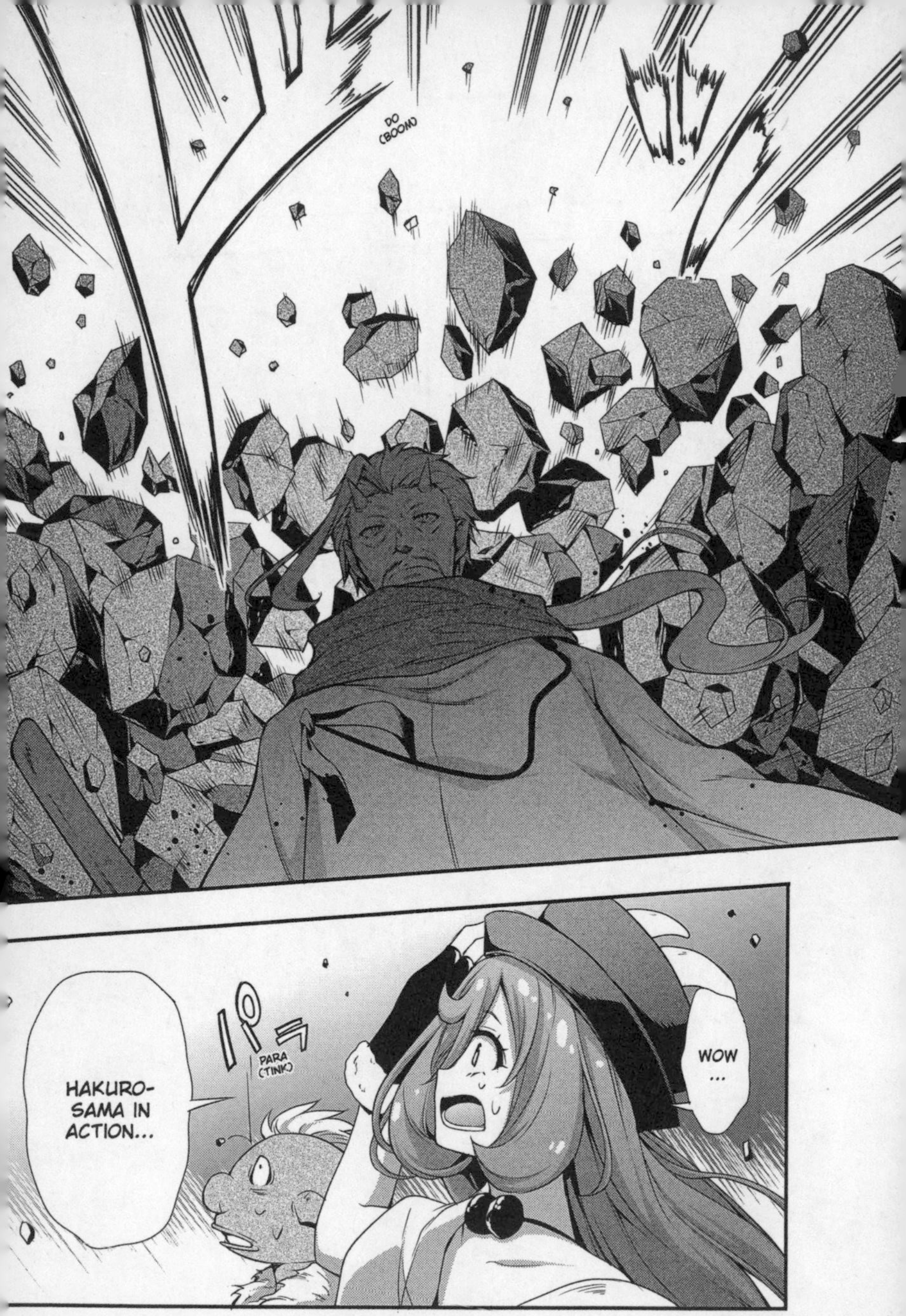
DO
(BOOM)
WOW ...
PARA
(TINK)
HAKURO-SAMA IN ACTION...

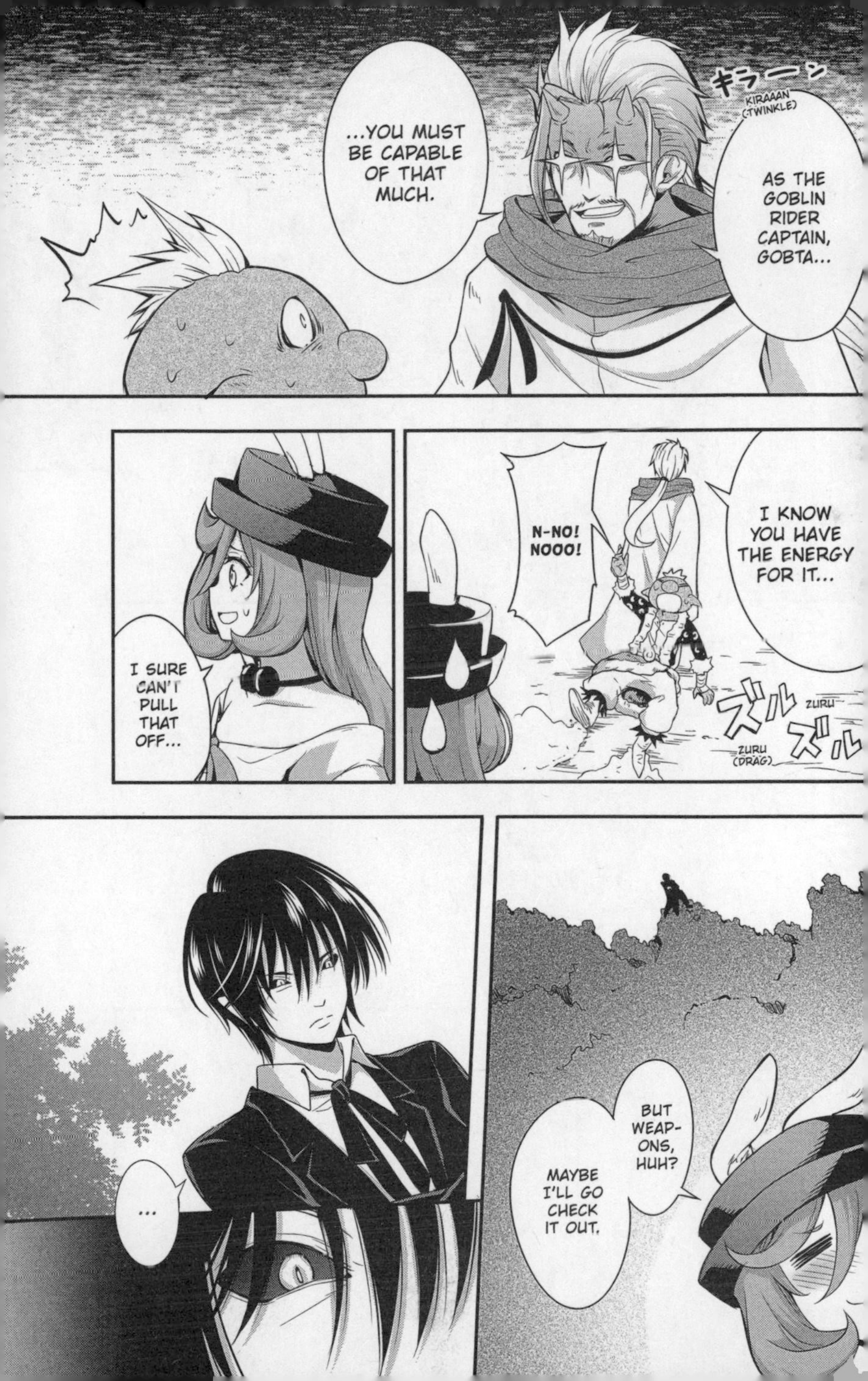
キラーン
KIRAAAN (TWINKLE)
AS THE GOBLIN RIDER CAPTAIN, GOBTA...
...YOU MUST BE CAPABLE OF THAT MUCH.
I KNOW YOU HAVE THE ENERGY FOR IT...
N-NO! NOOO!
ズルズル
ZURU ZURU (DRAG)
I SURE CAN'T PULL THAT OFF...
BUT WEAP-ONS, HUH?
MAYBE I'LL GO CHECK IT OUT.
...

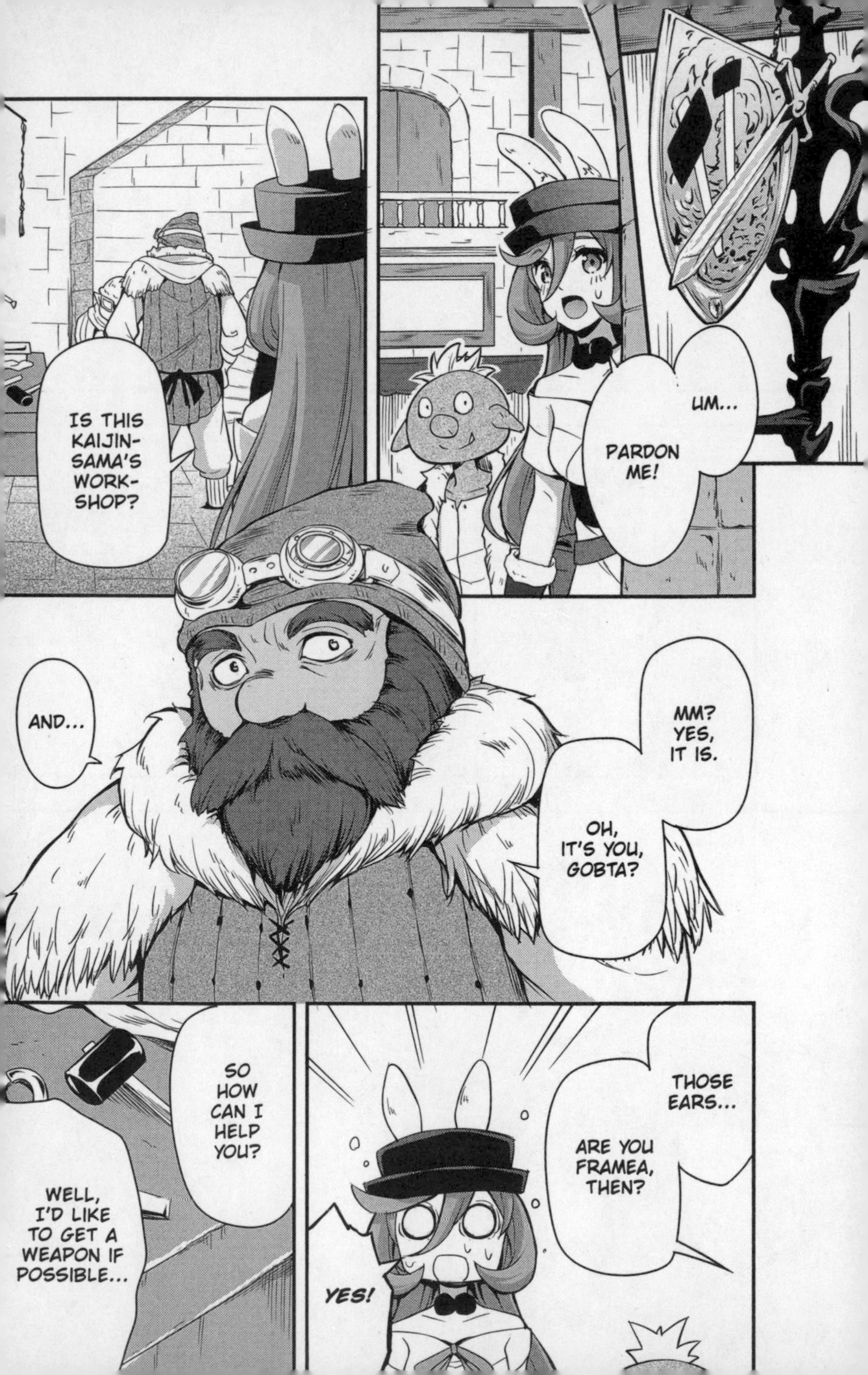
UM...
PARDON ME!
IS THIS KAIJIN-SAMA'S WORKSHOP?
MM? YES, IT IS.
OH, IT'S YOU, GOBTA?
AND...
THOSE EARS...
ARE YOU FRAMEA, THEN?
YES!
SO HOW CAN I HELP YOU?
WELL, I'D LIKE TO GET A WEAPON IF POSSIBLE...

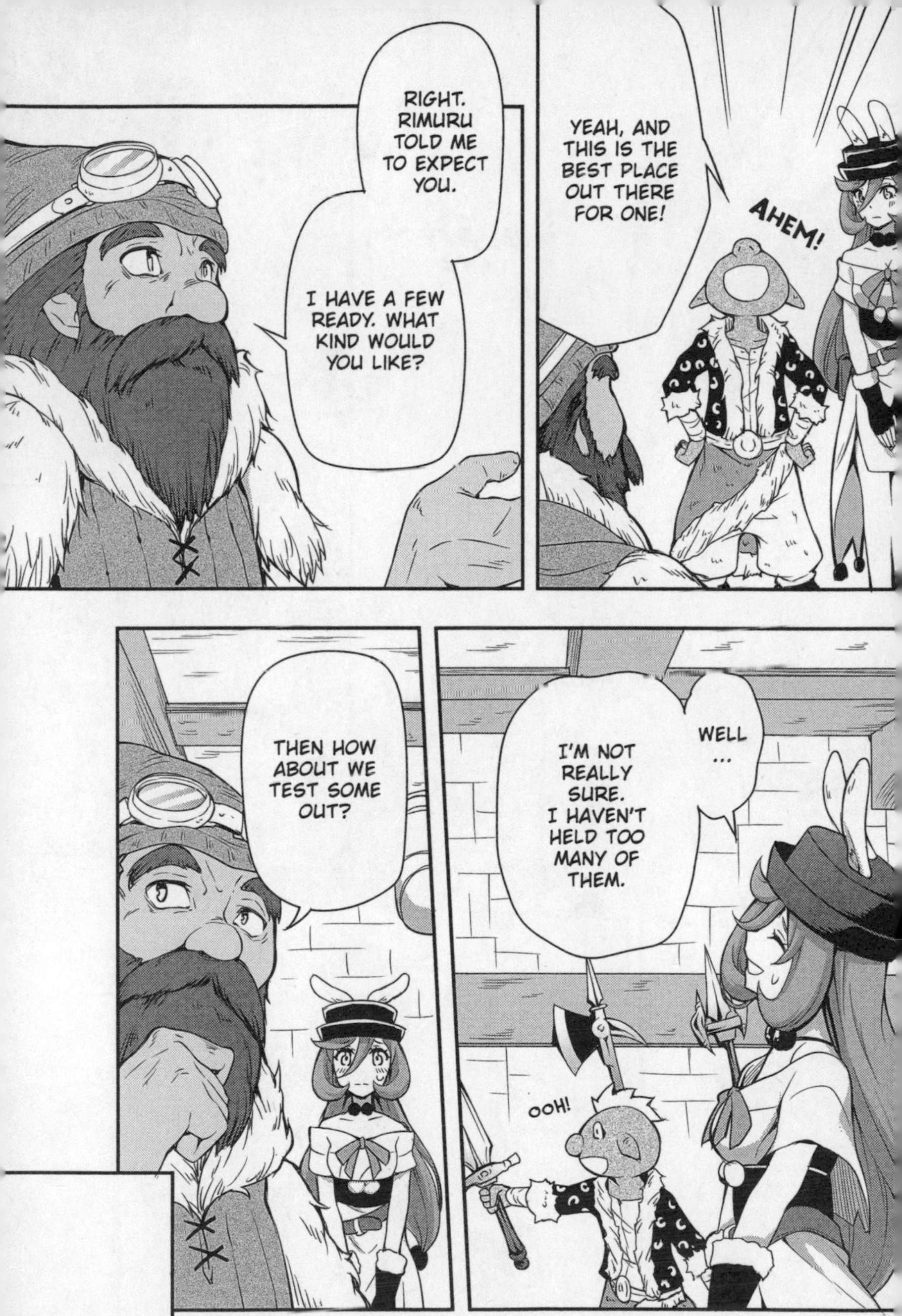
YEAH, AND THIS IS THE BEST PLACE OUT THERE FOR ONE!
AHEM!
RIGHT. RIMURU TOLD ME TO EXPECT YOU.
I HAVE A FEW READY. WHAT KIND WOULD YOU LIKE?
WELL ...
I'M NOT REALLY SURE. I HAVEN'T HELD TOO MANY OF THEM.
OOH!
THEN HOW ABOUT WE TEST SOME OUT?

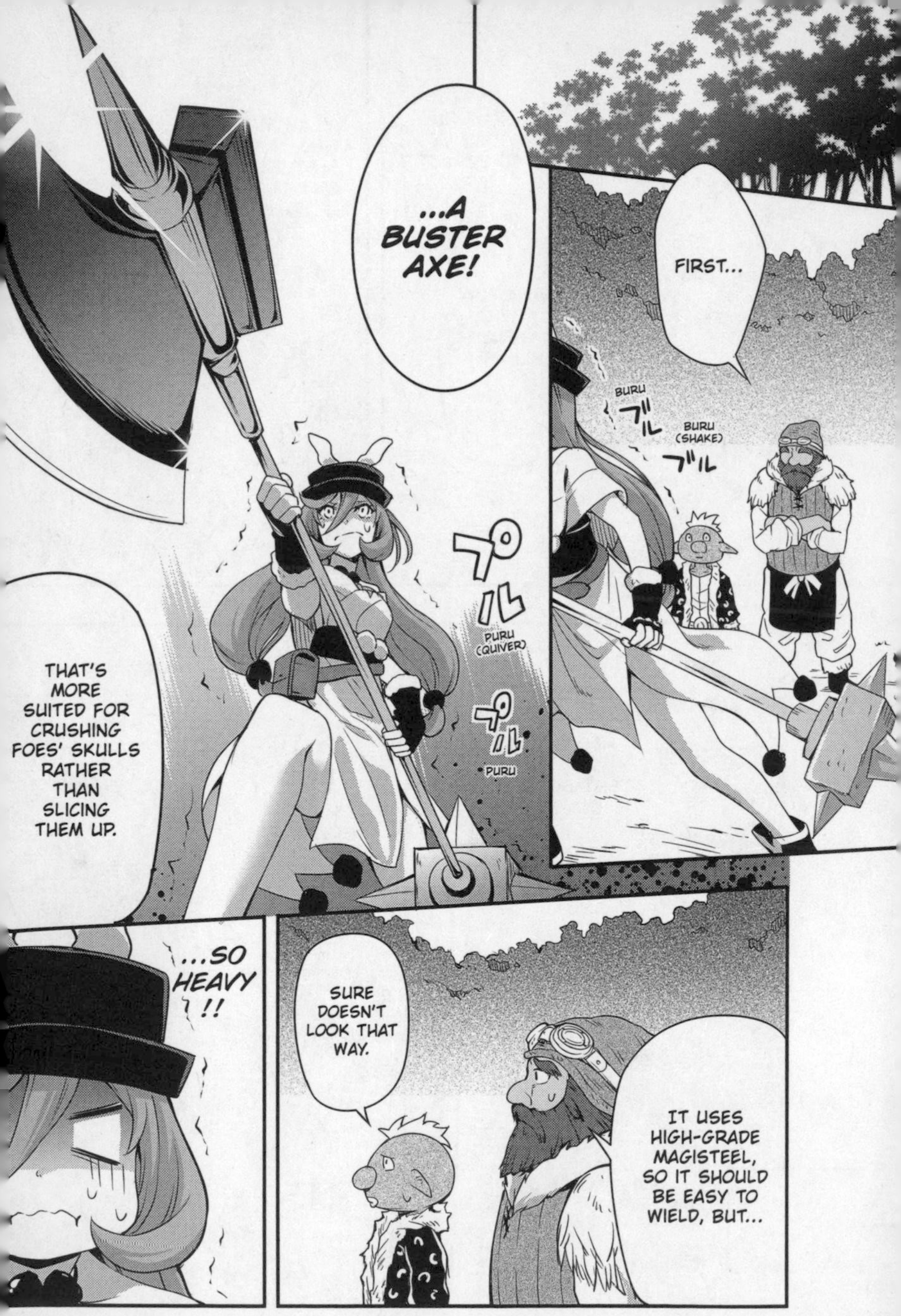
FIRST...
BURU ブル
BURU (SHAKE) ブル
...A BUSTER AXE!
プル PURU (QUIVER)
プル PURU
THAT'S MORE SUITED FOR CRUSHING FOES' SKULLS RATHER THAN SLICING THEM UP.
IT USES HIGH-GRADE MAGISTEEL, SO IT SHOULD BE EASY TO WIELD, BUT...
SURE DOESN'T LOOK THAT WAY.
...SO HEAVY!!

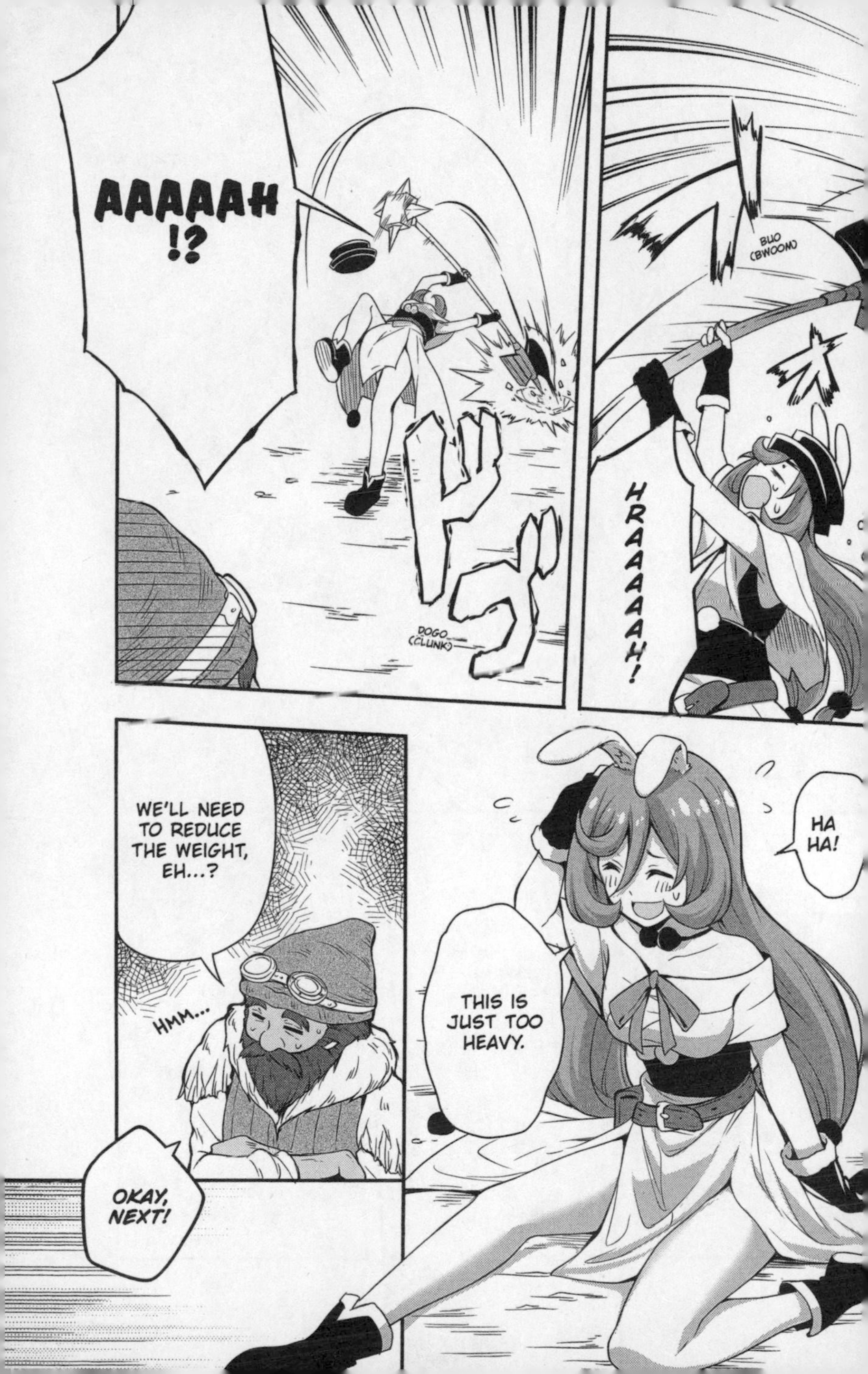
BUO
(BWOOM)
HRAAAAAAH!
AAAAAH
!?
DOGO
(CLUNK)
HA
HA!
THIS IS JUST TOO HEAVY.
WE'LL NEED TO REDUCE THE WEIGHT, EH...?
HMM...
OKAY, NEXT!

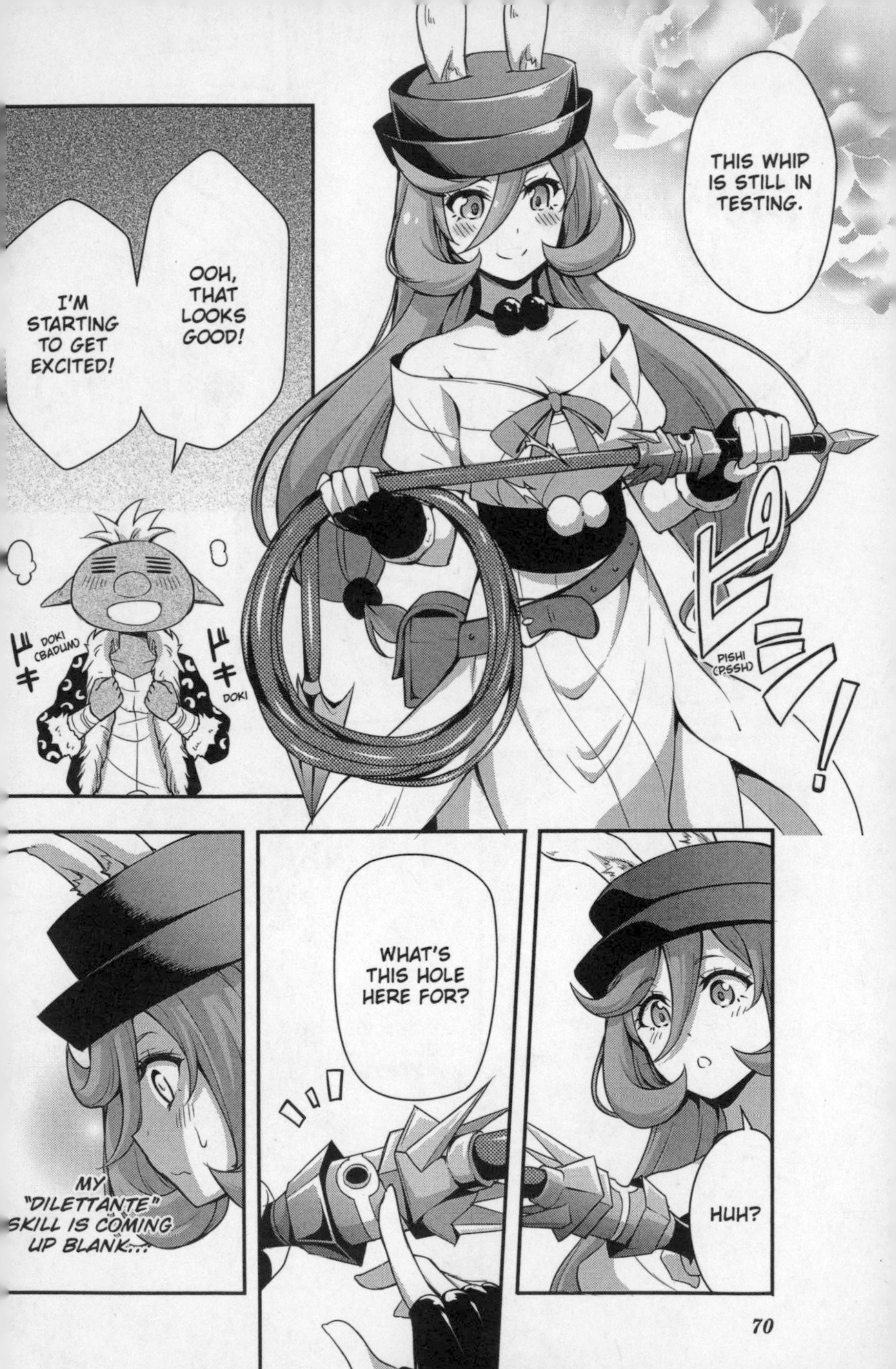
THIS WHIP IS STILL IN TESTING.
PISHI (P'SSH)
OOH, THAT LOOKS GOOD!
I'M STARTING TO GET EXCITED!
DOKI (BADUM)
DOKI
HUH?
WHAT'S THIS HOLE HERE FOR?
MY "DILETTANTE" SKILL IS COMING UP BLANK...

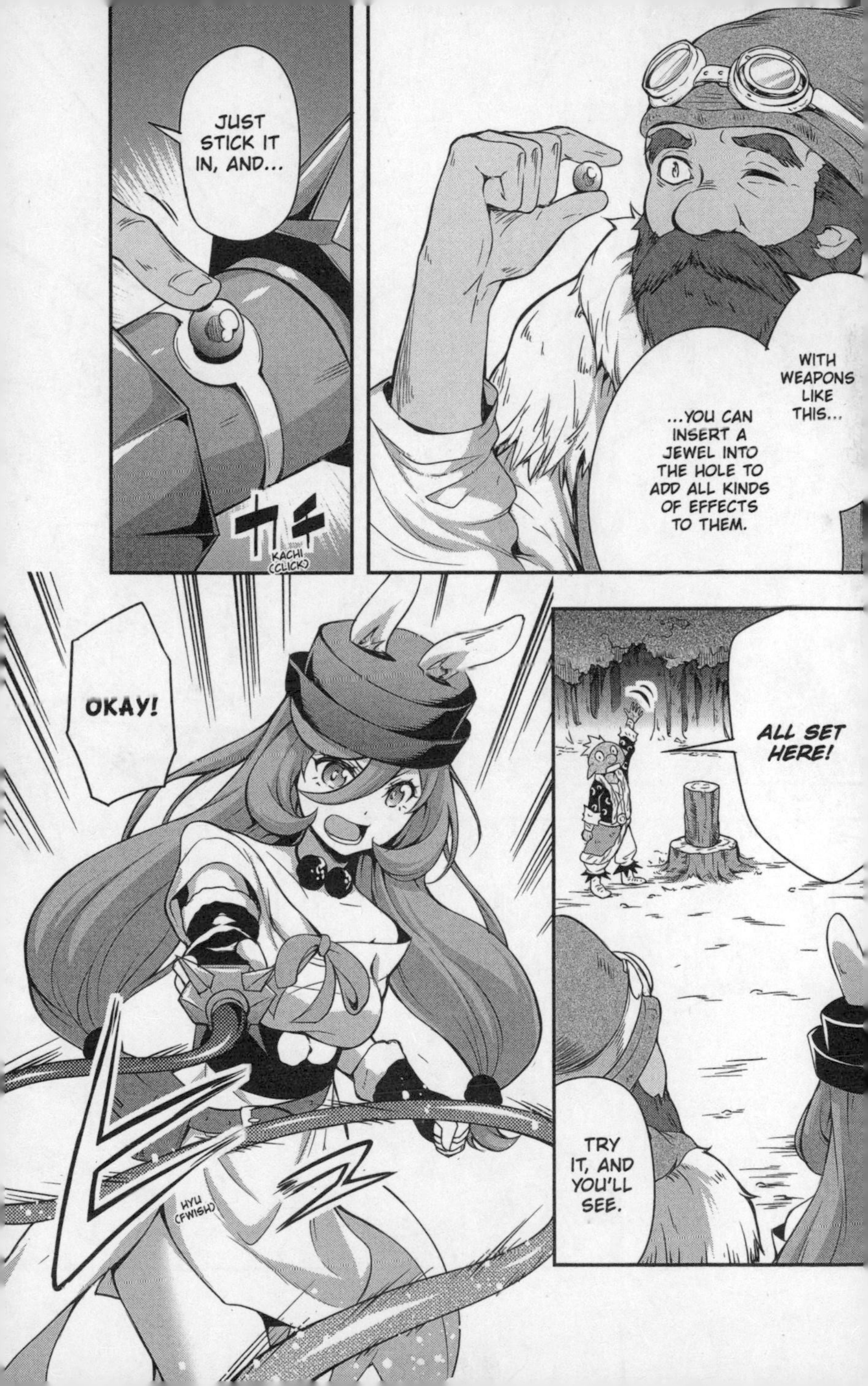
WITH WEAPONS LIKE THIS...
...YOU CAN INSERT A JEWEL INTO THE HOLE TO ADD ALL KINDS OF EFFECTS TO THEM.
JUST STICK IT IN, AND...
KACHI (CLICK)
ALL SET HERE!
TRY IT, AND YOU'LL SEE.
OKAY!
HYU (FWISH)

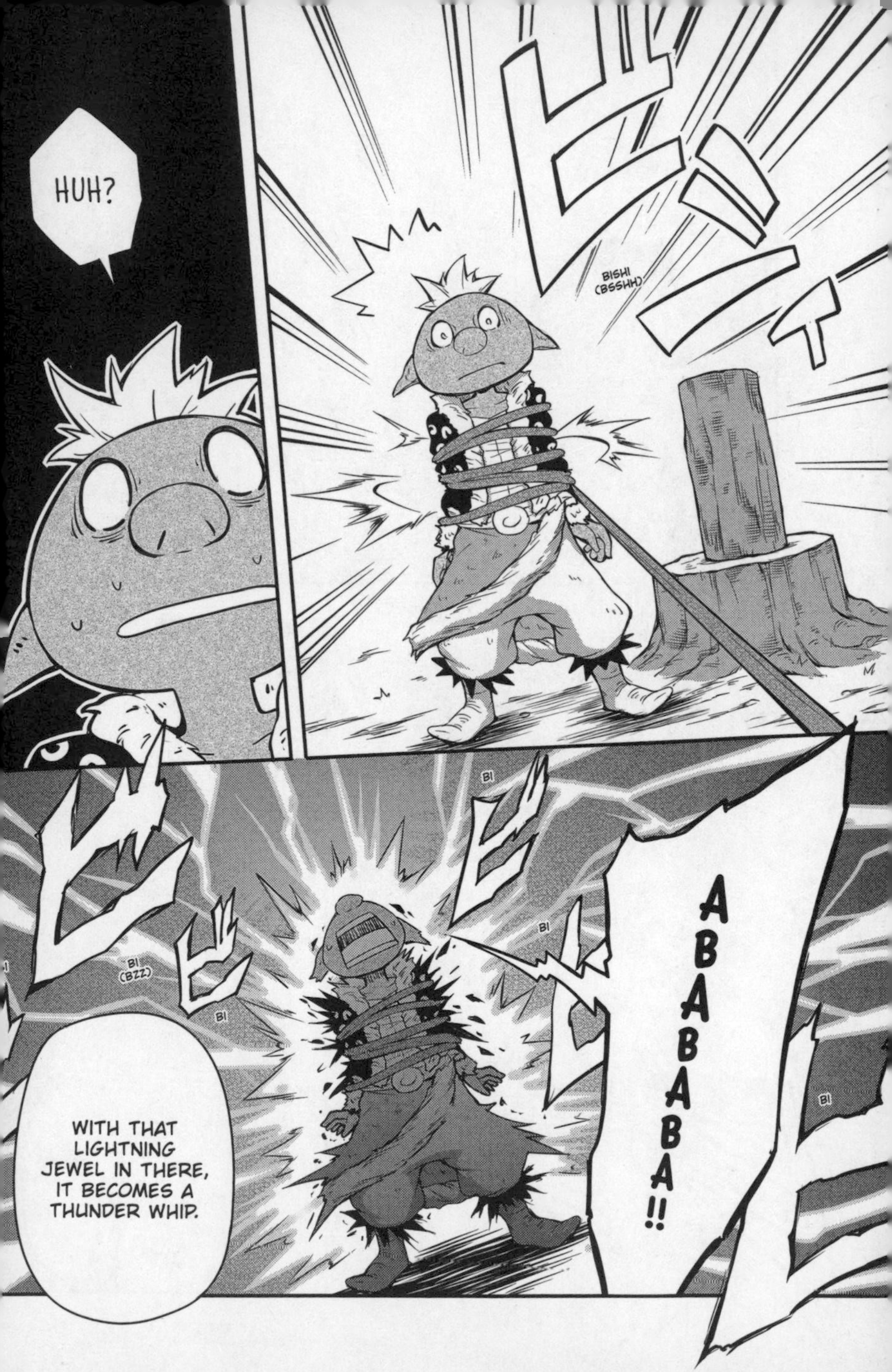
BISHI (BSSHH)
HUH?
BI
ABABABA!!
BI
BI
BI (BZZ)
BI
WITH THAT LIGHTNING JEWEL IN THERE, IT BECOMES A THUNDER WHIP.

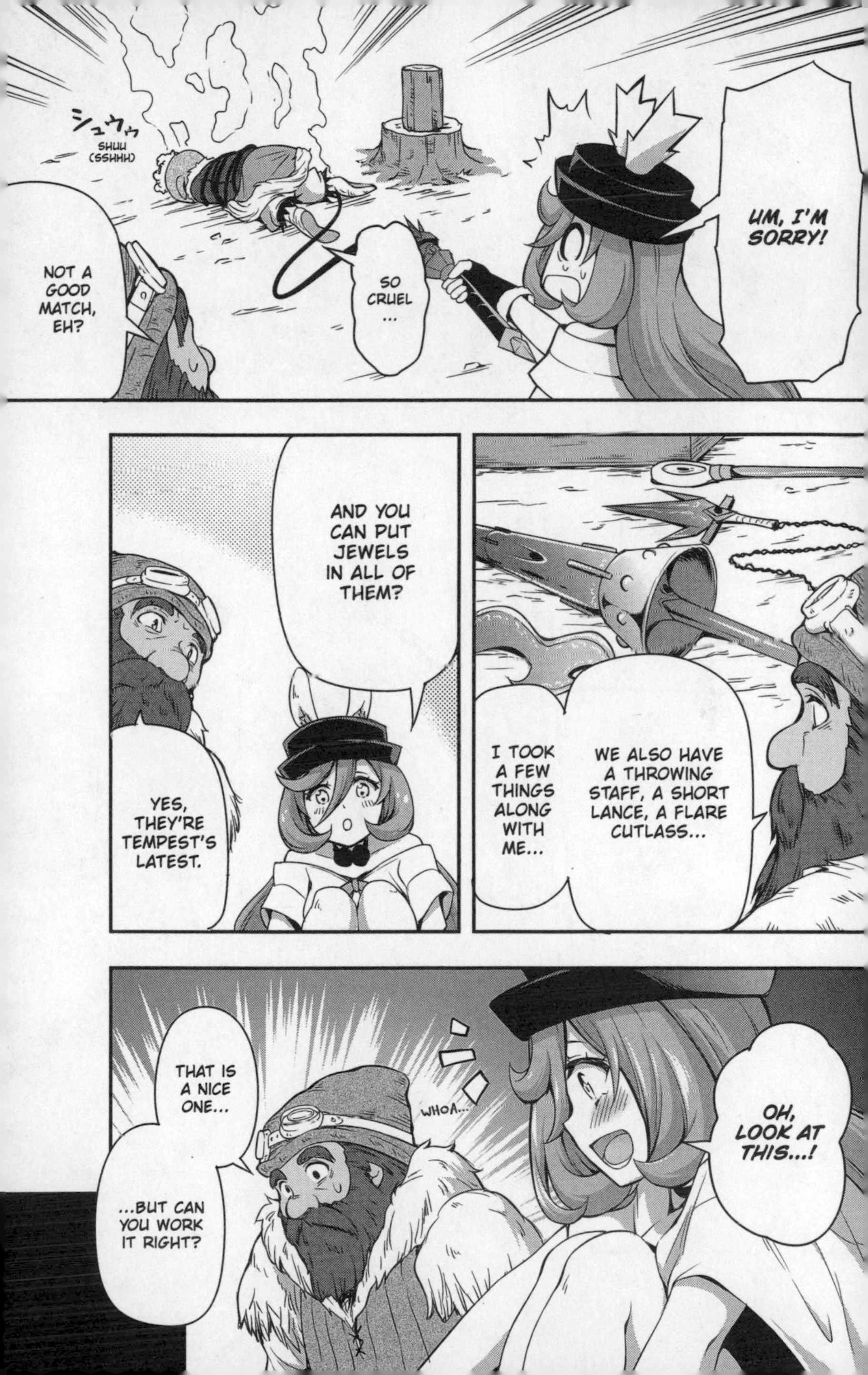
UM, I'M SORRY!
SO CRUEL ...
シュウゥ
SHUU (SSHHH)
NOT A GOOD MATCH, EH?
WE ALSO HAVE A THROWING STAFF, A SHORT LANCE, A FLARE CUTLASS...
I TOOK A FEW THINGS ALONG WITH ME...
AND YOU CAN PUT JEWELS IN ALL OF THEM?
YES, THEY'RE TEMPEST'S LATEST.
OH, LOOK AT THIS...!
WHOA...
THAT IS A NICE ONE...
...BUT CAN YOU WORK IT RIGHT?

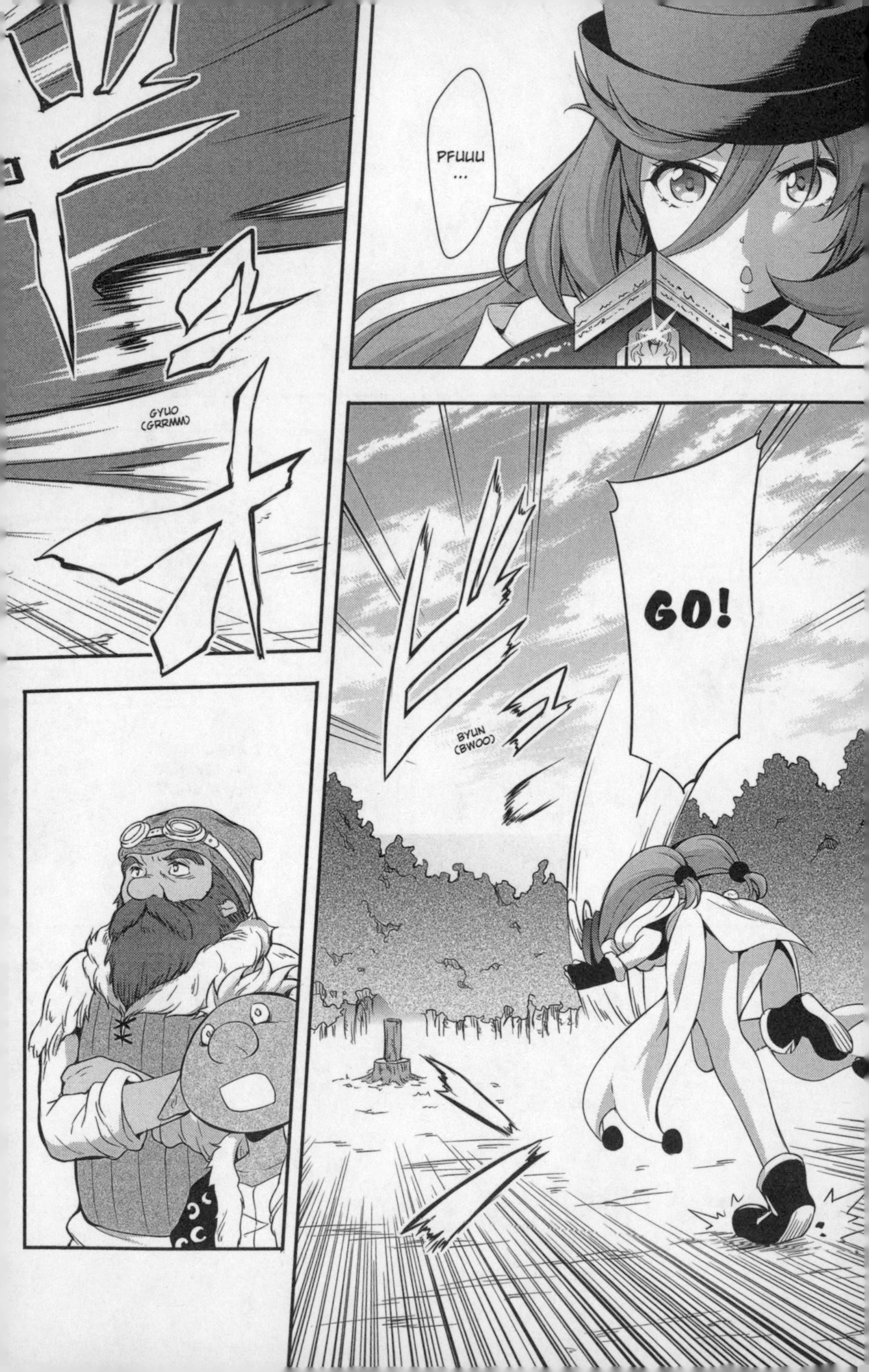
PFUUU
...
GYUO
(GRRMM)
GO!
BYUN
(BWOO)

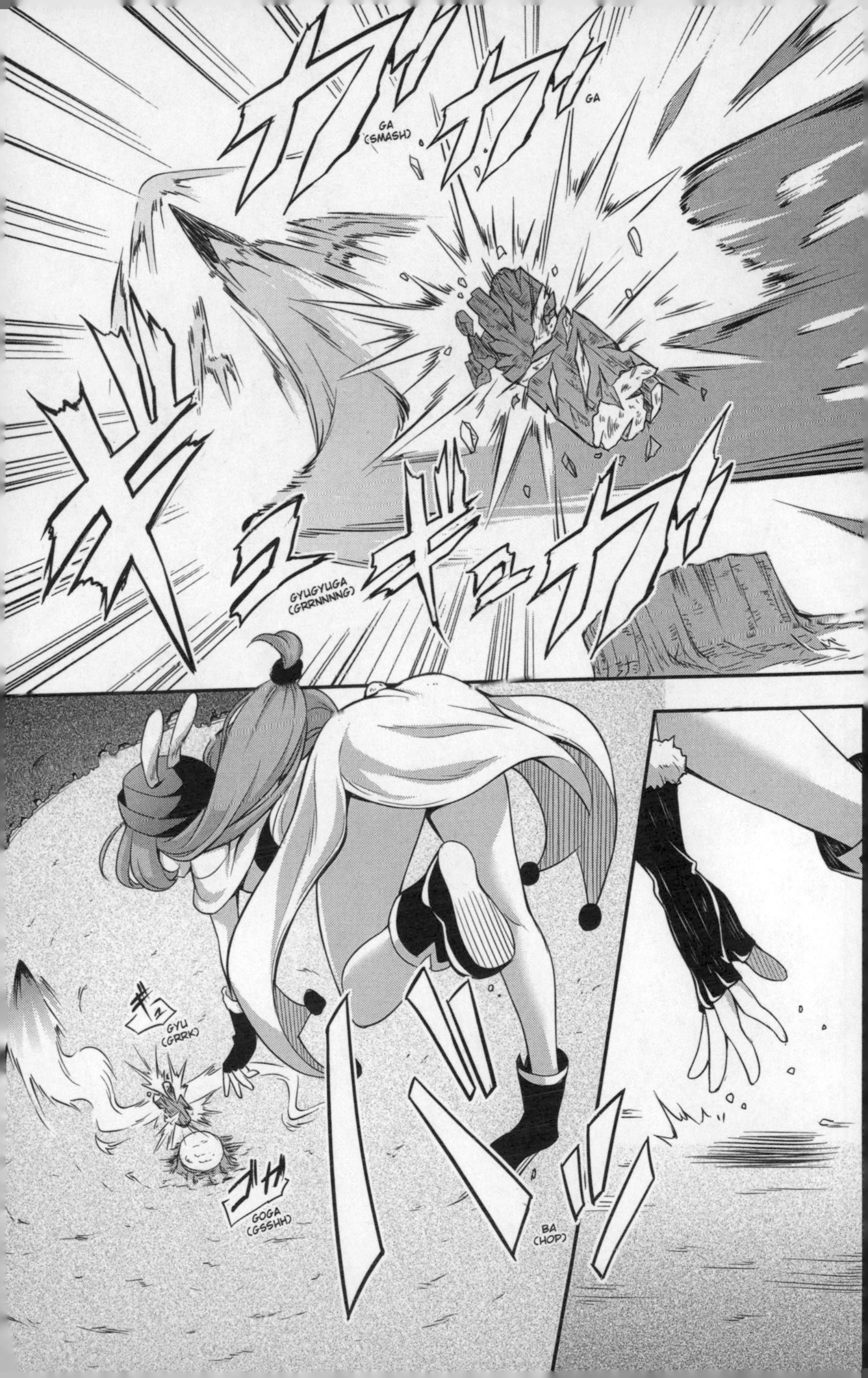
GA
GA
(SMASH)
GYUGYUGA
(GRRNNNNG)
BA
(HOP)
GYU
(GRRK)
GOGA
(GSSHH)

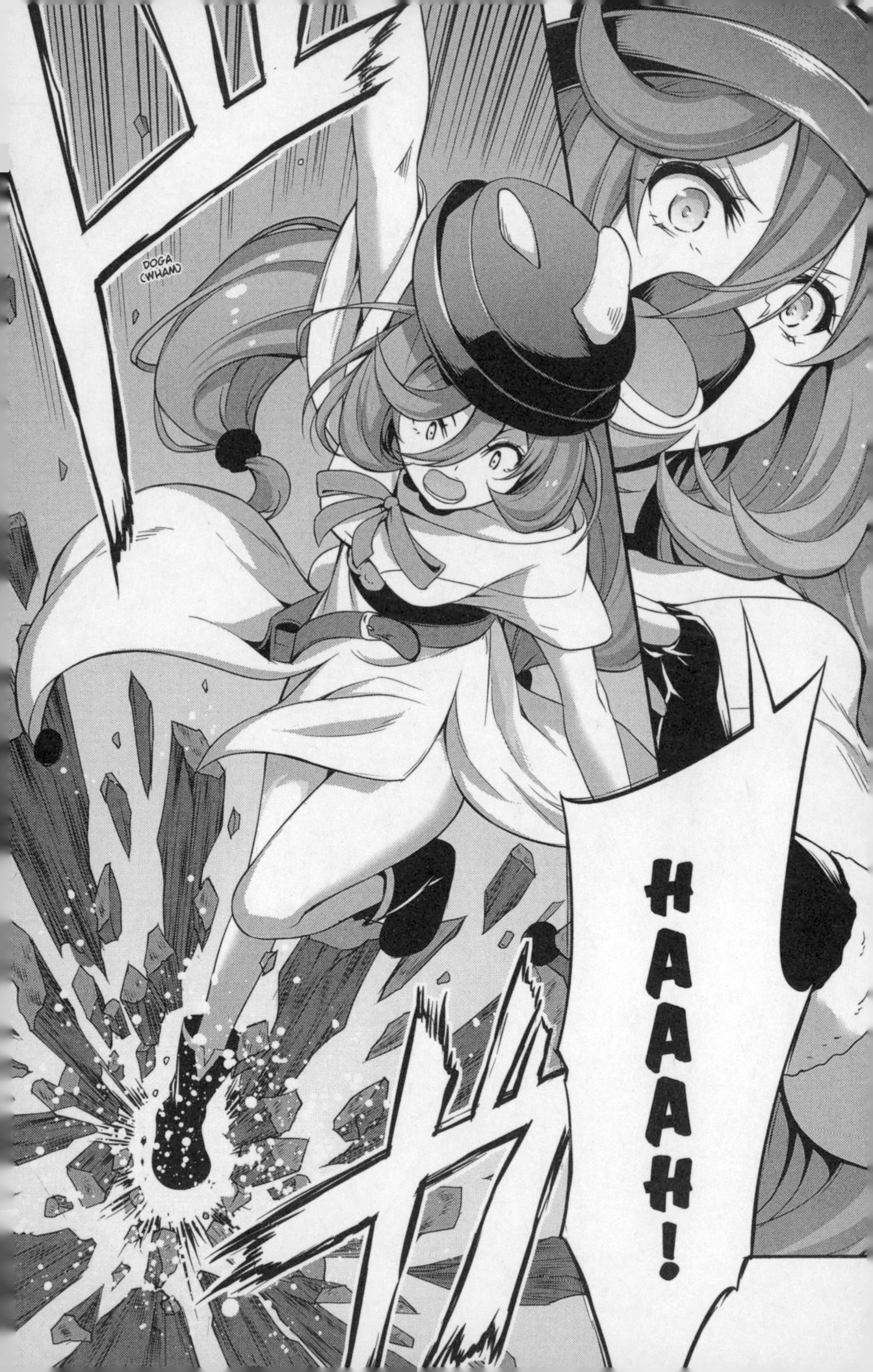
DOGA (WHAM)
HAAAAH!

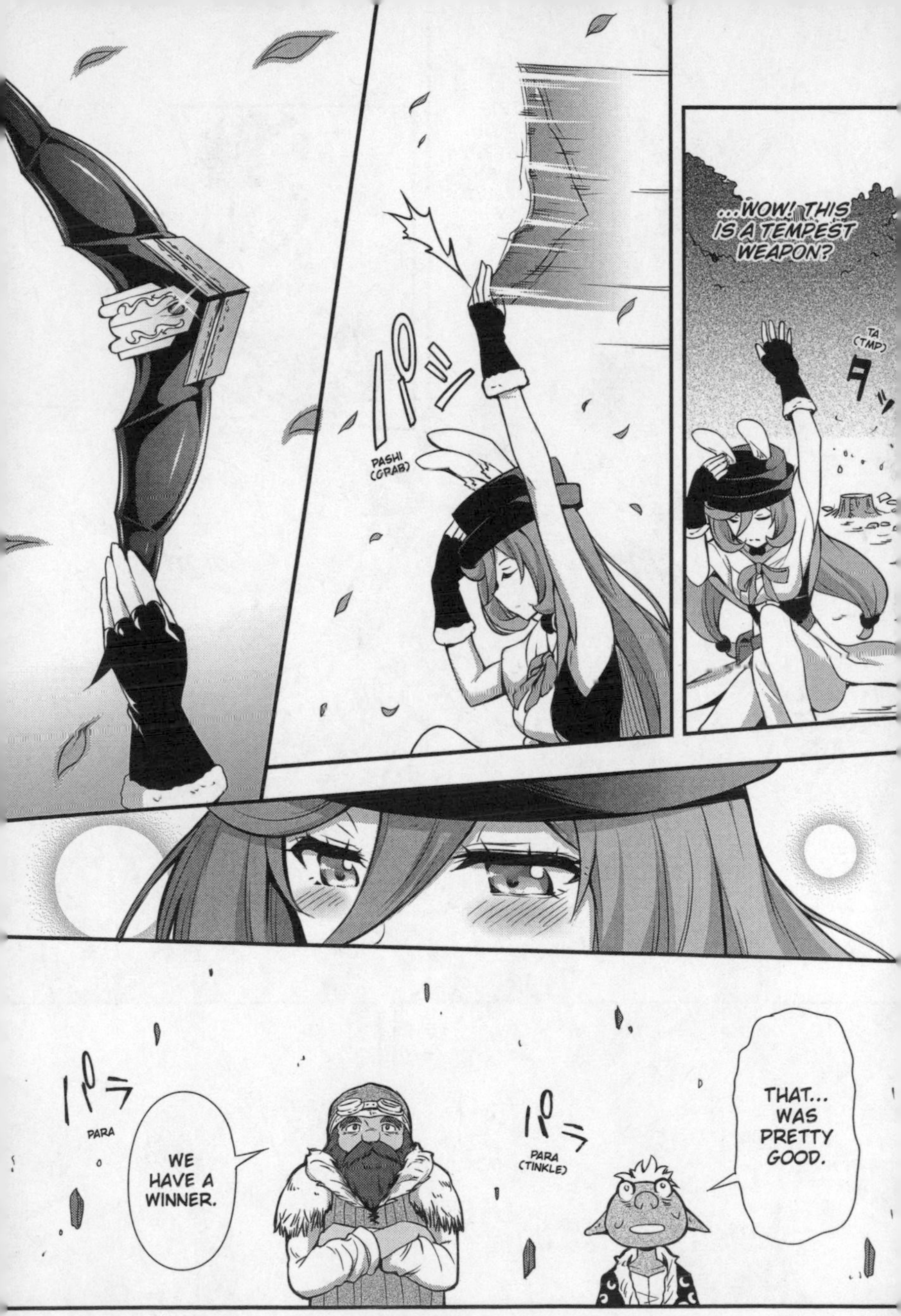
...WOW! THIS IS A TEMPEST WEAPON?
TA (TMP)
PASHI (GRAB)
THAT... WAS PRETTY GOOD.
PARA (TINKLE)
WE HAVE A WINNER.
PARA

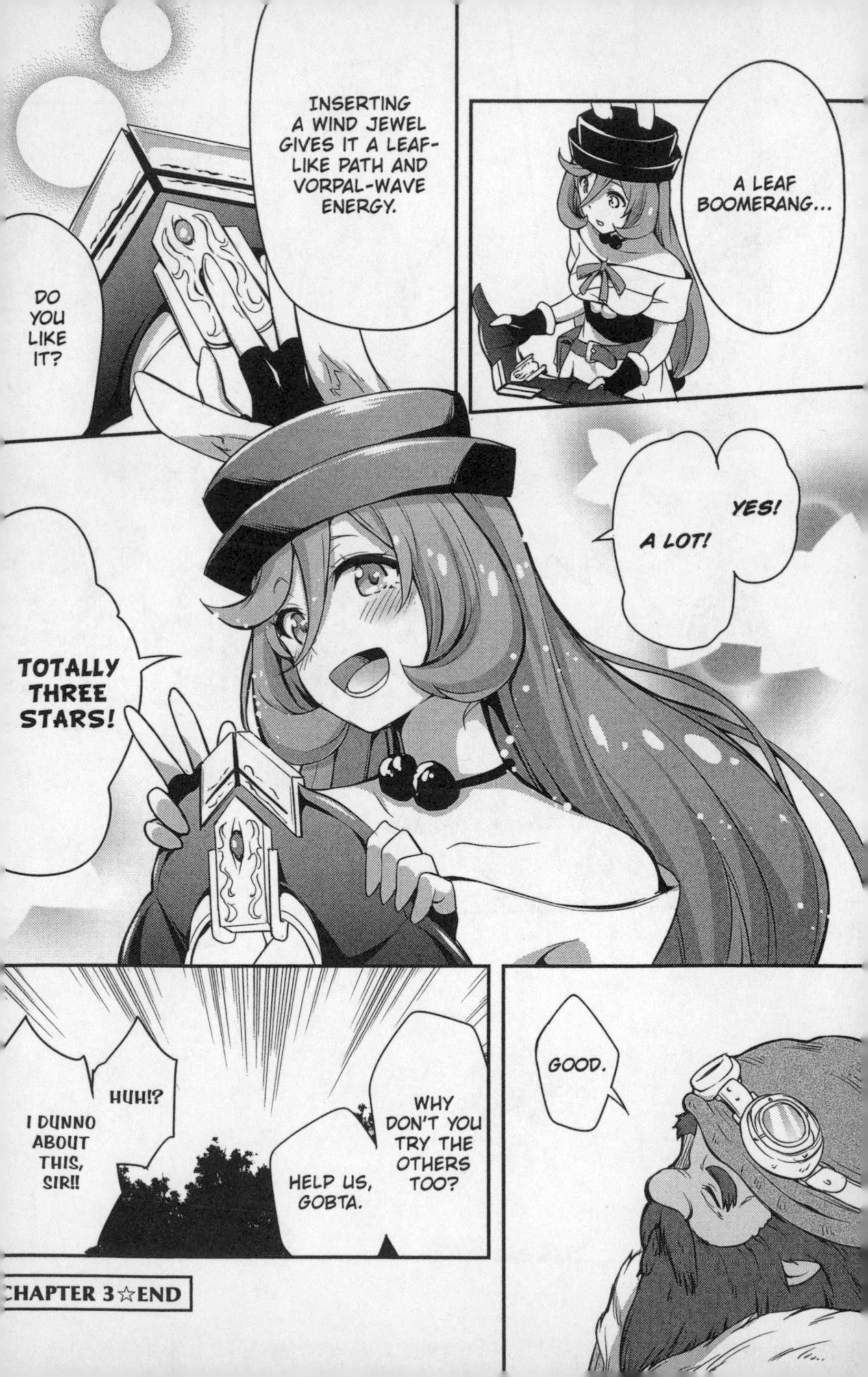
A LEAF BOOMERANG...
INSERTING A WIND JEWEL GIVES IT A LEAF-LIKE PATH AND VORPAL-WAVE ENERGY.
DO YOU LIKE IT?
YES! A LOT!
TOTALLY THREE STARS!
GOOD.
WHY DON'T YOU TRY THE OTHERS TOO?
HELP US, GOBTA.
HUH!?
I DUNNO ABOUT THIS, SIR!!
CHAPTER 3☆END

CHAPTER 4

HIGHWAY WAGON TRIP ☆ THREE STARS!!

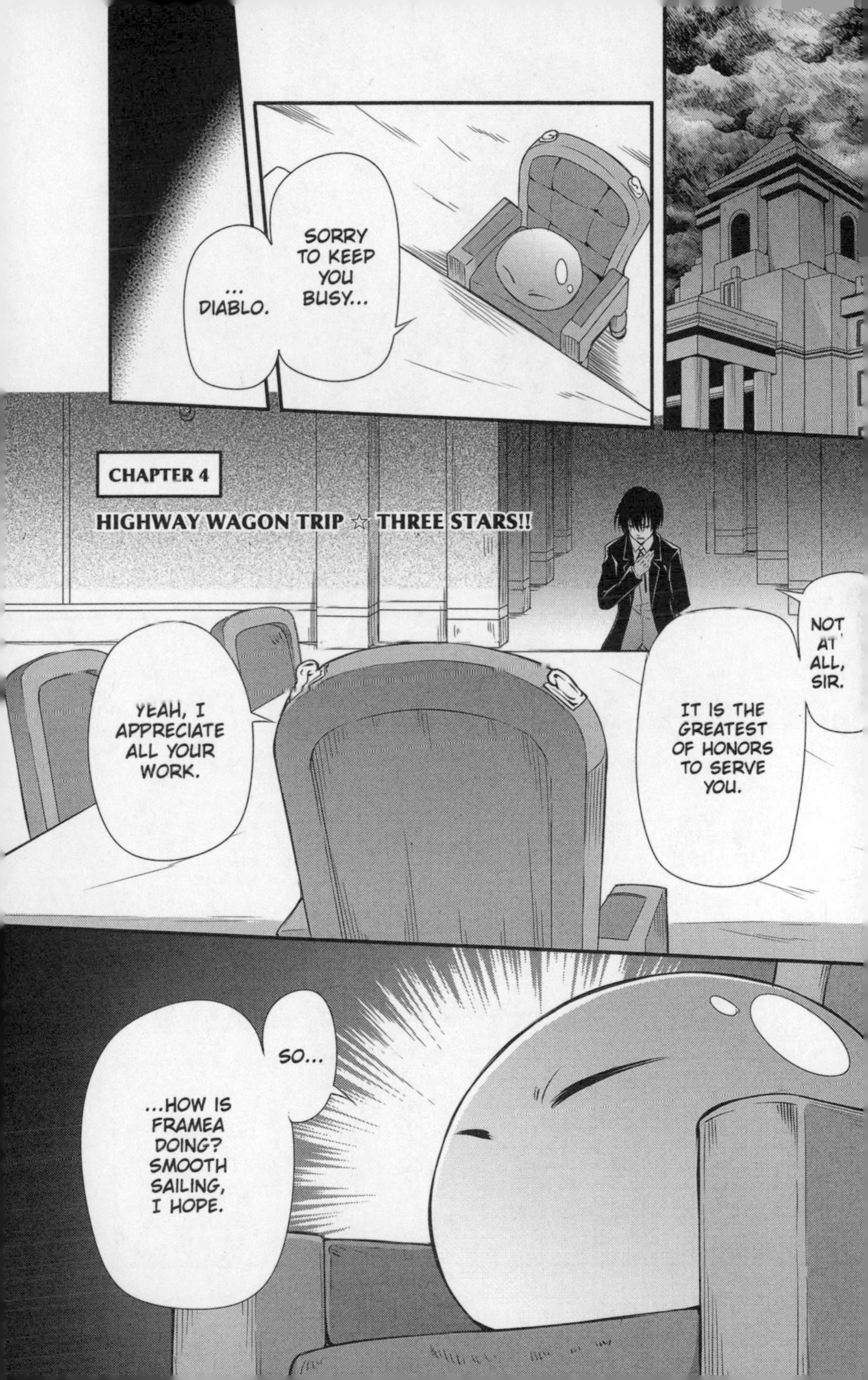
SORRY TO KEEP YOU BUSY...
... DIABLO.
NOT AT ALL, SIR.
IT IS THE GREATEST OF HONORS TO SERVE YOU.
YEAH, I APPRECIATE ALL YOUR WORK.
SO...
...HOW IS FRAMEA DOING? SMOOTH SAILING, I HOPE.

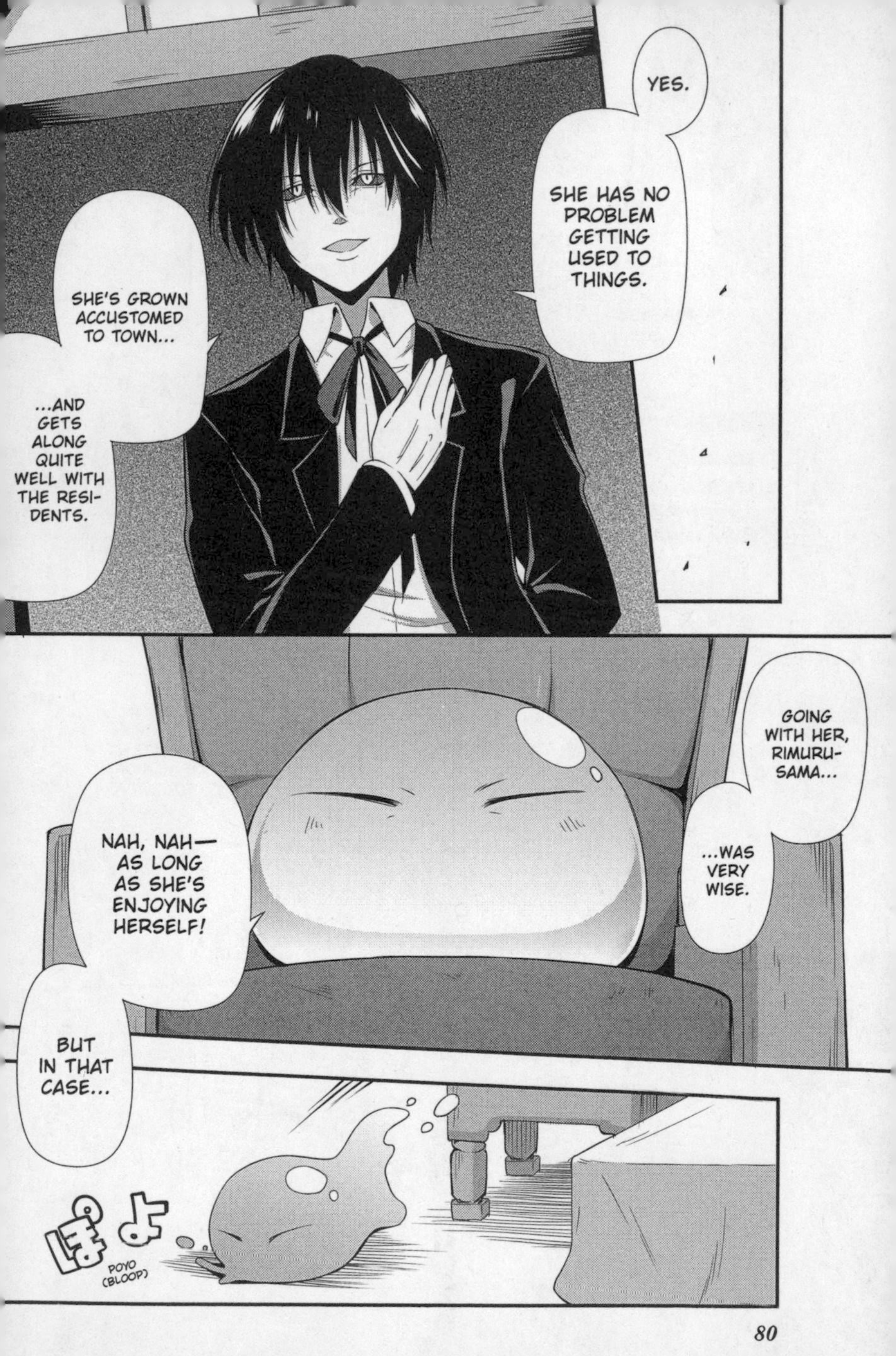
YES.
SHE HAS NO PROBLEM GETTING USED TO THINGS.
SHE'S GROWN ACCUSTOMED TO TOWN...
...AND GETS ALONG QUITE WELL WITH THE RESI-DENTS.
GOING WITH HER, RIMURU-SAMA...
...WAS VERY WISE.
NAH, NAH— AS LONG AS SHE'S ENJOYING HERSELF!
BUT IN THAT CASE...
ぽよ
POYO (BLOOP)

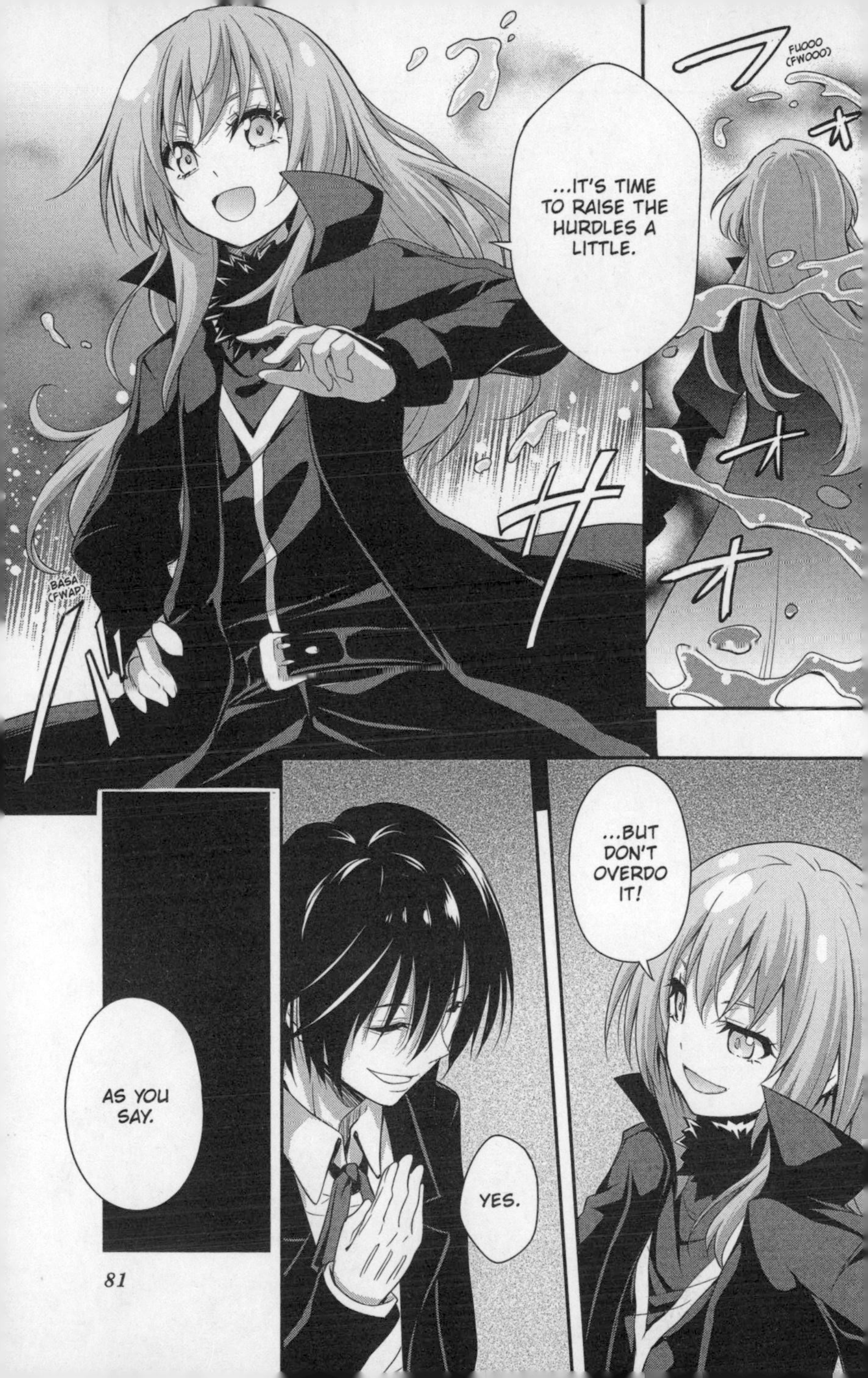
FUOOO
(FWOOO)
...IT'S TIME TO RAISE THE HURDLES A LITTLE.
BASA
(FWAP)
...BUT DON'T OVERDO IT!
YES.
AS YOU SAY.

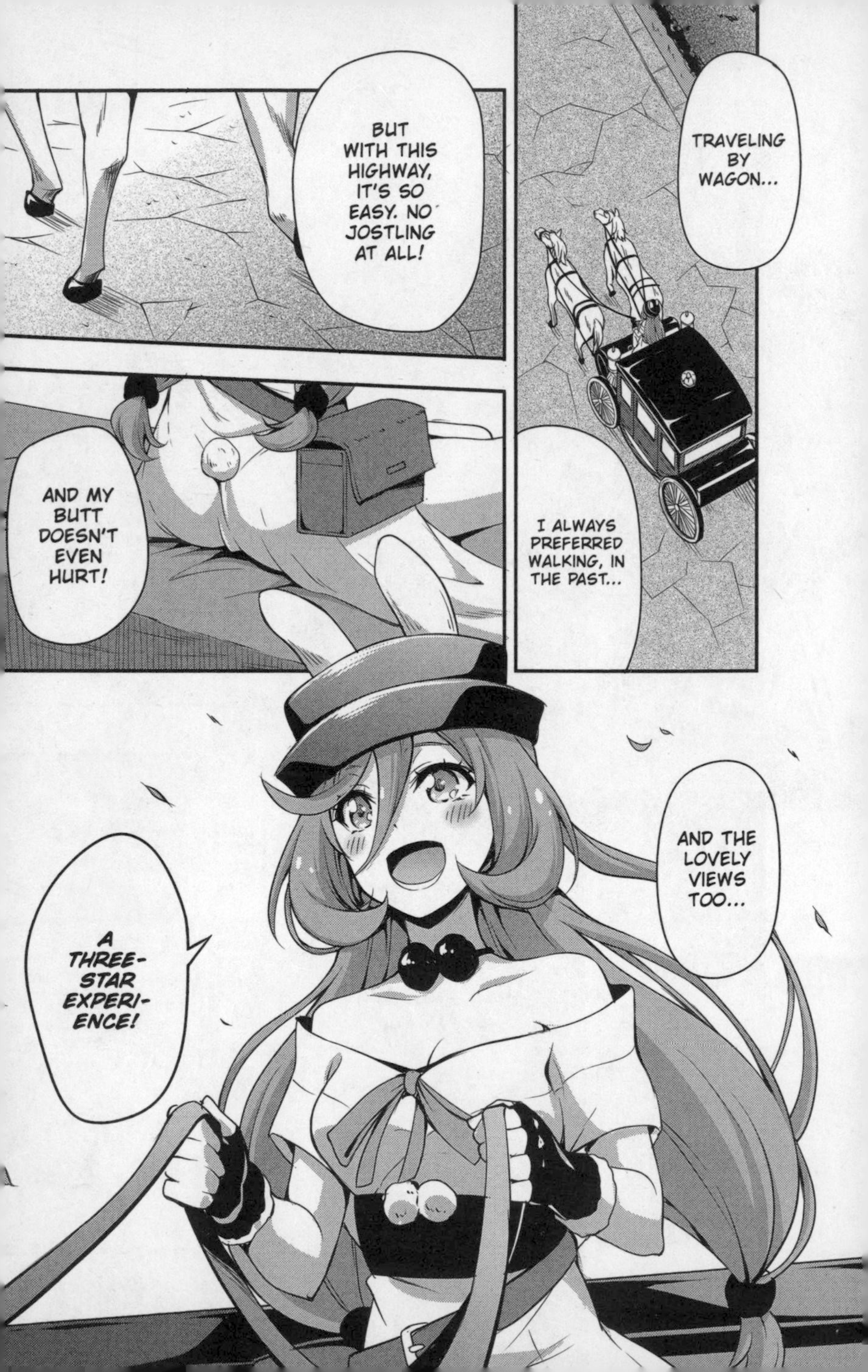
TRAVELING BY WAGON...
I ALWAYS PREFERRED WALKING, IN THE PAST...
BUT WITH THIS HIGHWAY, IT'S SO EASY. NO JOSTLING AT ALL!
AND MY BUTT DOESN'T EVEN HURT!
AND THE LOVELY VIEWS TOO...
A THREE-STAR EXPERIENCE!

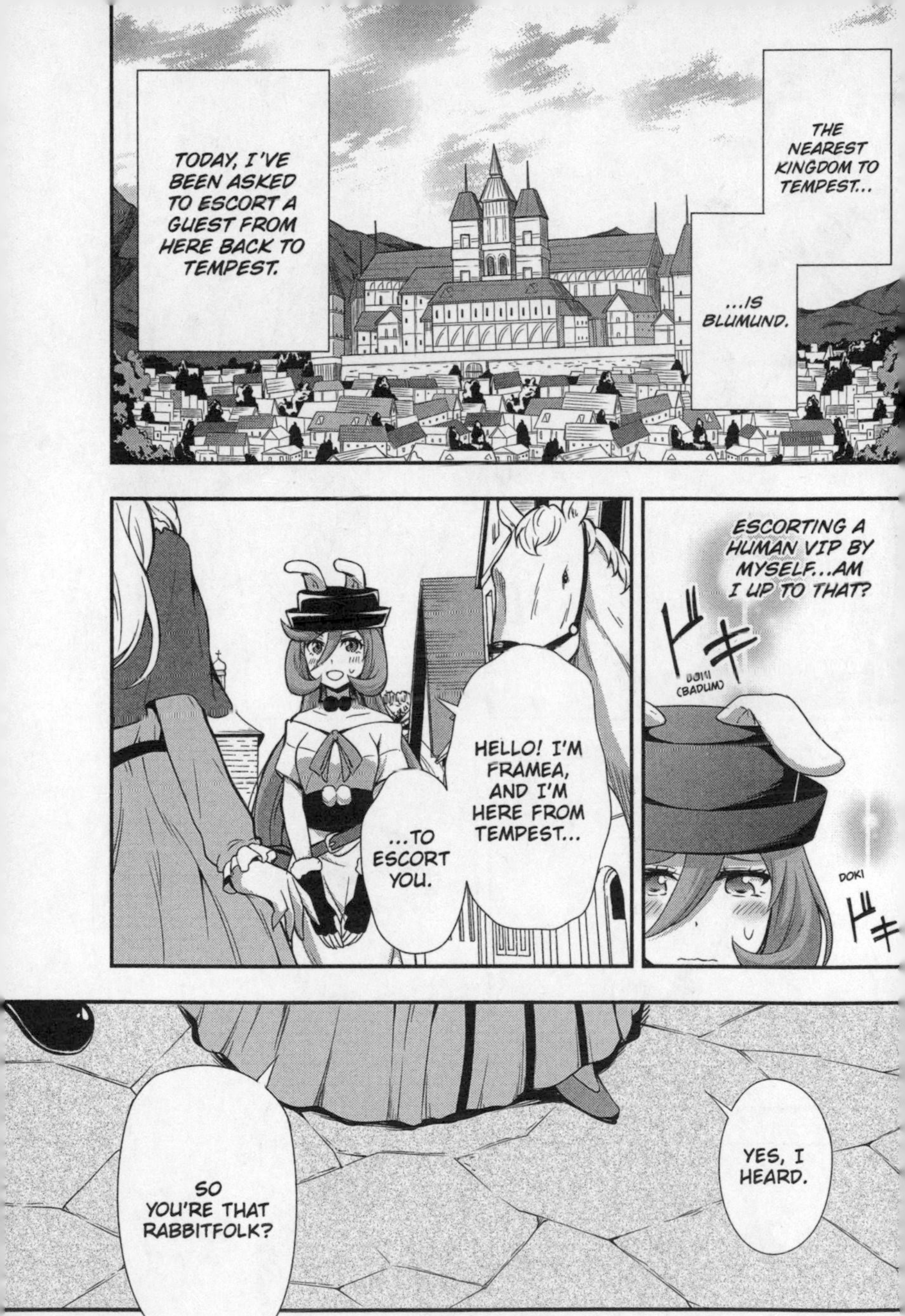
THE NEAREST KINGDOM TO TEMPEST...
...IS BLUMUND.
TODAY, I'VE BEEN ASKED TO ESCORT A GUEST FROM HERE BACK TO TEMPEST.
ESCORTING A HUMAN VIP BY MYSELF...AM I UP TO THAT?
DOKI (BADUM)
DOKI
HELLO! I'M FRAMEA, AND I'M HERE FROM TEMPEST...
...TO ESCORT YOU.
YES, I HEARD.
SO YOU'RE THAT RABBITFOLK?

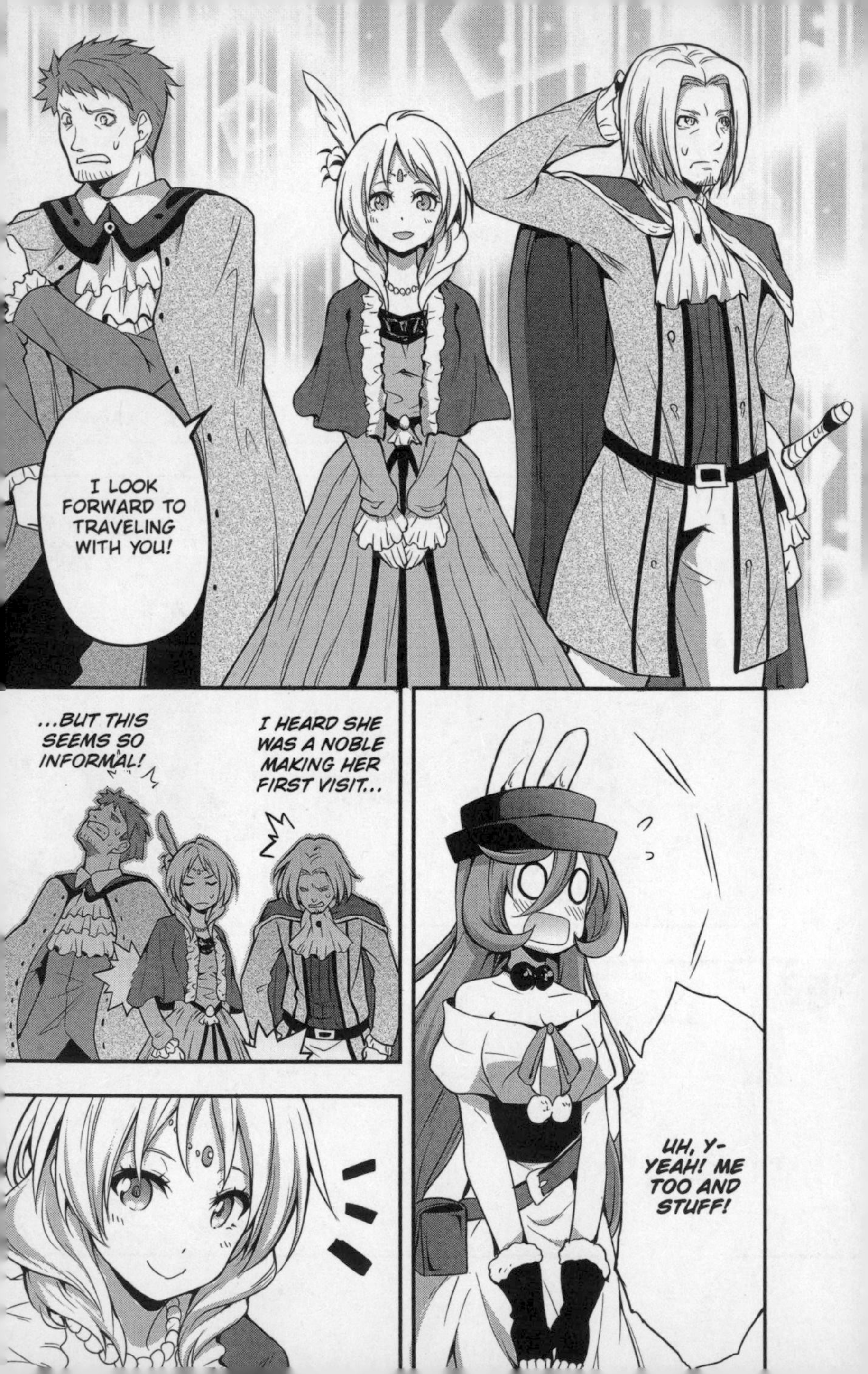
I LOOK FORWARD TO TRAVELING WITH YOU!
UH, Y-YEAH! ME TOO AND STUFF!
I HEARD SHE WAS A NOBLE MAKING HER FIRST VISIT...
...BUT THIS SEEMS SO INFORMAL!

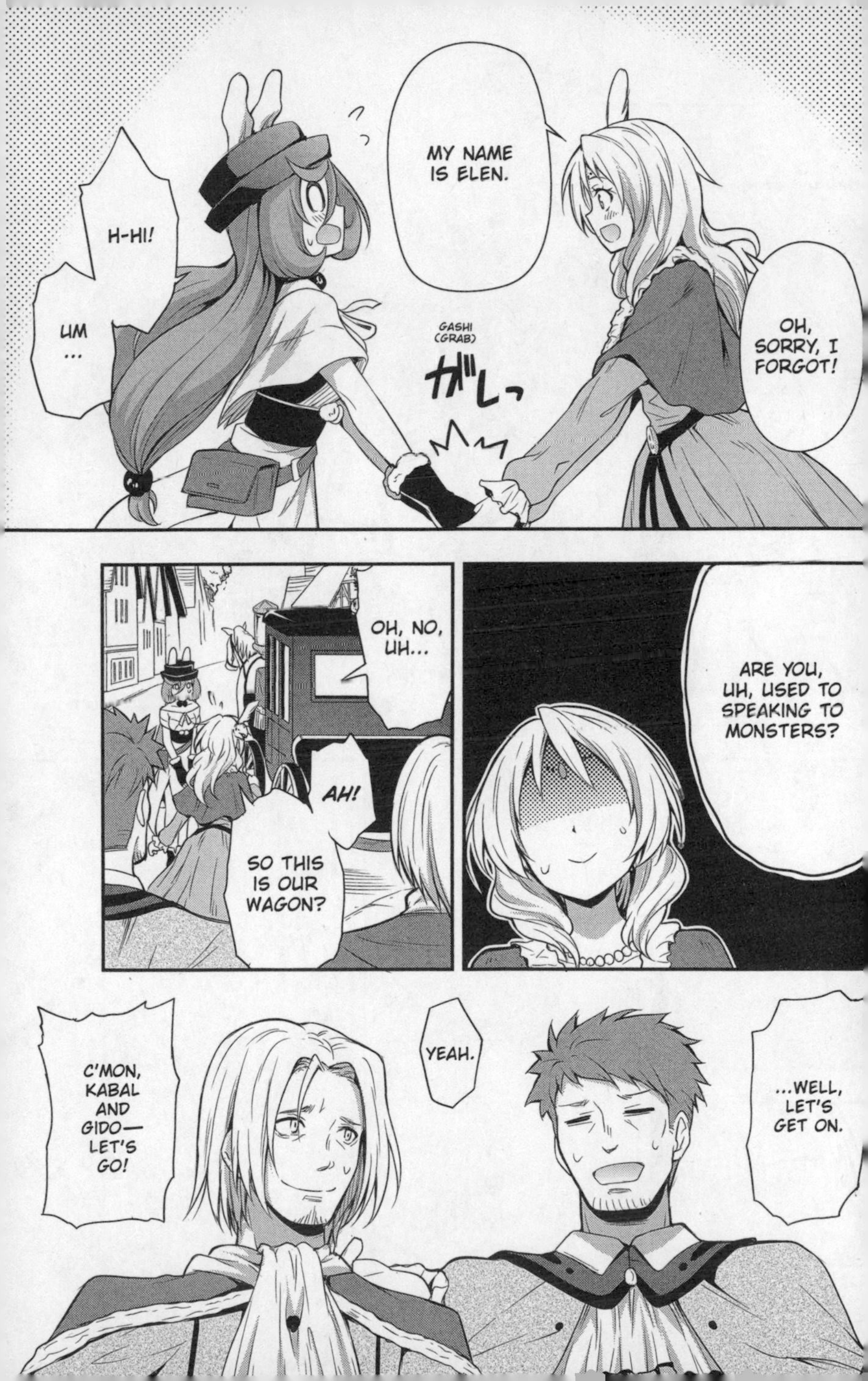
OH, SORRY, I FORGOT!
MY NAME IS ELEN.
GASHI (GRAB)
ガしっ
UM ...
H-HI!
ARE YOU, UH, USED TO SPEAKING TO MONSTERS?
OH, NO, UH...
AH!
SO THIS IS OUR WAGON?
...WELL, LET'S GET ON.
YEAH.
C'MON, KABAL AND GIDO—LET'S GO!

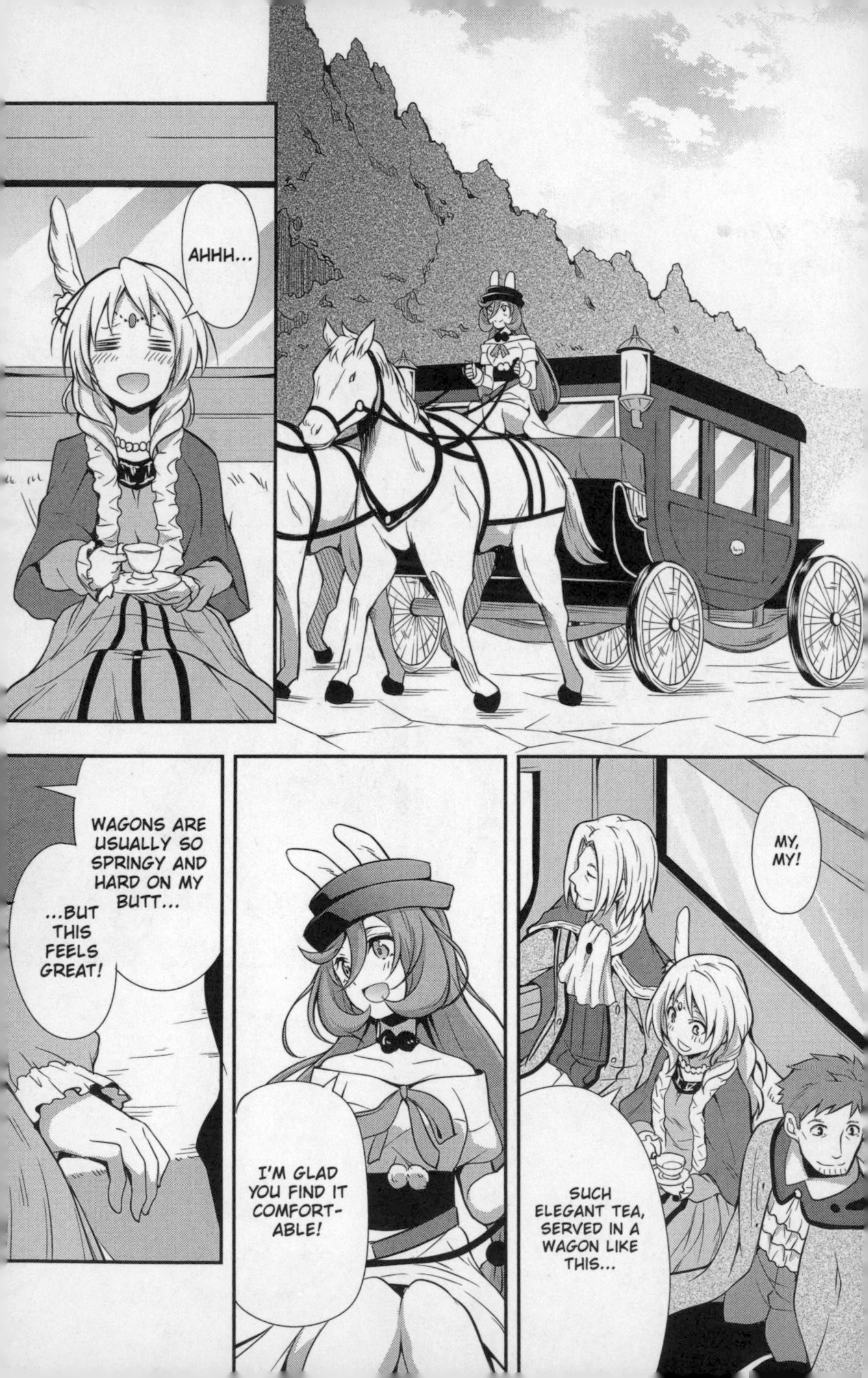
AHHH...
MY, MY!
SUCH ELEGANT TEA, SERVED IN A WAGON LIKE THIS...
I'M GLAD YOU FIND IT COMFORT-ABLE!
WAGONS ARE USUALLY SO SPRINGY AND HARD ON MY BUTT...
...BUT THIS FEELS GREAT!

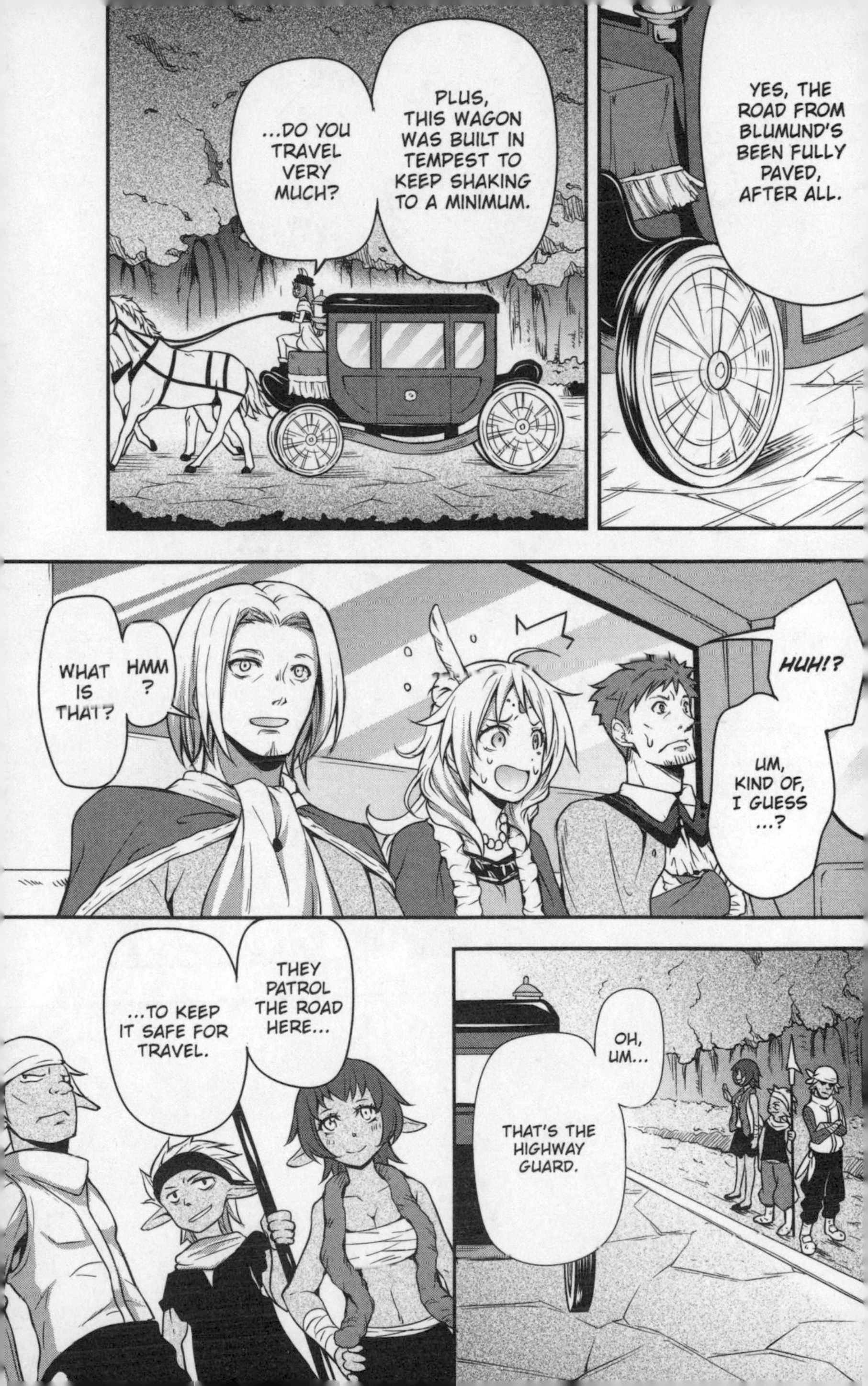
YES, THE ROAD FROM BLUMUND'S BEEN FULLY PAVED, AFTER ALL.
PLUS, THIS WAGON WAS BUILT IN TEMPEST TO KEEP SHAKING TO A MINIMUM.
...DO YOU TRAVEL VERY MUCH?
HUH!?
UM, KIND OF, I GUESS ...?
HMM ?
WHAT IS THAT?
OH, UM...
THAT'S THE HIGHWAY GUARD.
THEY PATROL THE ROAD HERE...
...TO KEEP IT SAFE FOR TRAVEL.

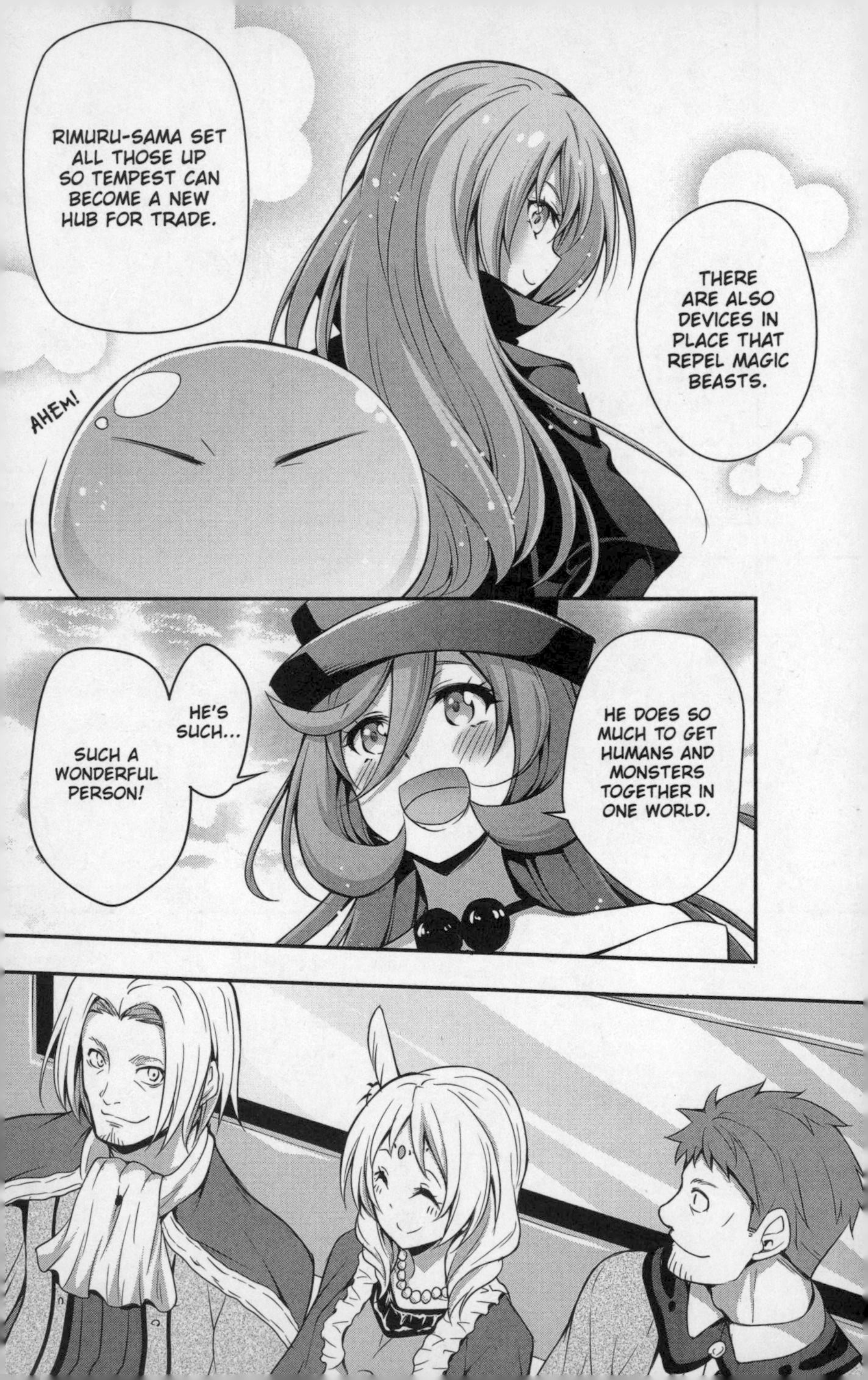
THERE ARE ALSO DEVICES IN PLACE THAT REPEL MAGIC BEASTS.
RIMURU-SAMA SET ALL THOSE UP SO TEMPEST CAN BECOME A NEW HUB FOR TRADE.
AHEM!
HE DOES SO MUCH TO GET HUMANS AND MONSTERS TOGETHER IN ONE WORLD.
HE'S SUCH...
SUCH A WONDERFUL PERSON!

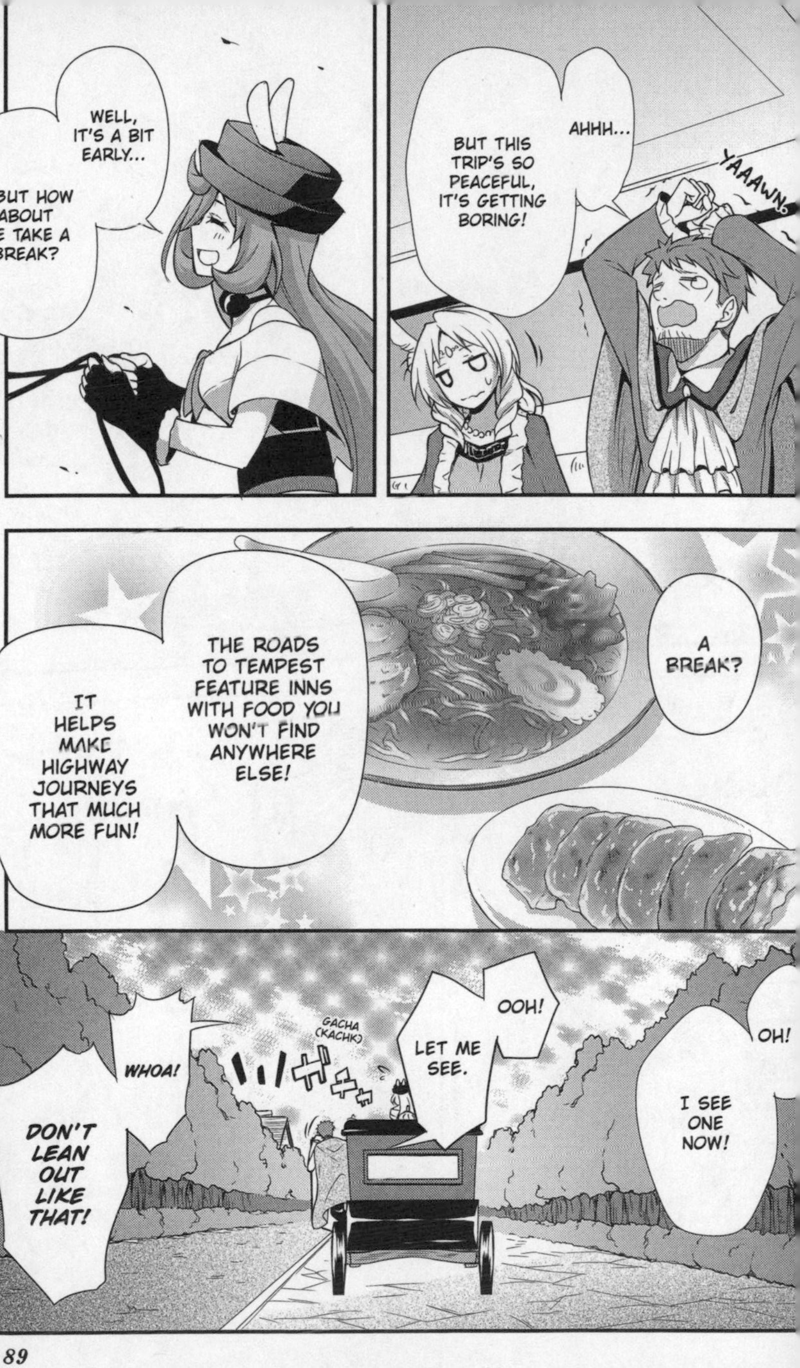
AHHH...
BUT THIS TRIP'S SO PEACEFUL, IT'S GETTING BORING!
YAAAWN
WELL, IT'S A BIT EARLY...
...BUT HOW ABOUT WE TAKE A BREAK?
A BREAK?
THE ROADS TO TEMPEST FEATURE INNS WITH FOOD YOU WON'T FIND ANYWHERE ELSE!
IT HELPS MAKE HIGHWAY JOURNEYS THAT MUCH MORE FUN!
OH!
I SEE ONE NOW!
OOH!
LET ME SEE.
GACHA (KACHK)
WHOA!
DON'T LEAN OUT LIKE THAT!

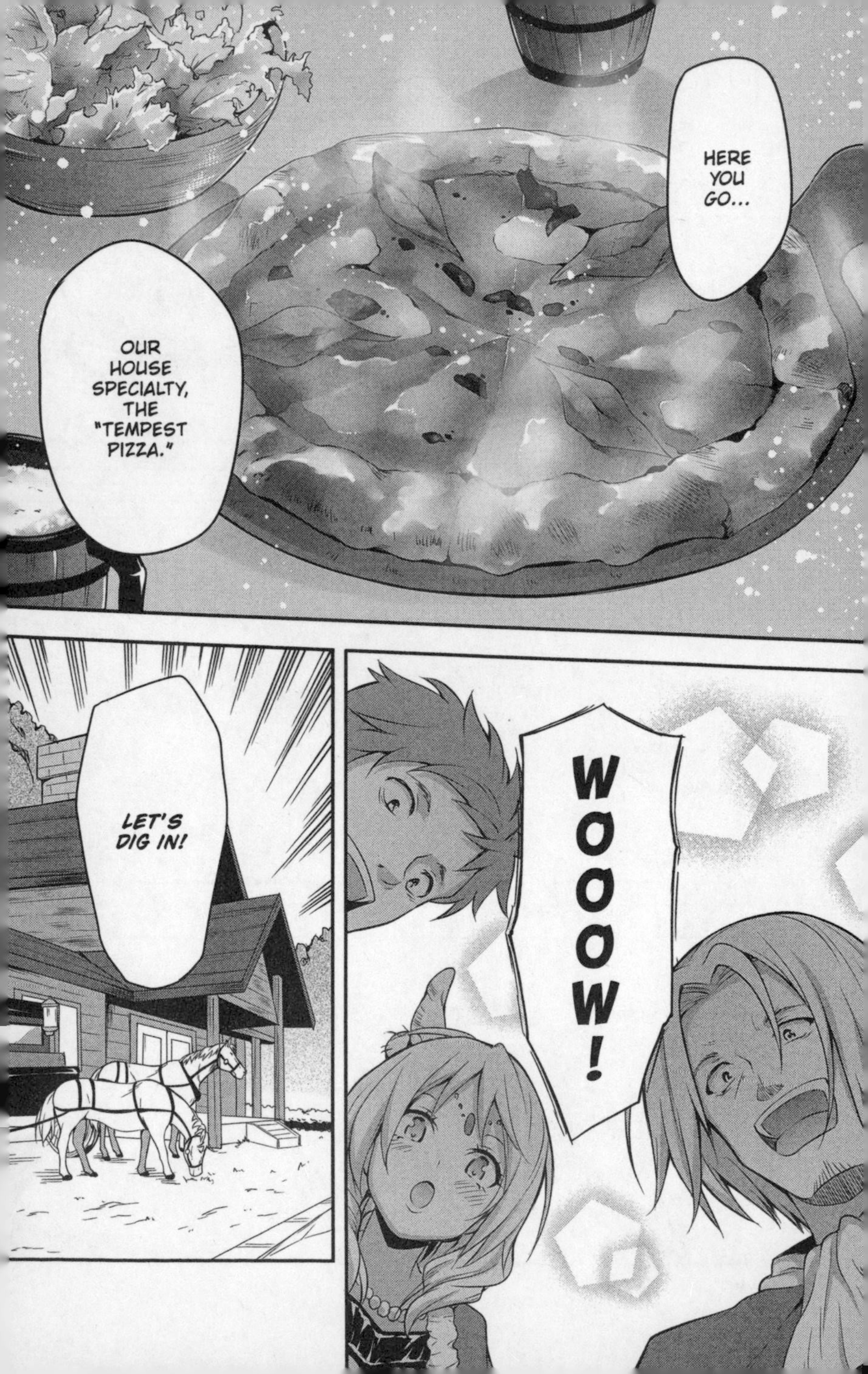
HERE YOU GO...
OUR HOUSE SPECIALTY, THE "TEMPEST PIZZA."
WOOOW!
LET'S DIG IN!

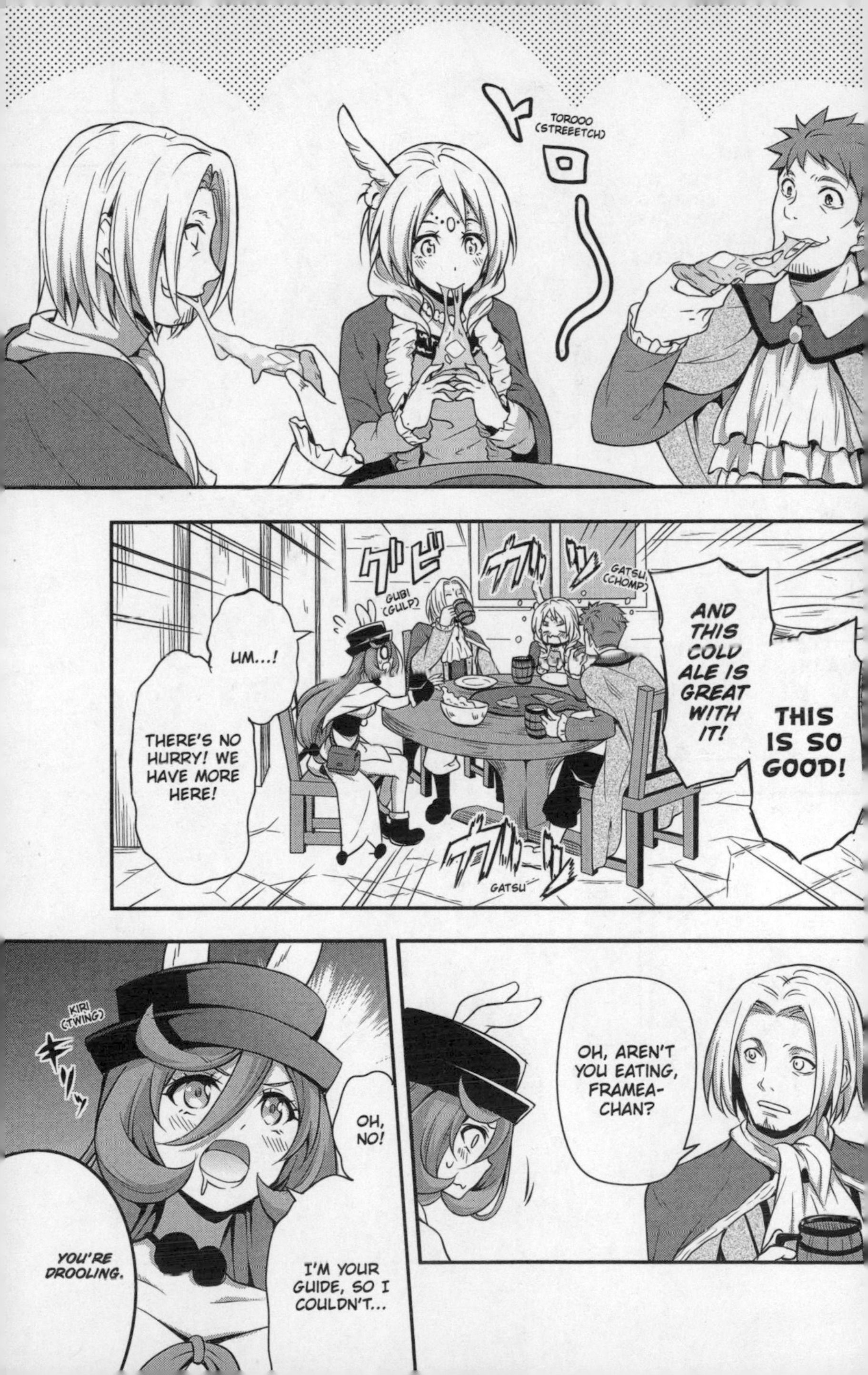

トロ
TOROOO (STREEETCH)
THIS IS SO GOOD!
AND THIS COLD ALE IS GREAT WITH IT!
ガツッ
GATSU (CHOMP)
グビ
GUBI (GULP)
UM...!
THERE'S NO HURRY! WE HAVE MORE HERE!
ガツッ
GATSU
OH, AREN'T YOU EATING, FRAMEA-CHAN?
キリッ
KIRI (TWING)
OH, NO!
I'M YOUR GUIDE, SO I COULDN'T...
YOU'RE DROOLING.

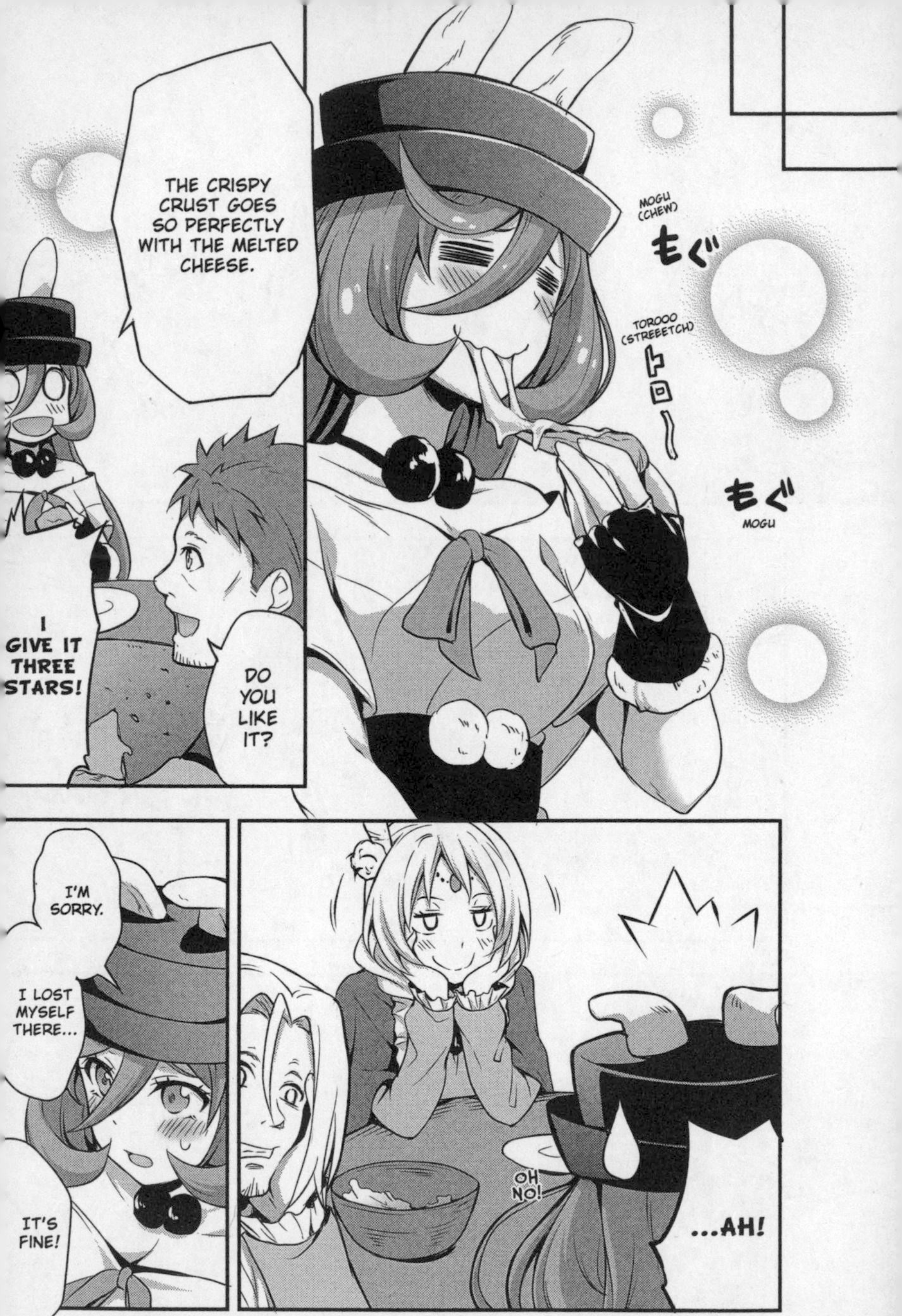
MOGU (CHEW)
もぐ
TOROOO (STREEETCH)
トロ〜
もぐ
MOGU
THE CRISPY CRUST GOES SO PERFECTLY WITH THE MELTED CHEESE.
DO YOU LIKE IT?
I GIVE IT THREE STARS!
...AH!
OH NO!
I'M SORRY.
I LOST MYSELF THERE...
IT'S FINE!

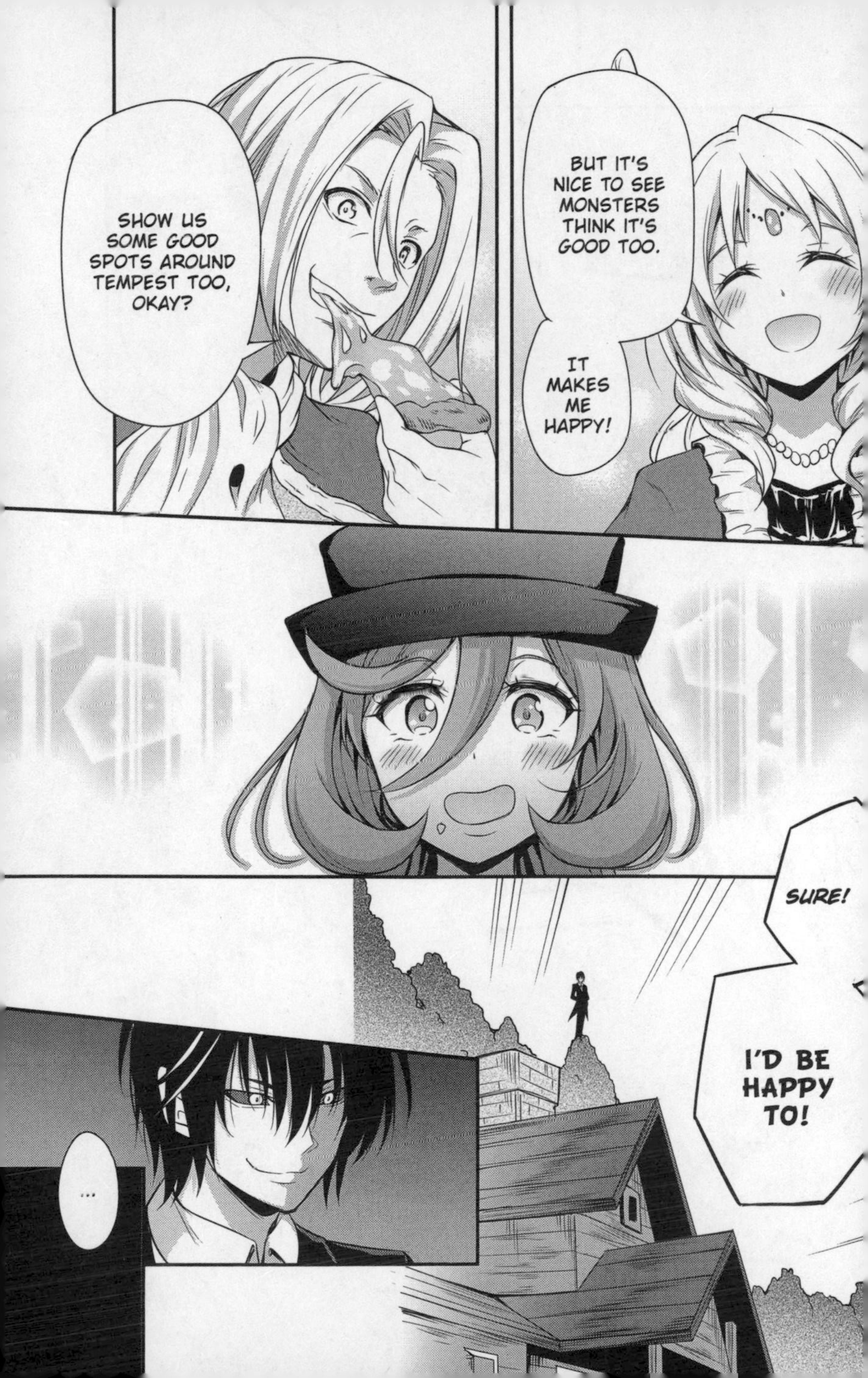
BUT IT'S NICE TO SEE MONSTERS THINK IT'S GOOD TOO.
IT MAKES ME HAPPY!
SHOW US SOME GOOD SPOTS AROUND TEMPEST TOO, OKAY?
SURE!
I'D BE HAPPY TO!
...

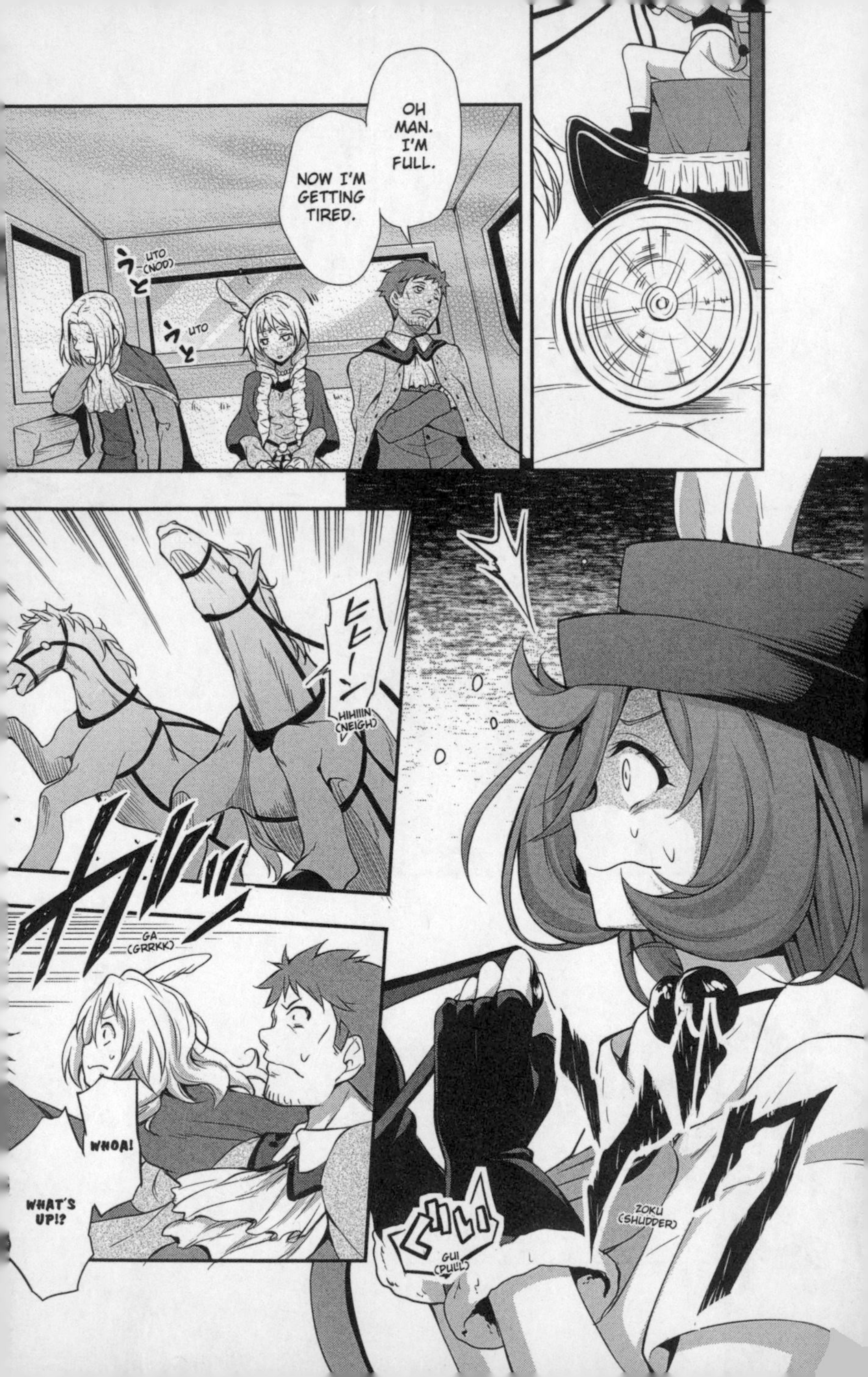
OH MAN. I'M FULL.
NOW I'M GETTING TIRED.
うと
UTO (NOD)
うと
UTO
ヒヒーン
HIHIIIN (NEIGH)
GA (GRRKK)
WHOA!
WHAT'S UP!?
ZOKU (SHUDDER)
GUI (PULL)

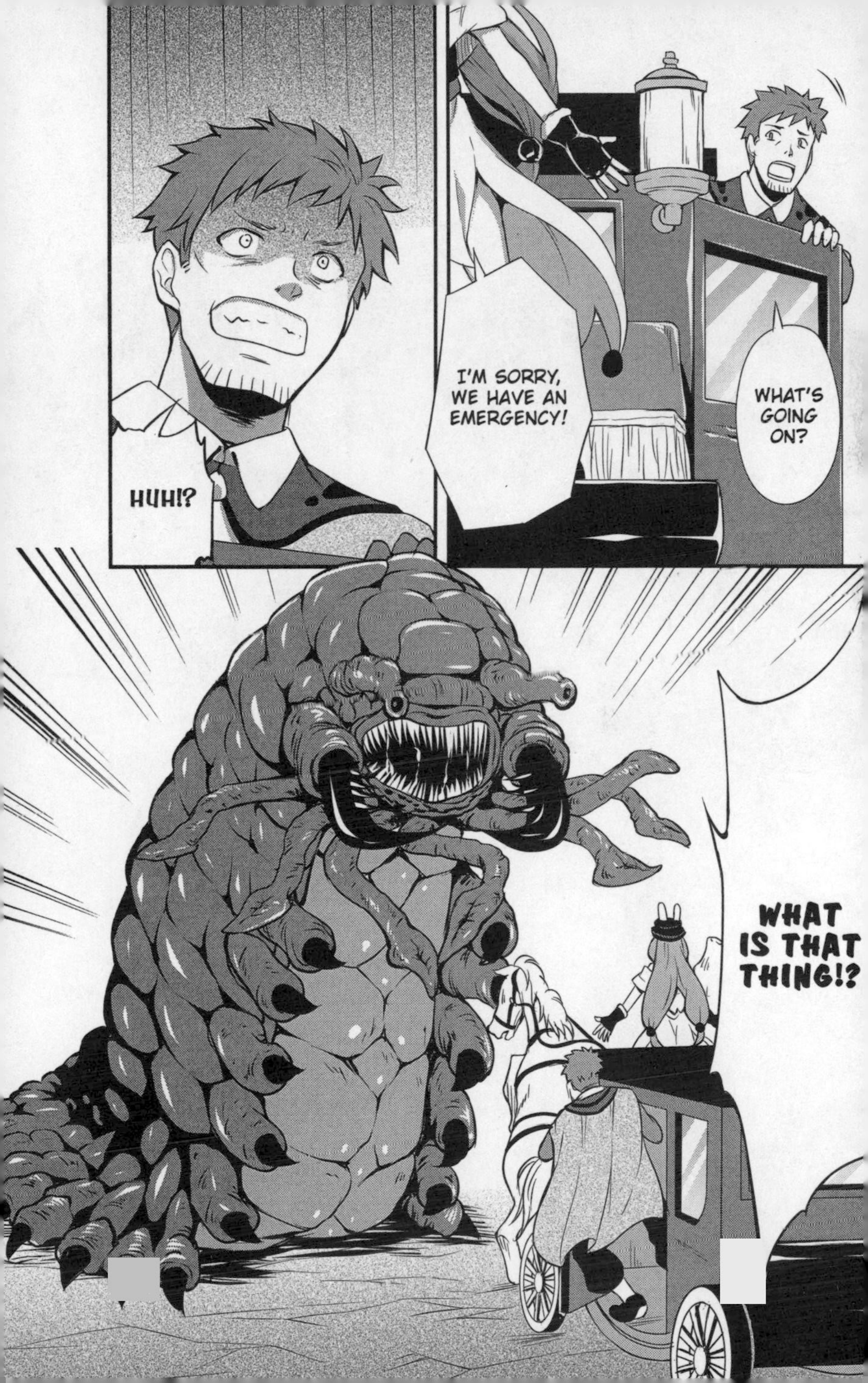
WHAT'S GOING ON?
I'M SORRY, WE HAVE AN EMERGENCY!
HUH!?
WHAT IS THAT THING!?

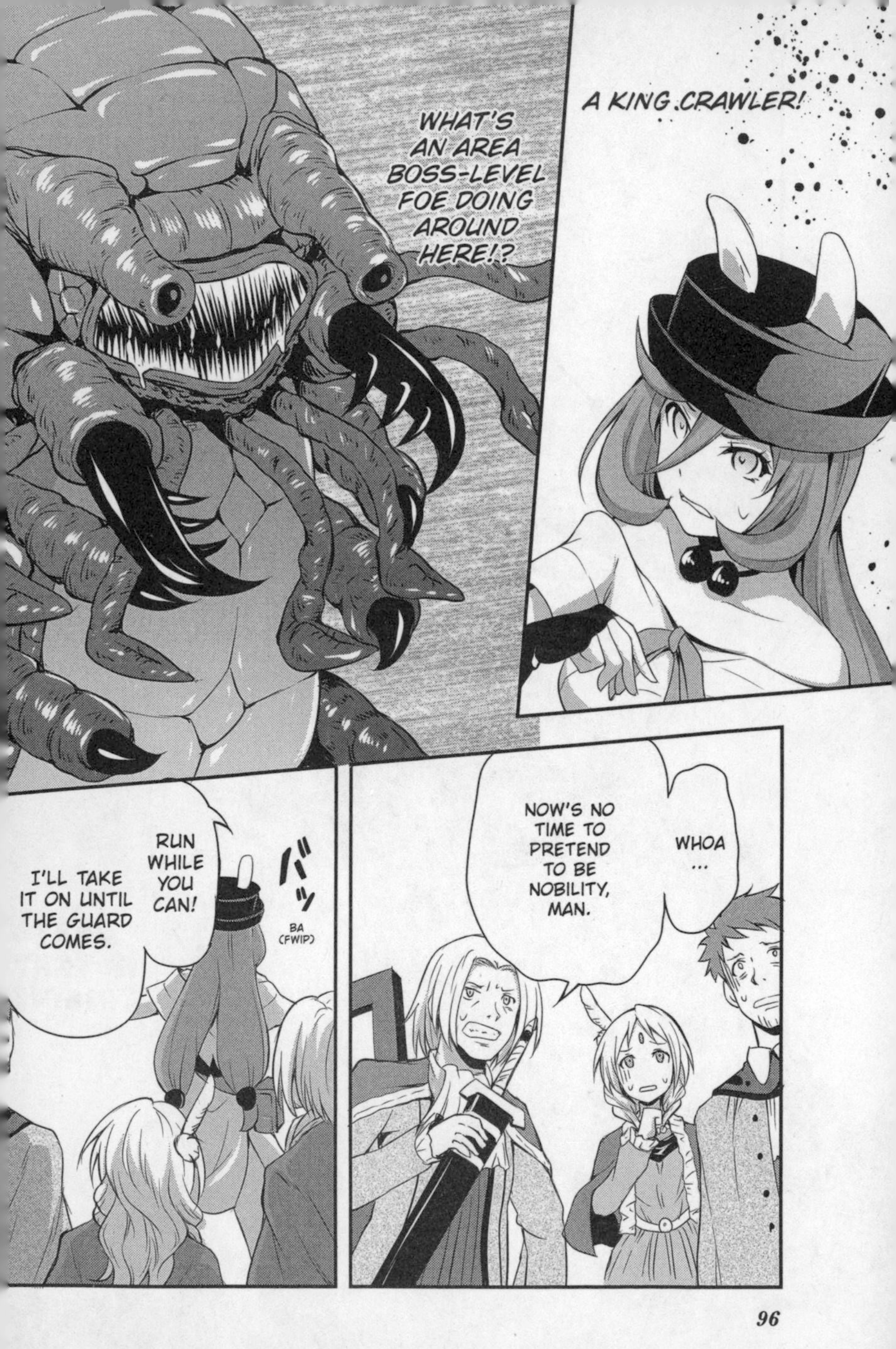
A KING CRAWLER!
WHAT'S AN AREA BOSS-LEVEL FOE DOING AROUND HERE!?
WHOA ...
NOW'S NO TIME TO PRETEND TO BE NOBILITY, MAN.
バッ
BA (FWIP)
RUN WHILE YOU CAN!
I'LL TAKE IT ON UNTIL THE GUARD COMES.

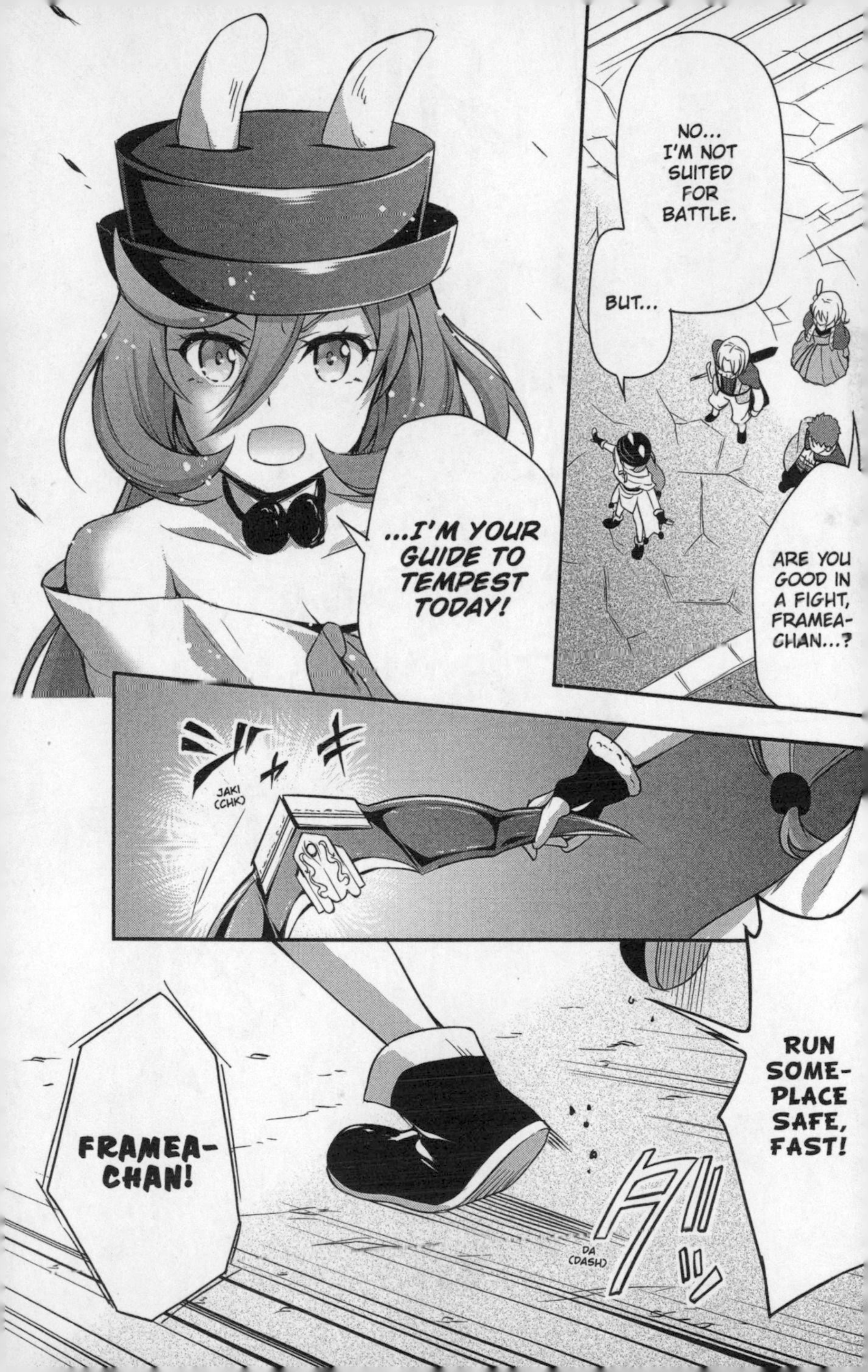
ARE YOU GOOD IN A FIGHT, FRAMEA-CHAN...?
NO... I'M NOT SUITED FOR BATTLE.
BUT...
...I'M YOUR GUIDE TO TEMPEST TODAY!
JAKI (CHK)
RUN SOME-PLACE SAFE, FAST!
DA (DASH)
FRAMEA-CHAN!

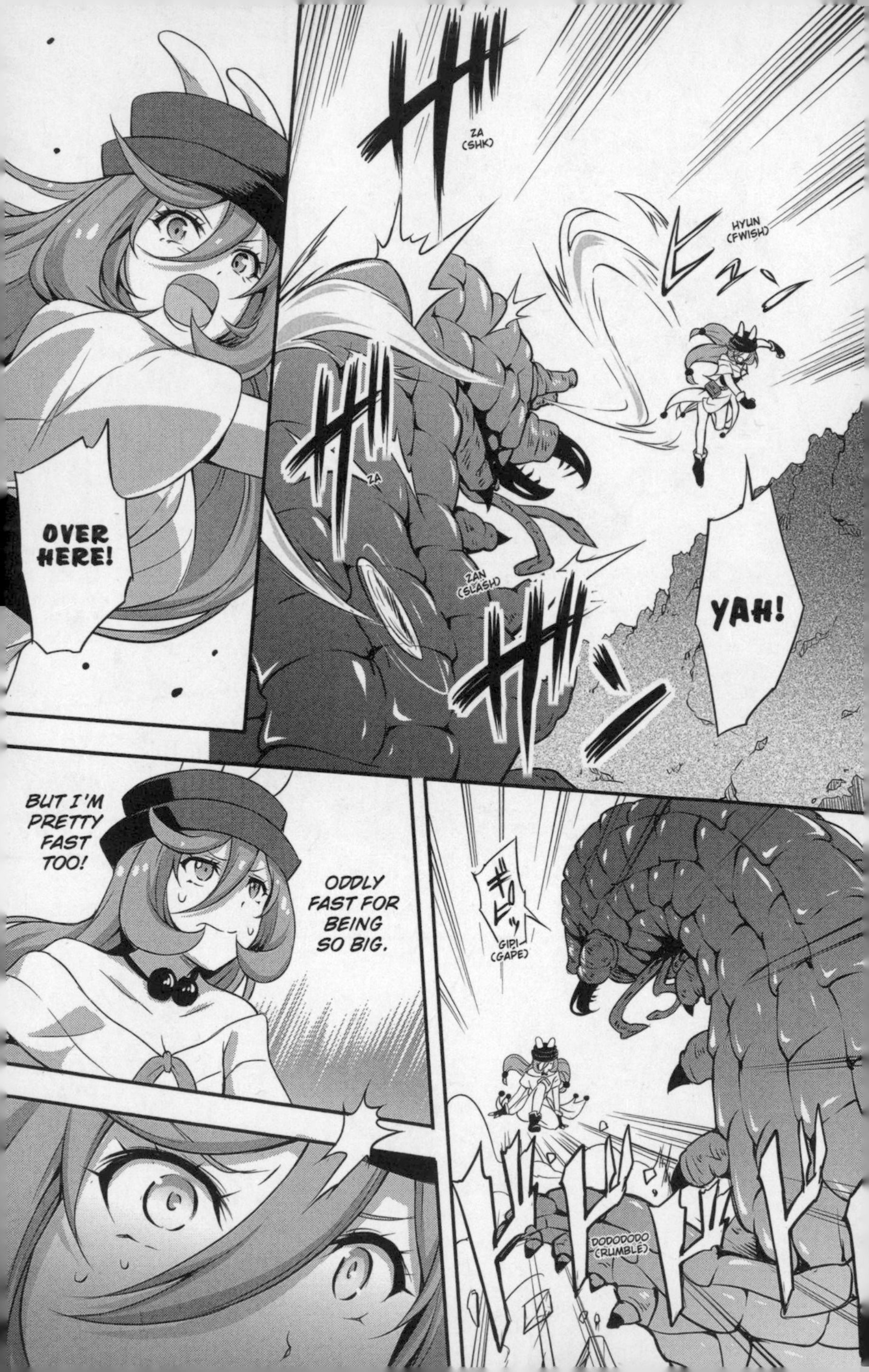
ZA (SHK)
HYUN (FWISH)
YAH!
ZA
ZAN (SLASH)
OVER HERE!
GIPI (GAPE)
DODODODO (RUMBLE)
ODDLY FAST FOR BEING SO BIG.
BUT I'M PRETTY FAST TOO!

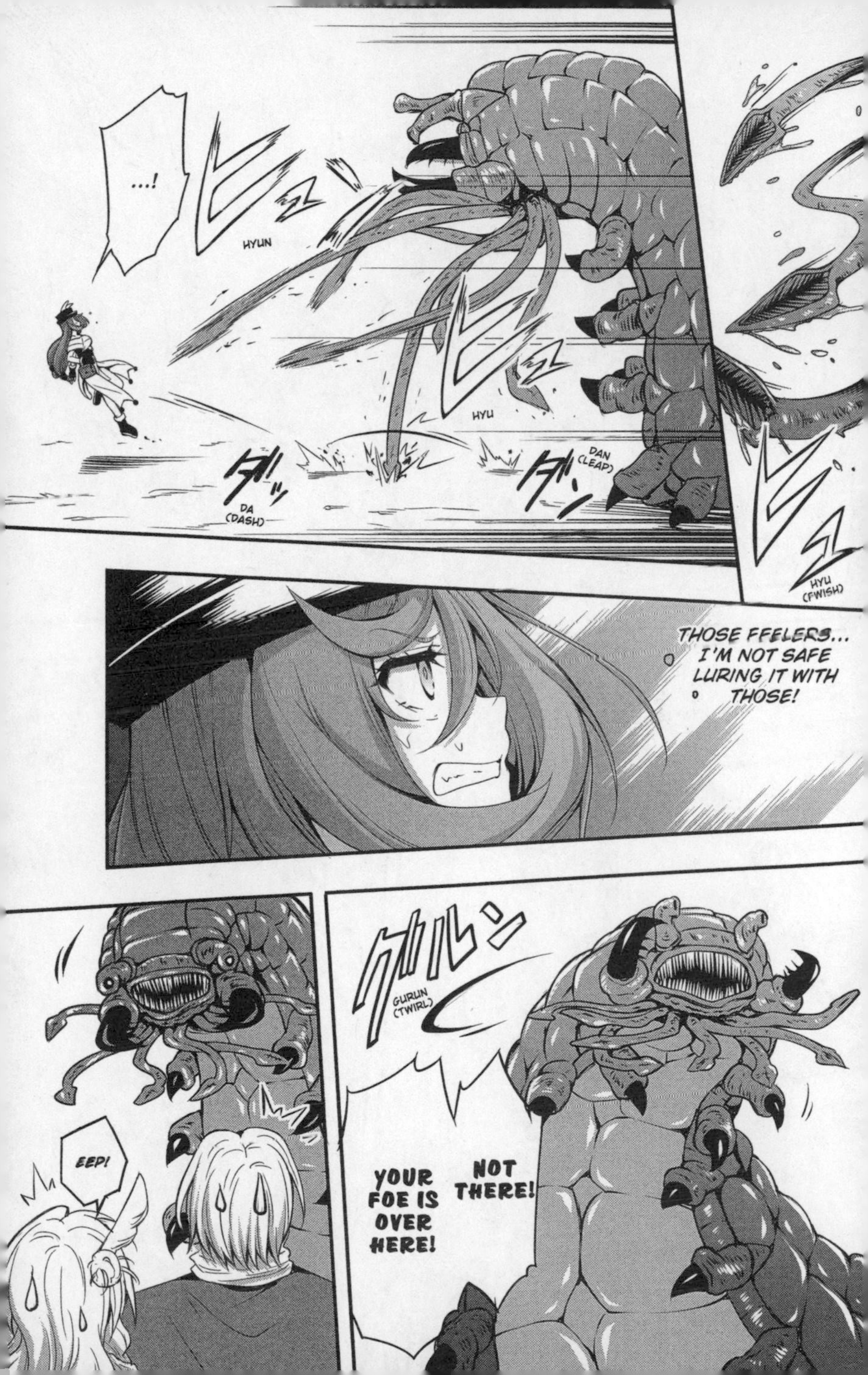
HYU
(FWISH)
...!
HYUN
HYU
DAN
(LEAP)
DA
(DASH)
THOSE FFELERS... I'M NOT SAFE LURING IT WITH THOSE!
GURUN
(TWIRL)
NOT THERE!
YOUR FOE IS OVER HERE!
EEP!

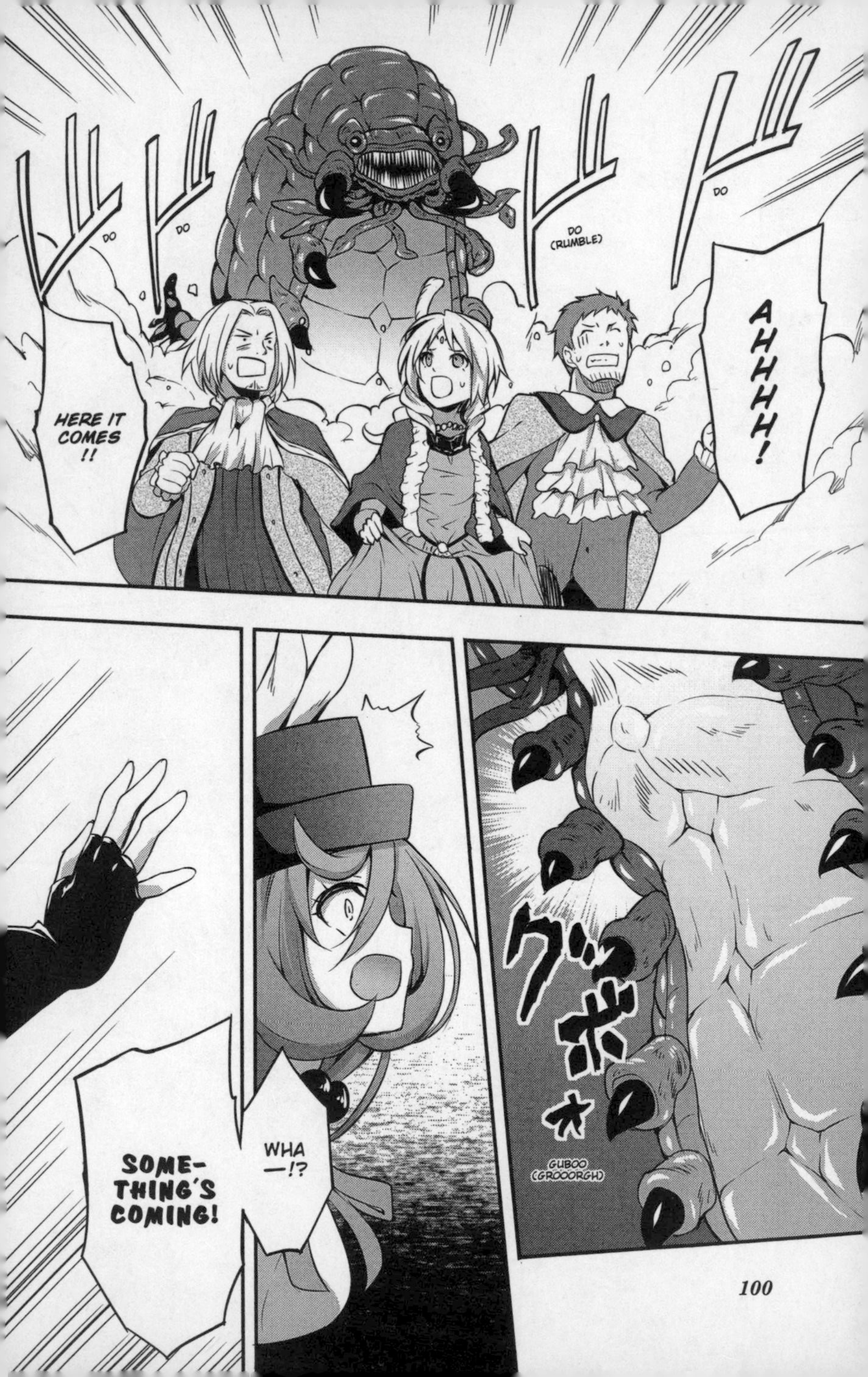
DO
DO (RUMBLE)
AHHHH!
DO
DO
HERE IT COMES!!
GUBOO (GROOORGH)
WHA—!?
SOME-THING'S COMING!

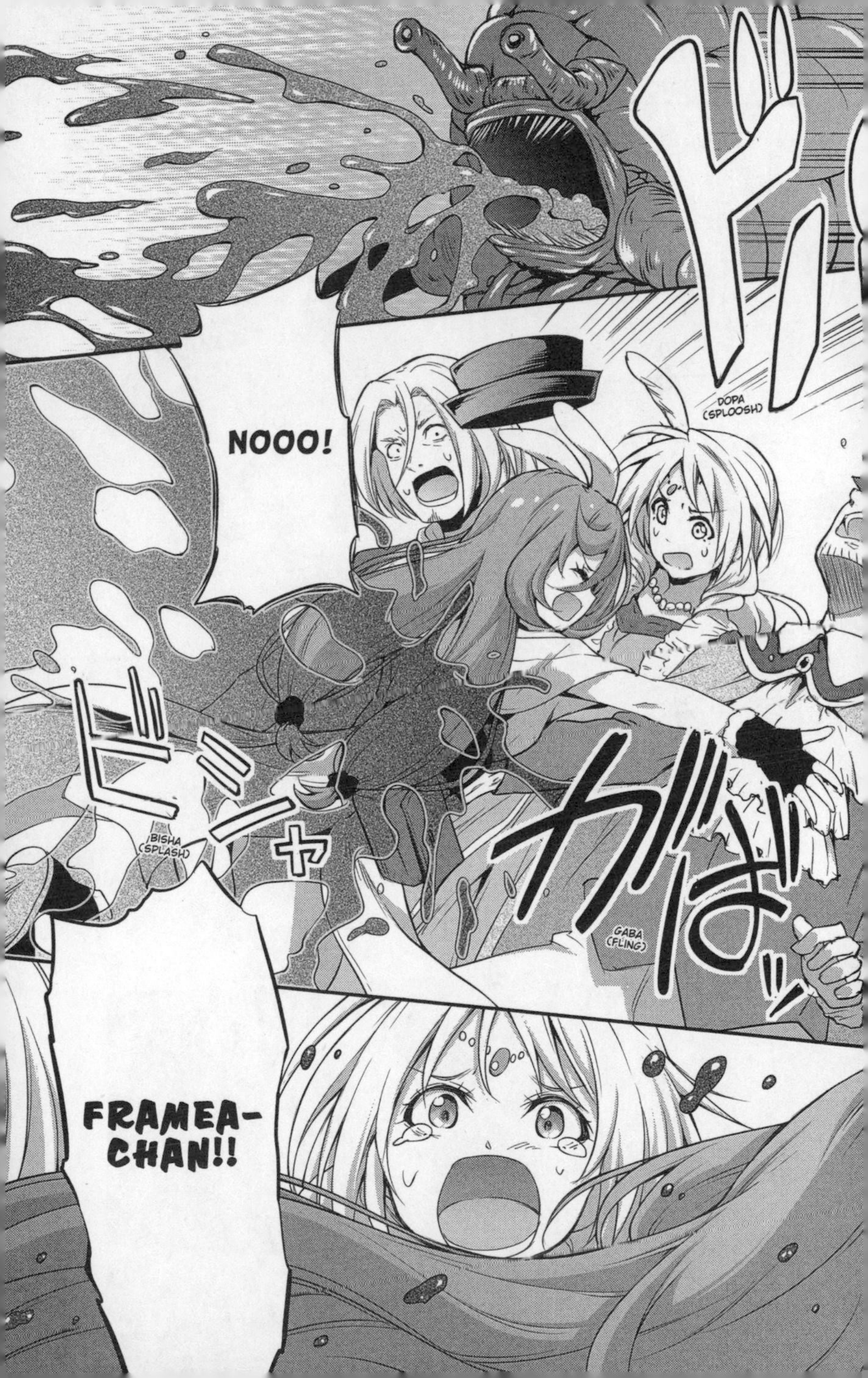
DOPA
(SPLOOSH)
NOOO!
GABA
(FLING)
BISHA
(SPLASH)
FRAMEA-
CHAN!!

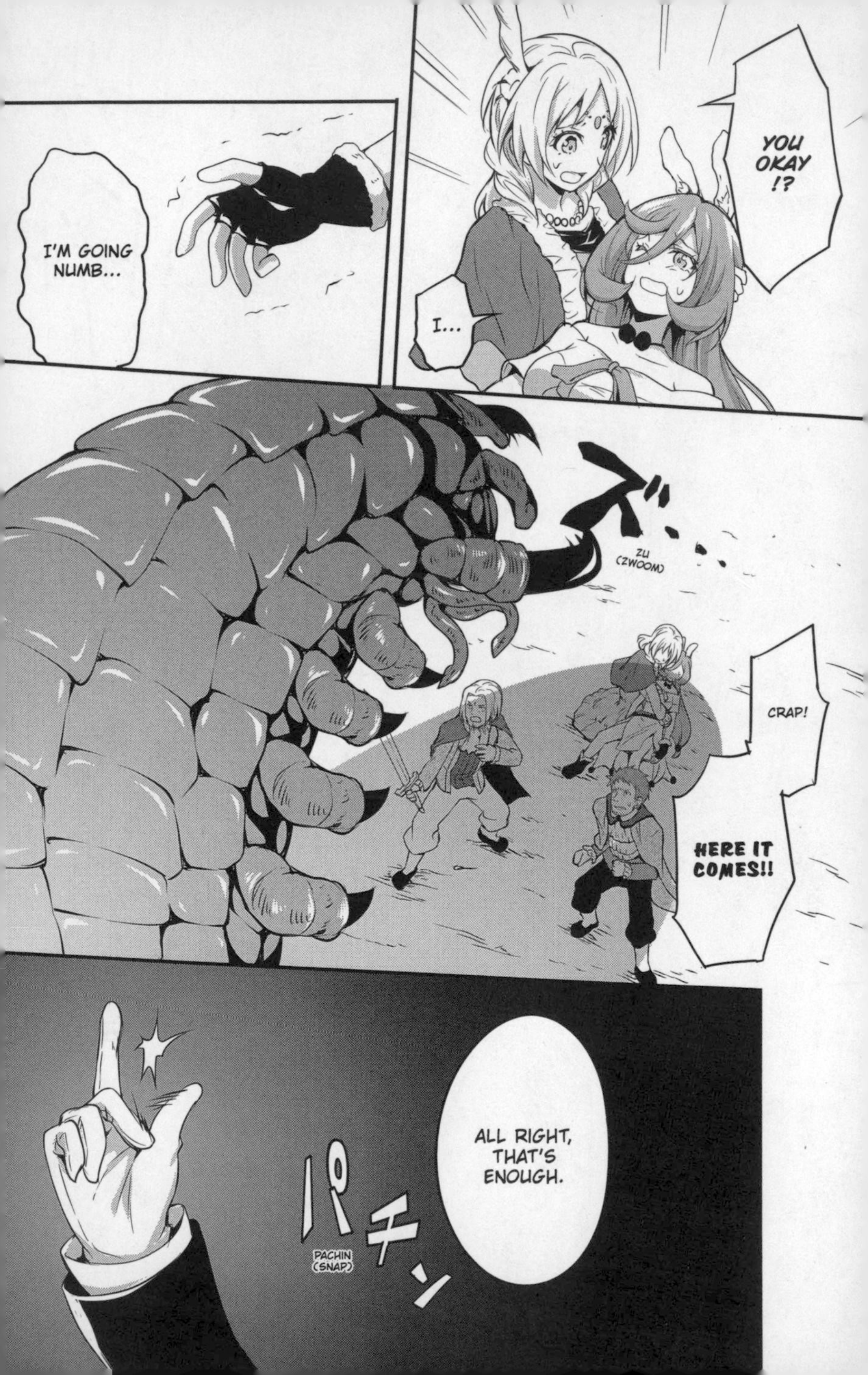
YOU OKAY !?
I...
I'M GOING NUMB...
ズ
ZU (ZWOOM)
CRAP!
HERE IT COMES!!
ALL RIGHT, THAT'S ENOUGH.
パチン
PACHIN (SNAP)

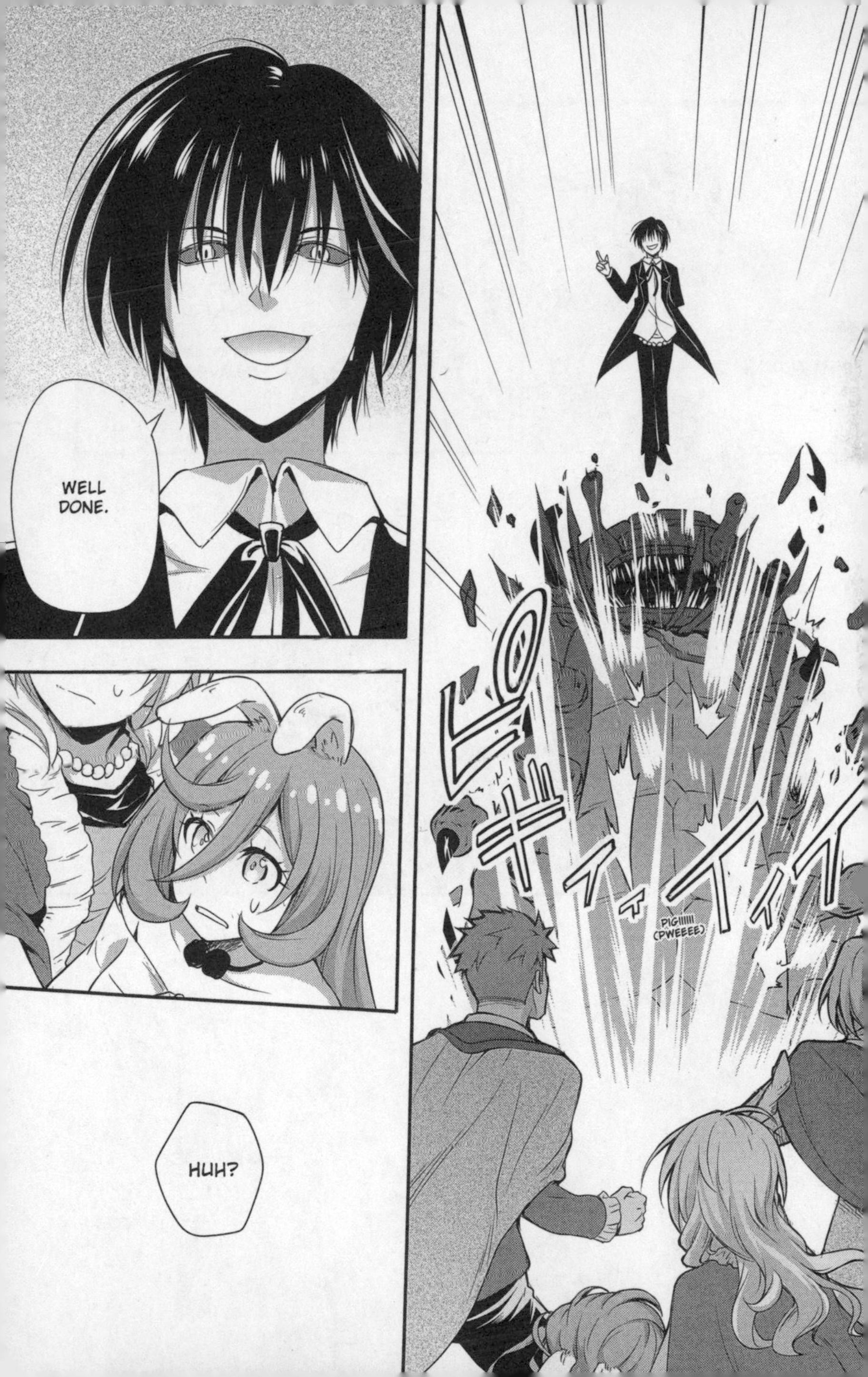
ピギィィィ
PIGIIIIIII
(PWEEEEE)
WELL DONE.
HUH?

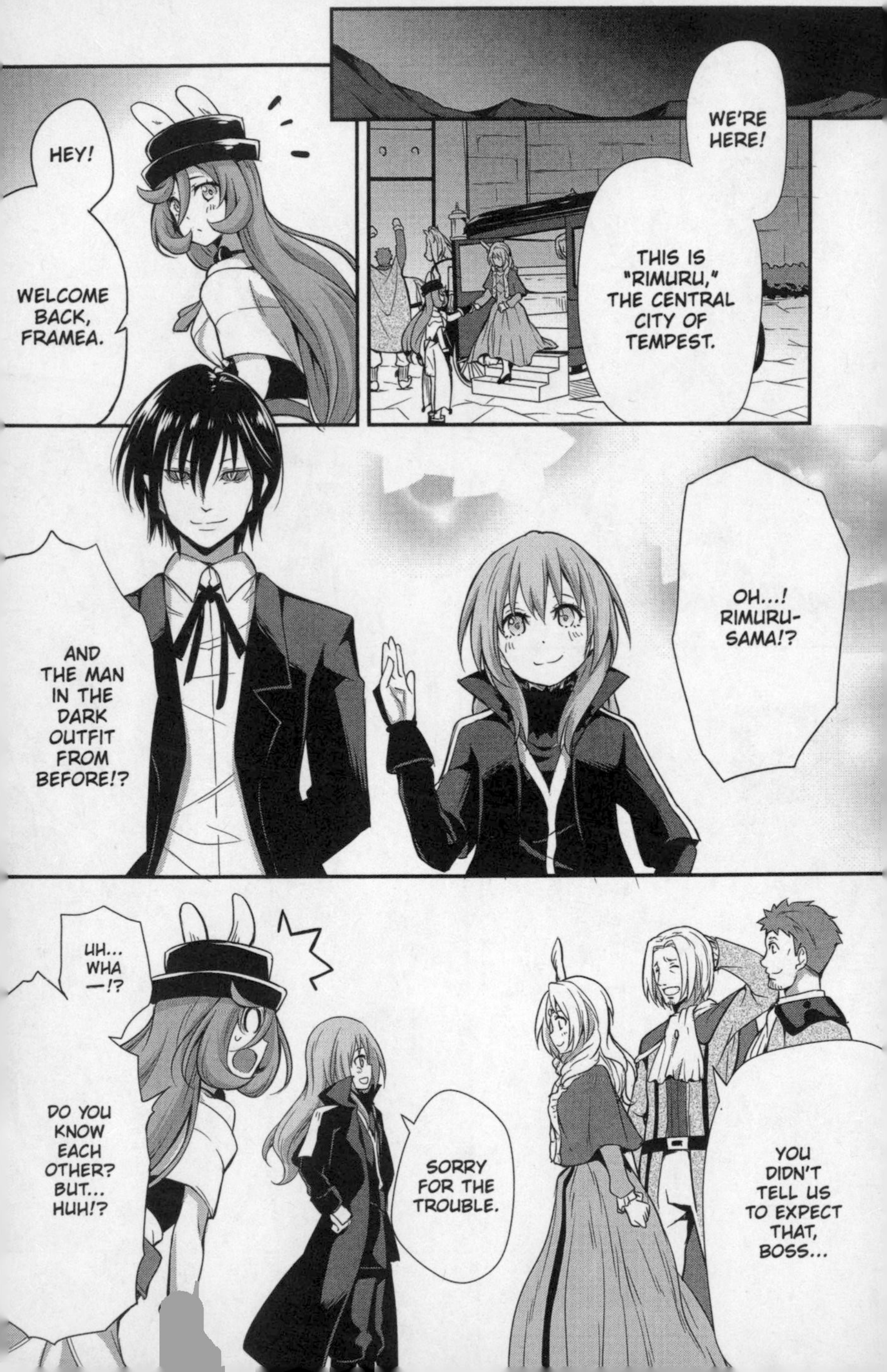
WE'RE HERE!
THIS IS "RIMURU," THE CENTRAL CITY OF TEMPEST.
HEY!
WELCOME BACK, FRAMEA.
OH...! RIMURU-SAMA!?
AND THE MAN IN THE DARK OUTFIT FROM BEFORE!?
YOU DIDN'T TELL US TO EXPECT THAT, BOSS...
SORRY FOR THE TROUBLE.
UH... WHA—!?
DO YOU KNOW EACH OTHER? BUT... HUH!?

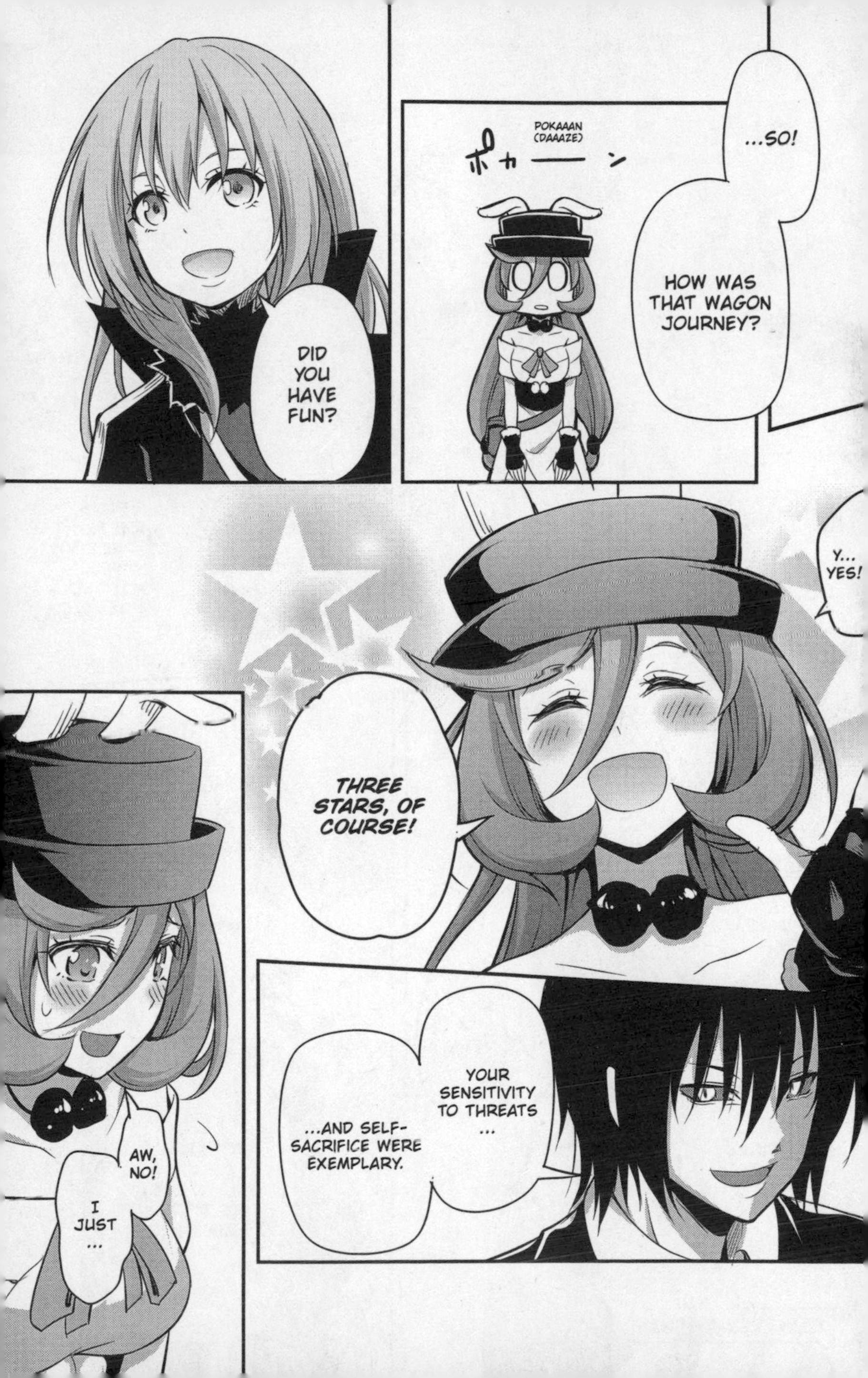
...SO!
HOW WAS THAT WAGON JOURNEY?
ポカーーン
POKAAAN (DAAAZE)
DID YOU HAVE FUN?
Y... YES!
THREE STARS, OF COURSE!
YOUR SENSITIVITY TO THREATS ...
...AND SELF-SACRIFICE WERE EXEMPLARY.
AW, NO!
I JUST ...

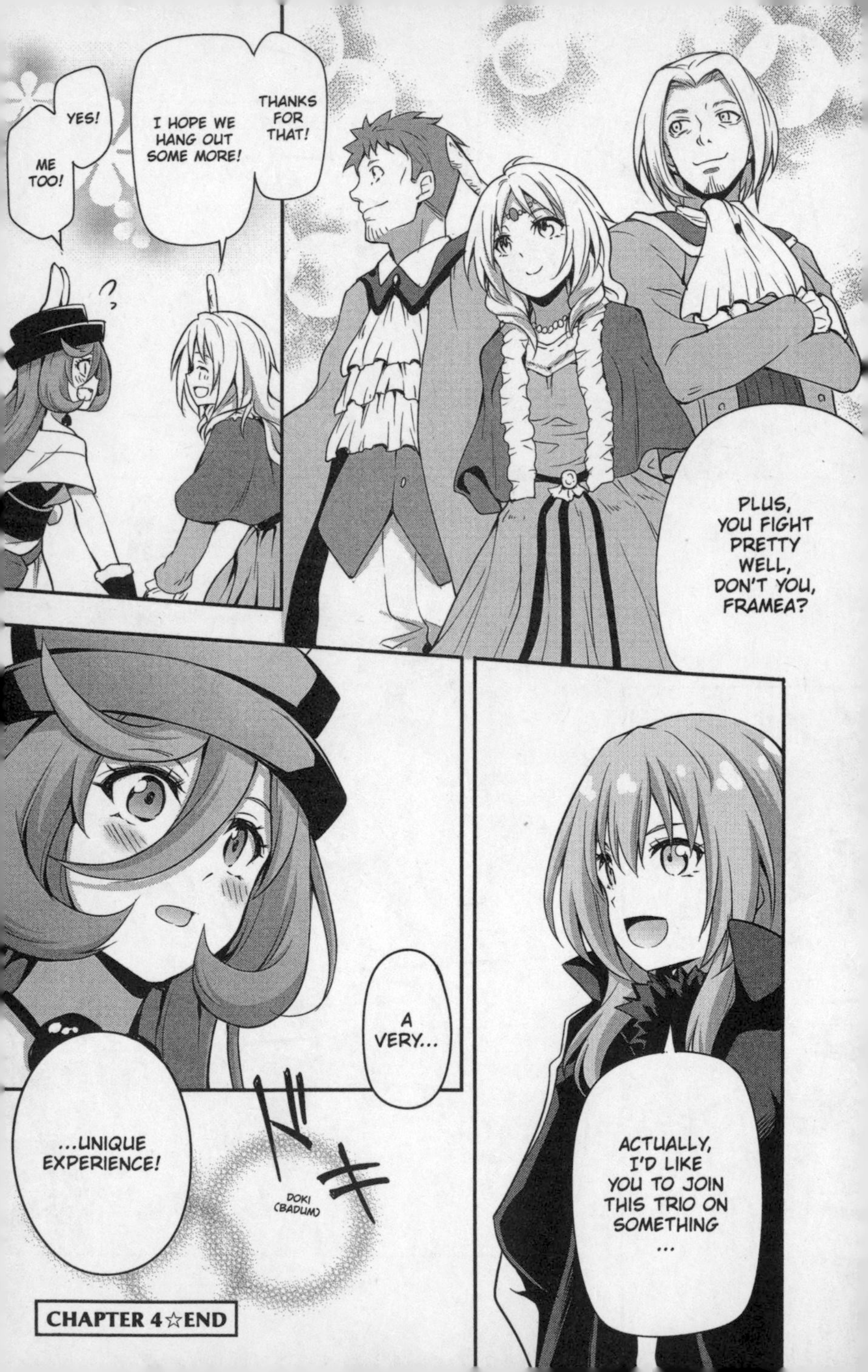
THANKS FOR THAT!
PLUS, YOU FIGHT PRETTY WELL, DON'T YOU, FRAMEA?
I HOPE WE HANG OUT SOME MORE!
YES!
ME TOO!
ACTUALLY, I'D LIKE YOU TO JOIN THIS TRIO ON SOMETHING ...
A VERY...
...UNIQUE EXPERIENCE!
DOKI (BADUM)
CHAPTER 4☆END

CHAPTER 5

THAT LIGHT FEELING OF INEBRIATION ☆ THREE STARS!!

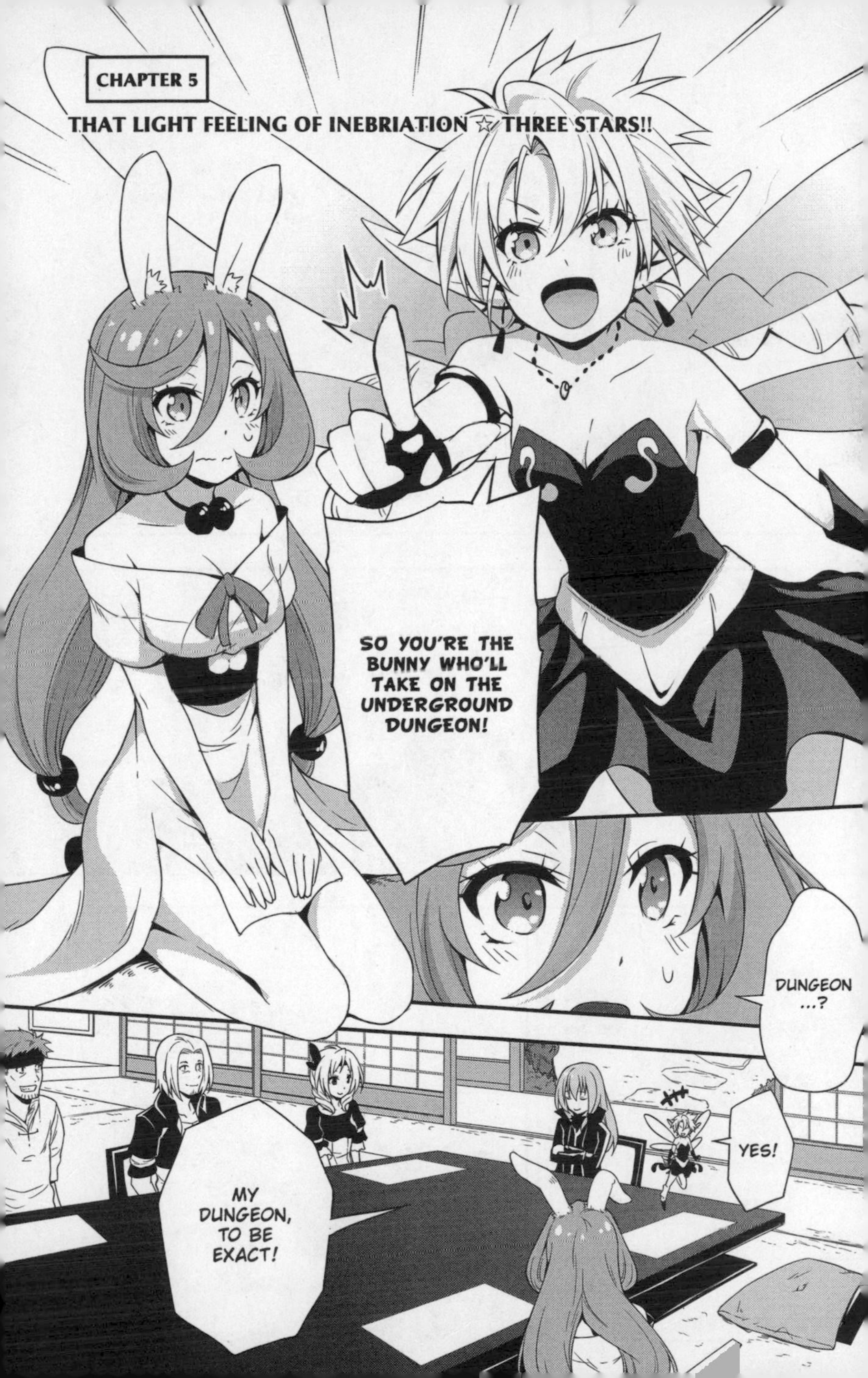
SO YOU'RE THE BUNNY WHO'LL TAKE ON THE UNDERGROUND DUNGEON!
DUNGEON ...?
YES!
MY DUNGEON, TO BE EXACT!

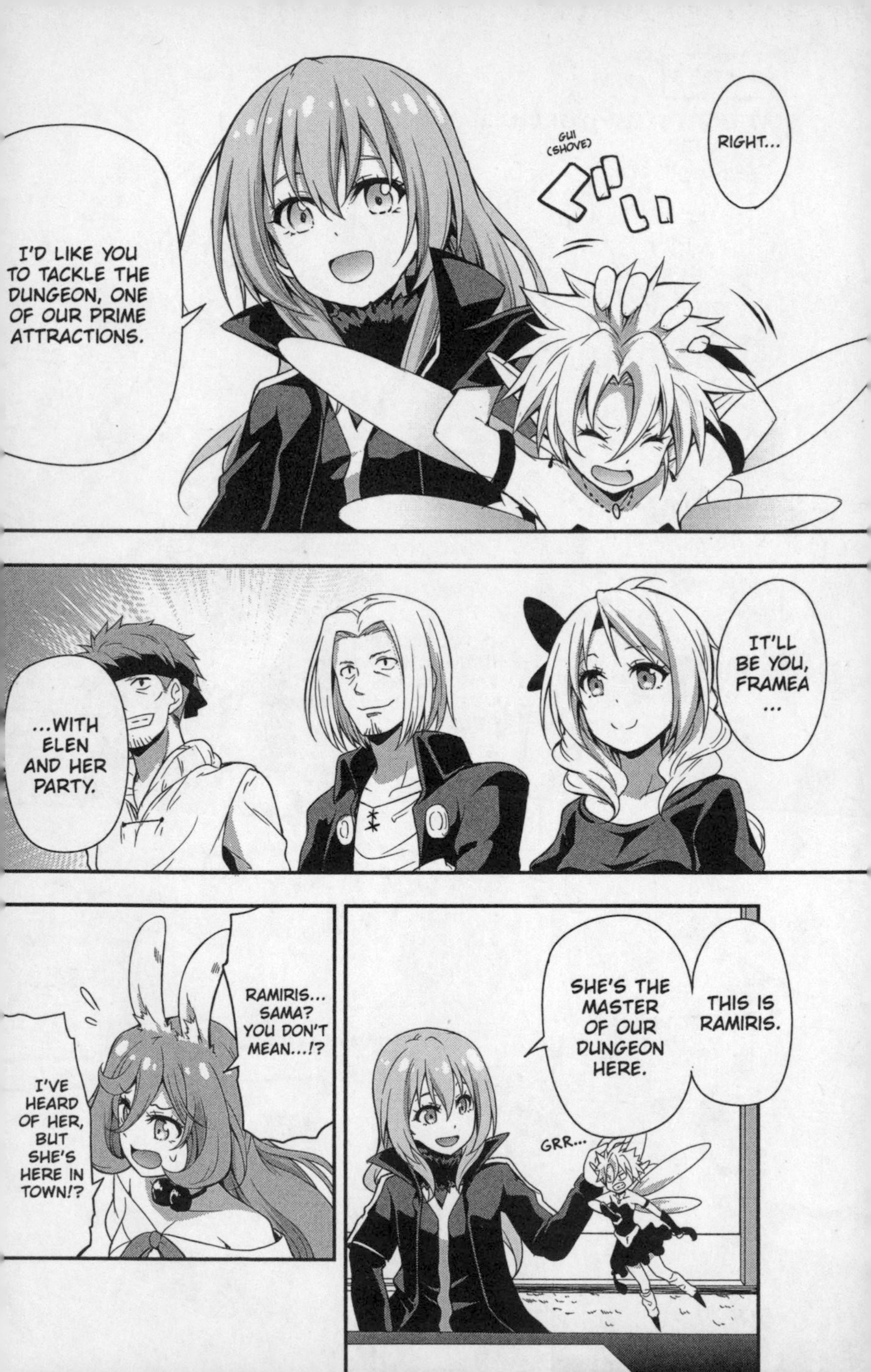
RIGHT...
GUI (SHOVE)
I'D LIKE YOU TO TACKLE THE DUNGEON, ONE OF OUR PRIME ATTRACTIONS.
IT'LL BE YOU, FRAMEA...
...WITH ELEN AND HER PARTY.
THIS IS RAMIRIS.
SHE'S THE MASTER OF OUR DUNGEON HERE.
GRR...
RAMIRIS... SAMA? YOU DON'T MEAN...!?
I'VE HEARD OF HER, BUT SHE'S HERE IN TOWN!?

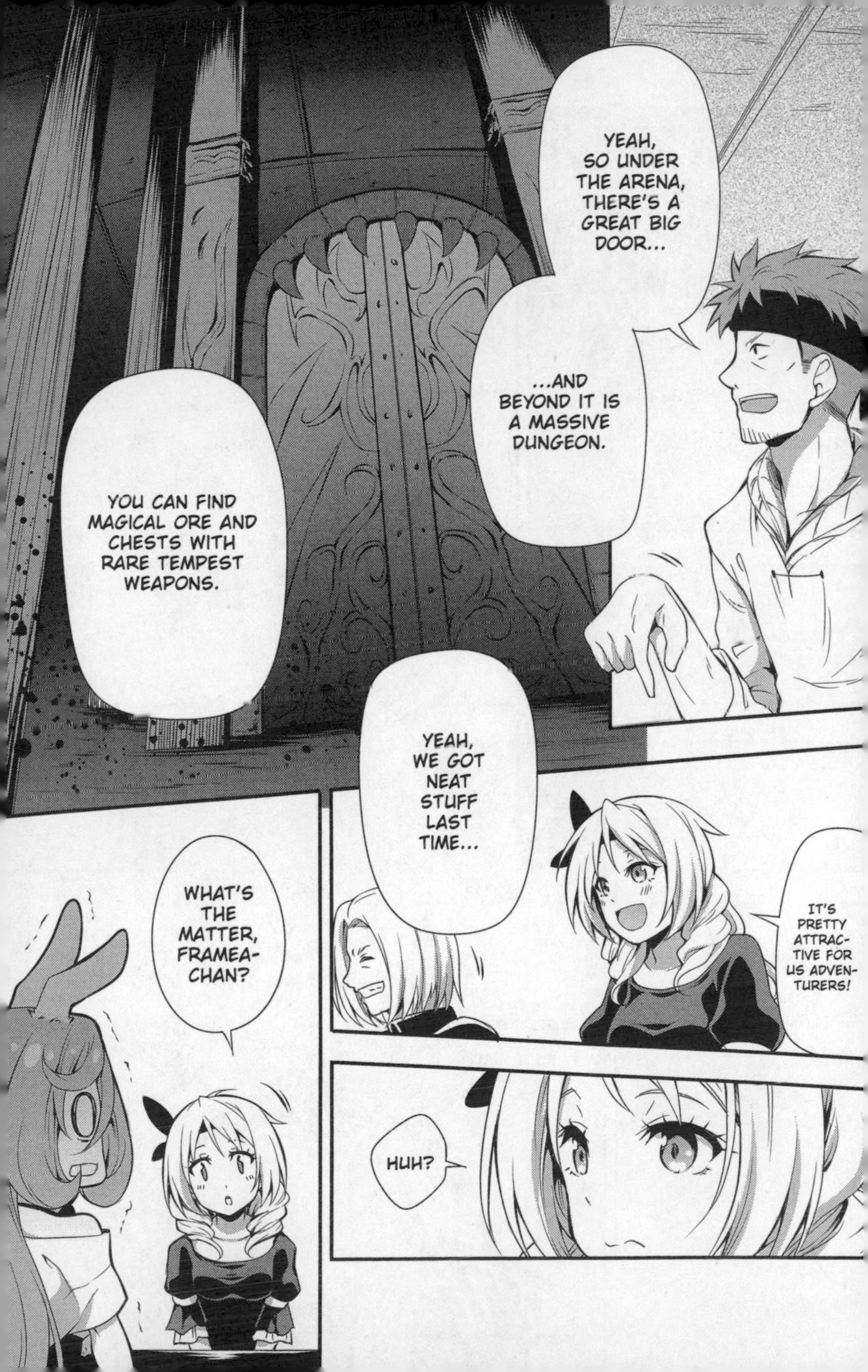
YEAH, SO UNDER THE ARENA, THERE'S A GREAT BIG DOOR...
...AND BEYOND IT IS A MASSIVE DUNGEON.
YOU CAN FIND MAGICAL ORE AND CHESTS WITH RARE TEMPEST WEAPONS.
YEAH, WE GOT NEAT STUFF LAST TIME...
IT'S PRETTY ATTRACTIVE FOR US ADVENTURERS!
HUH?
WHAT'S THE MATTER, FRAMEA-CHAN?

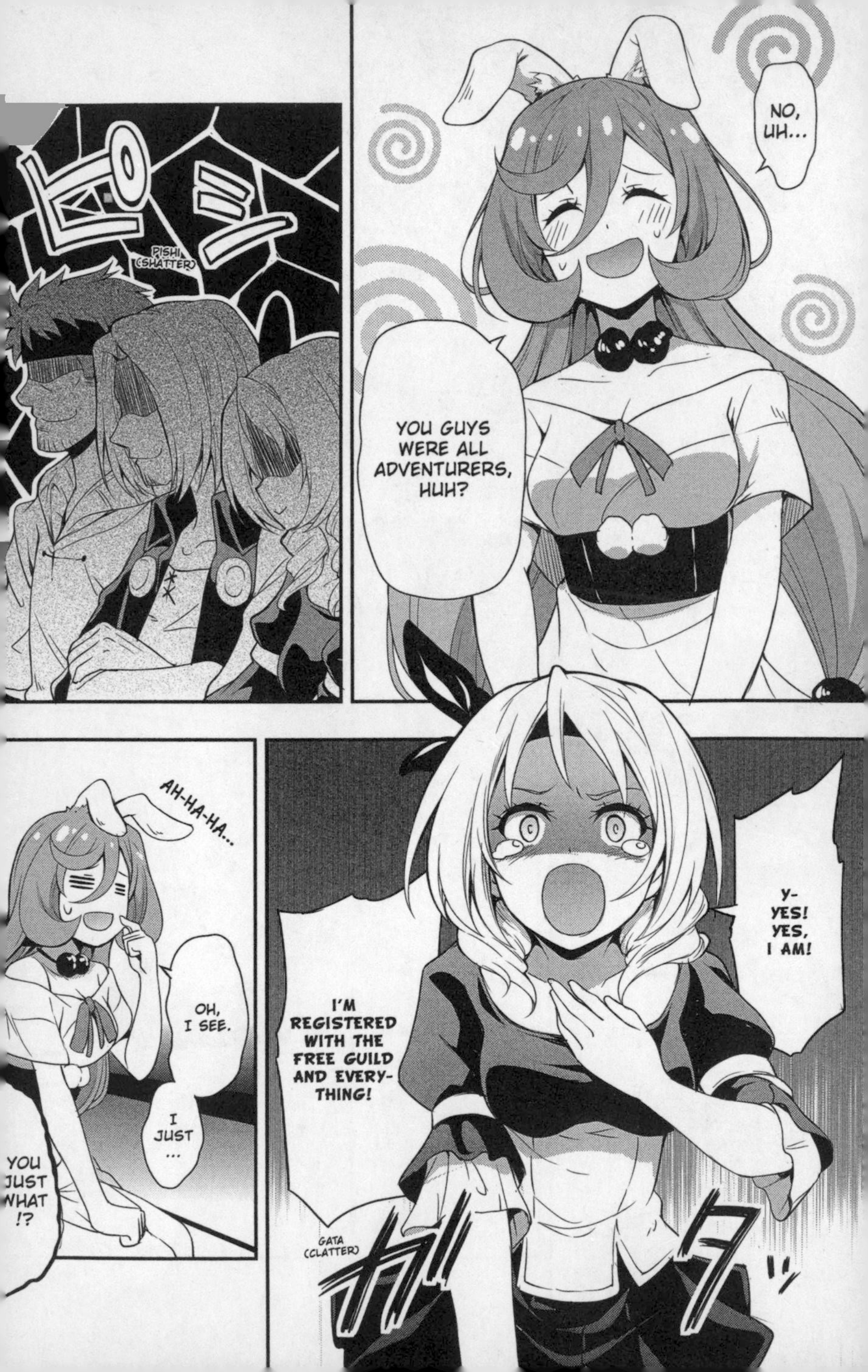
NO, UH...
YOU GUYS WERE ALL ADVENTURERS, HUH?
PISHI (SHATTER)
Y-YES! YES, I AM!
I'M REGISTERED WITH THE FREE GUILD AND EVERY-THING!
GATA (CLATTER)
AH-HA-HA...
OH, I SEE.
I JUST ...
YOU JUST WHAT !?

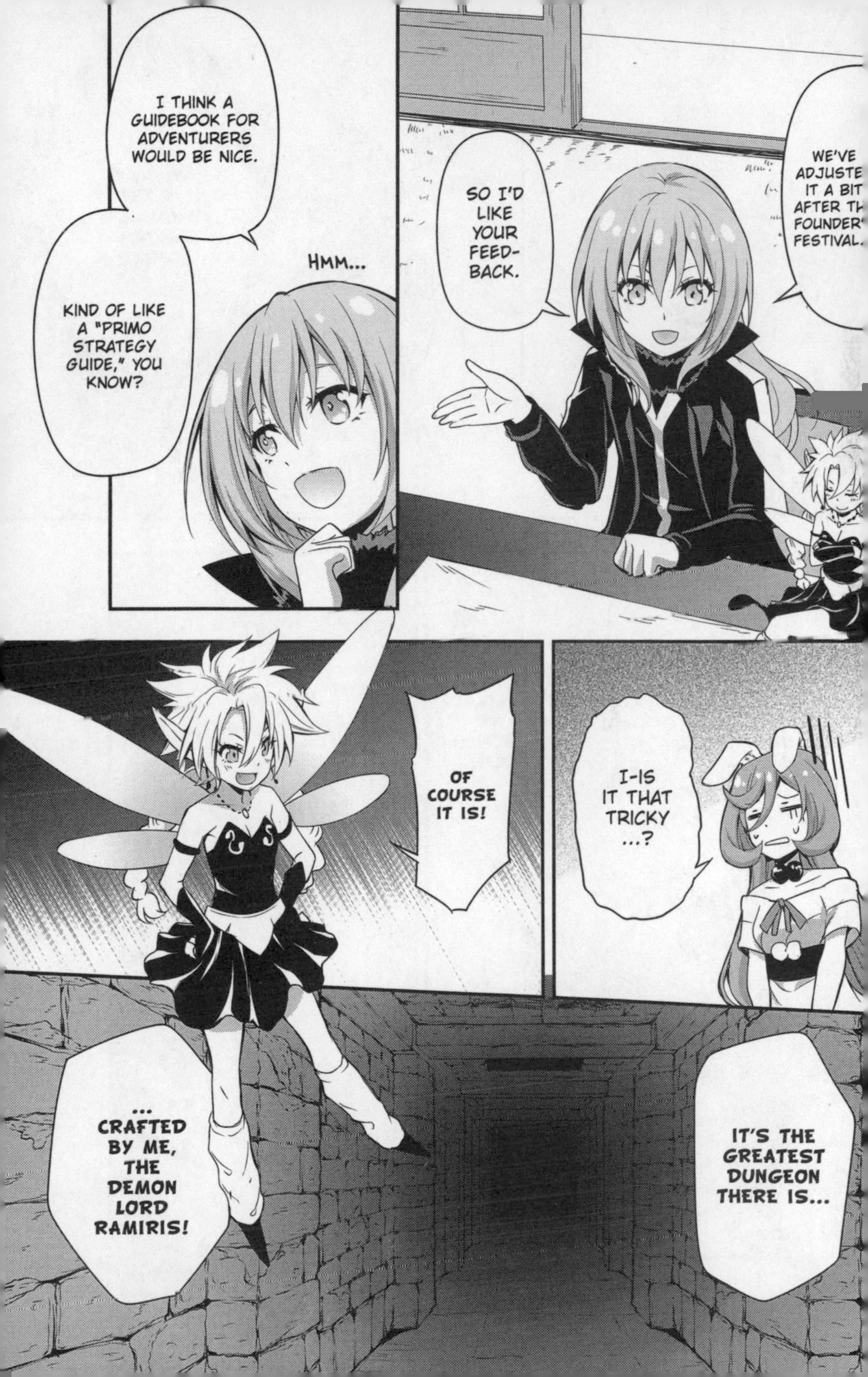
WE'VE ADJUSTE IT A BIT AFTER TH FOUNDER' FESTIVAL.
SO I'D LIKE YOUR FEED-BACK.
HMM...
I THINK A GUIDEBOOK FOR ADVENTURERS WOULD BE NICE.
KIND OF LIKE A "PRIMO STRATEGY GUIDE," YOU KNOW?
I-IS IT THAT TRICKY ...?
OF COURSE IT IS!
IT'S THE GREATEST DUNGEON THERE IS...
... CRAFTED BY ME, THE DEMON LORD RAMIRIS!

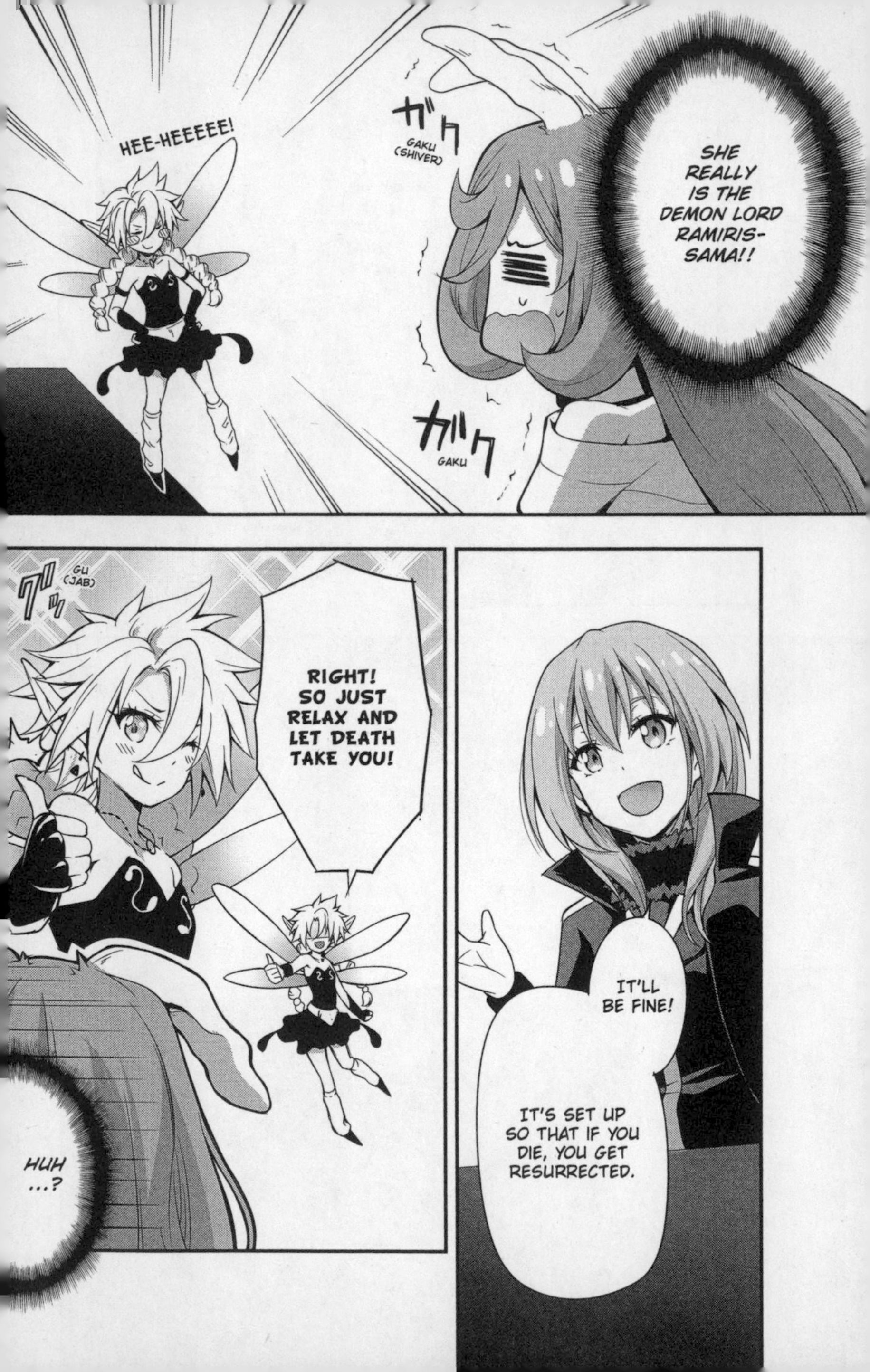
SHE REALLY IS THE DEMON LORD RAMIRIS-SAMA!!
ガク
GAKU (SHIVER)
HEE-HEEEEE!
ガク
GAKU
IT'LL BE FINE!
IT'S SET UP SO THAT IF YOU DIE, YOU GET RESURRECTED.
グッ
GU (JAB)
RIGHT! SO JUST RELAX AND LET DEATH TAKE YOU!
HUH ...?

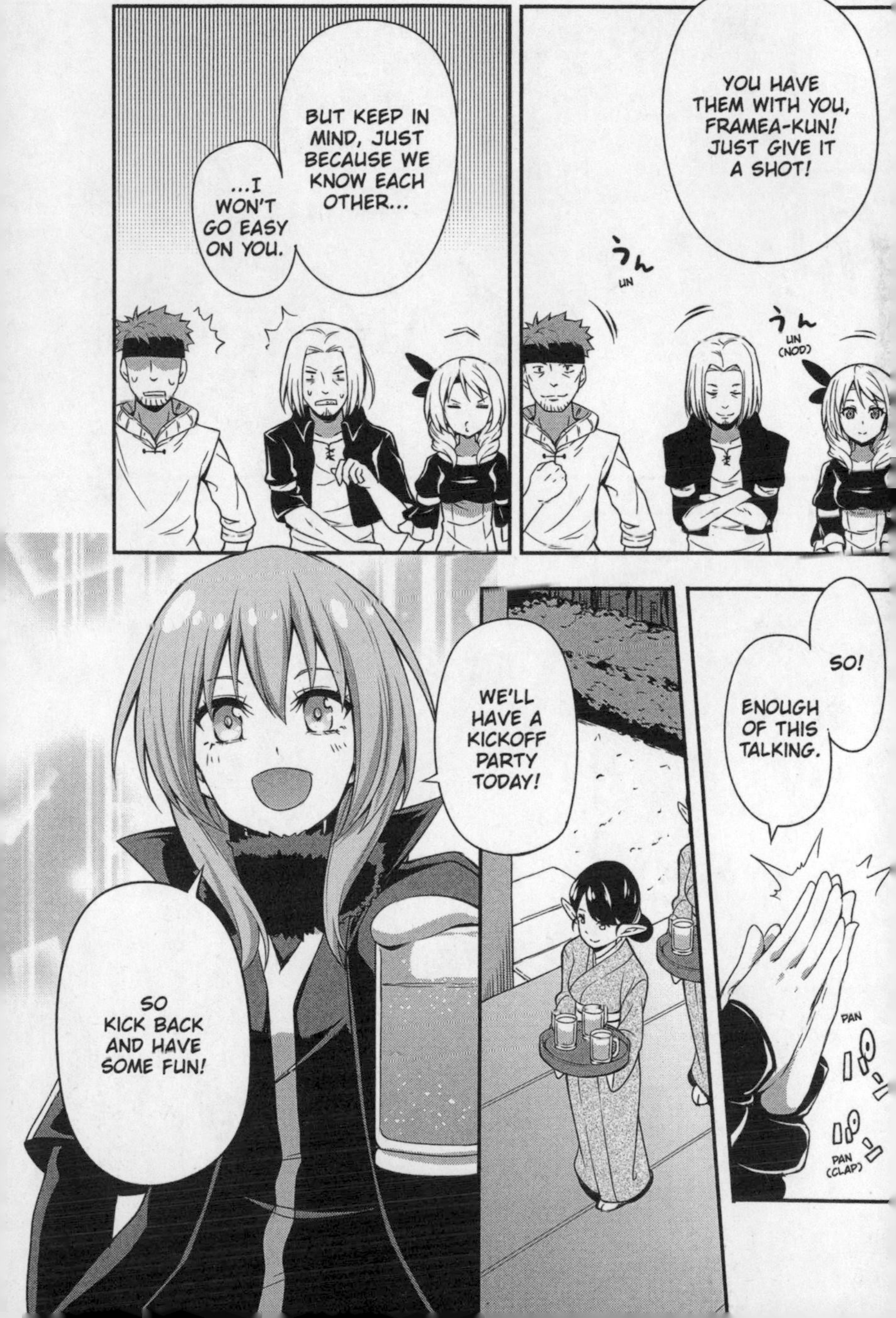
YOU HAVE THEM WITH YOU, FRAMEA-KUN! JUST GIVE IT A SHOT!
うん
UN
うん
UN (NOD)
BUT KEEP IN MIND, JUST BECAUSE WE KNOW EACH OTHER...
...I WON'T GO EASY ON YOU.
SO!
ENOUGH OF THIS TALKING.
PAN
PAN (CLAP)
WE'LL HAVE A KICKOFF PARTY TODAY!
SO KICK BACK AND HAVE SOME FUN!

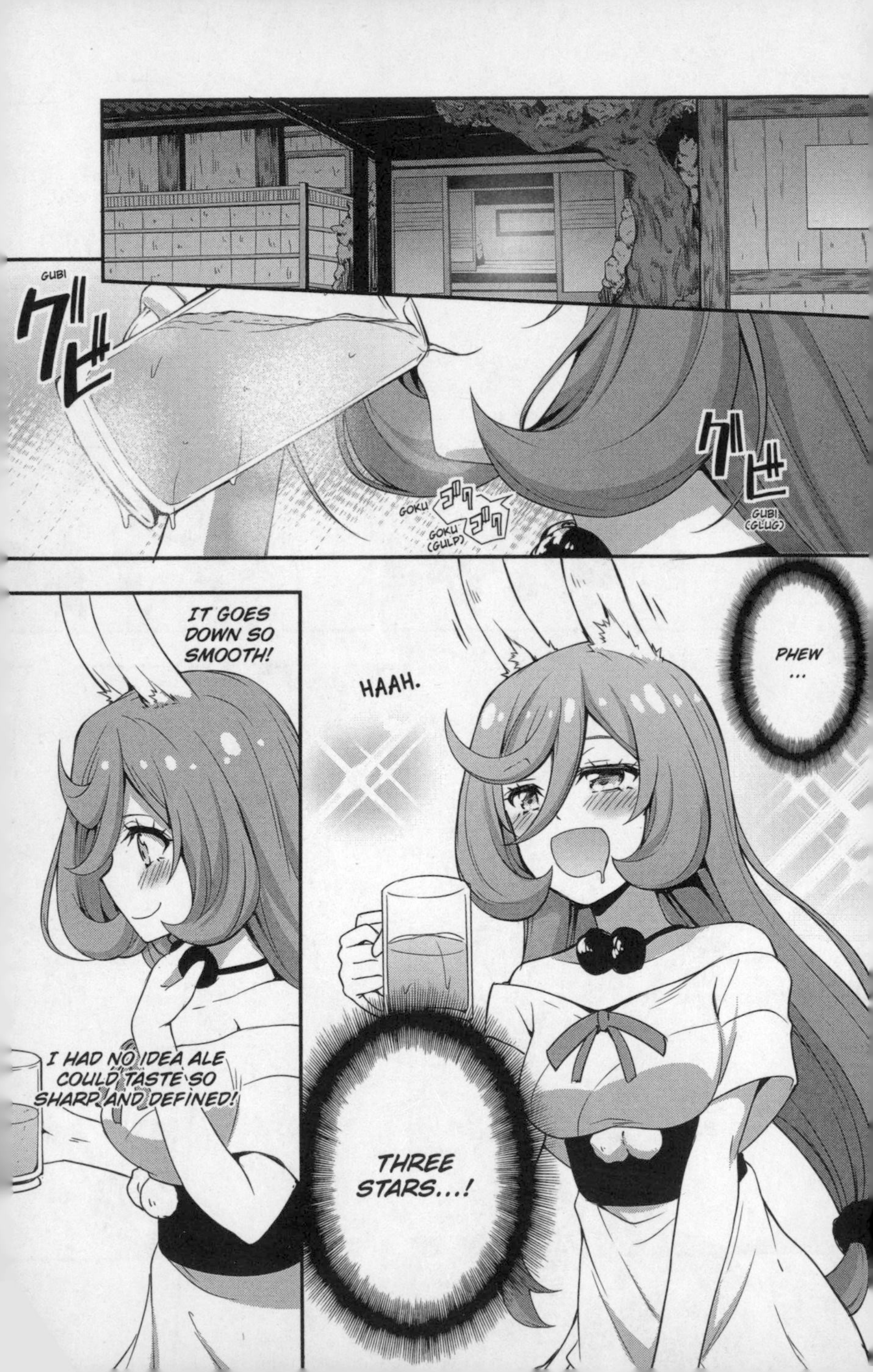
グビ
GUBI (GLUG)
ゴク ゴク
GOKU GOKU (GULP)
グビ
GUBI
PHEW...
HAAH.
THREE STARS...!
IT GOES DOWN SO SMOOTH!
I HAD NO IDEA ALE COULD TASTE SO SHARP AND DEFINED!

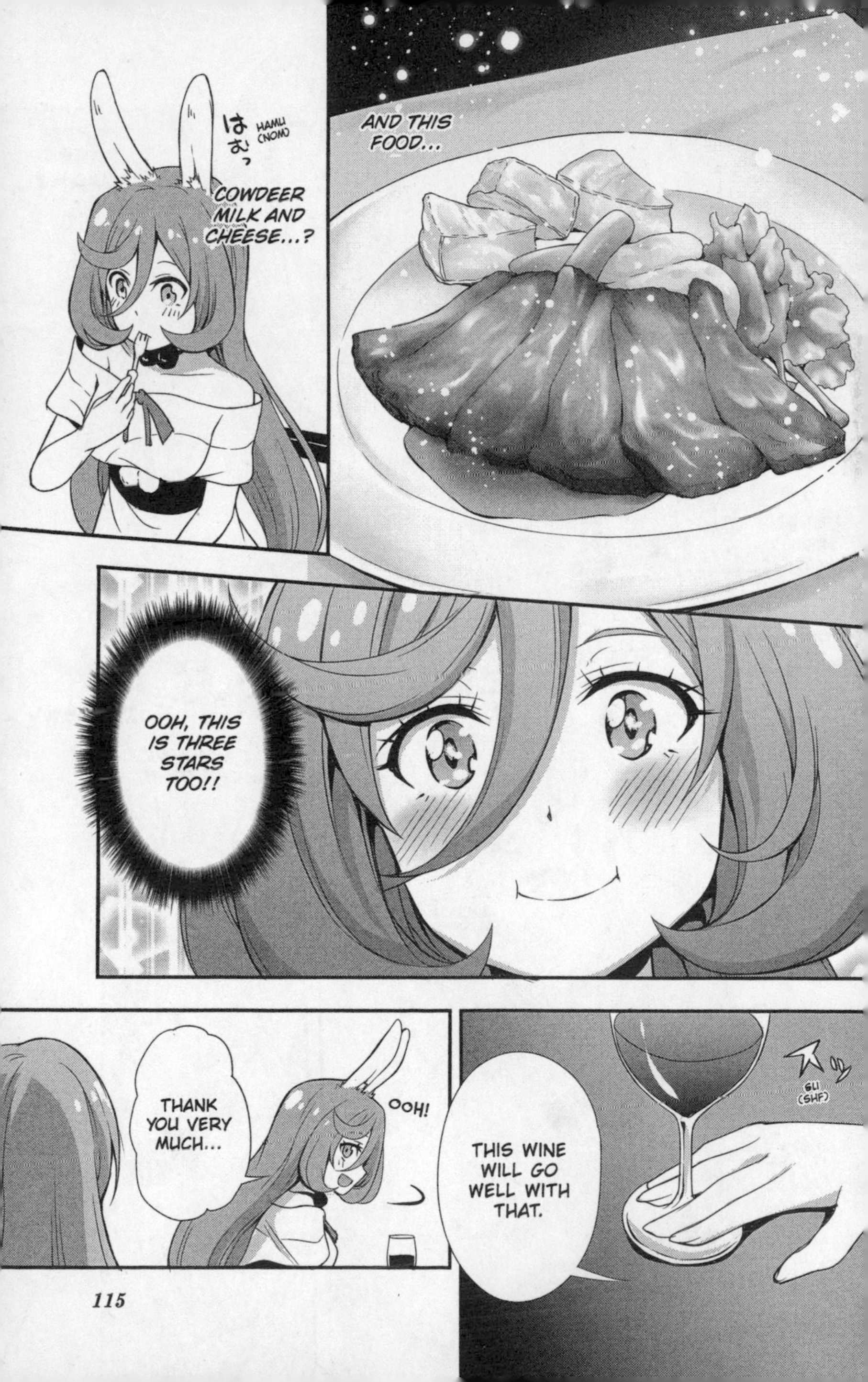
AND THIS FOOD...
はむっ
HAMU (NOM)
COWDEER MILK AND CHEESE...?
OOH, THIS IS THREE STARS TOO!!
GLI (SHF)
THIS WINE WILL GO WELL WITH THAT.
OOH!
THANK YOU VERY MUCH...

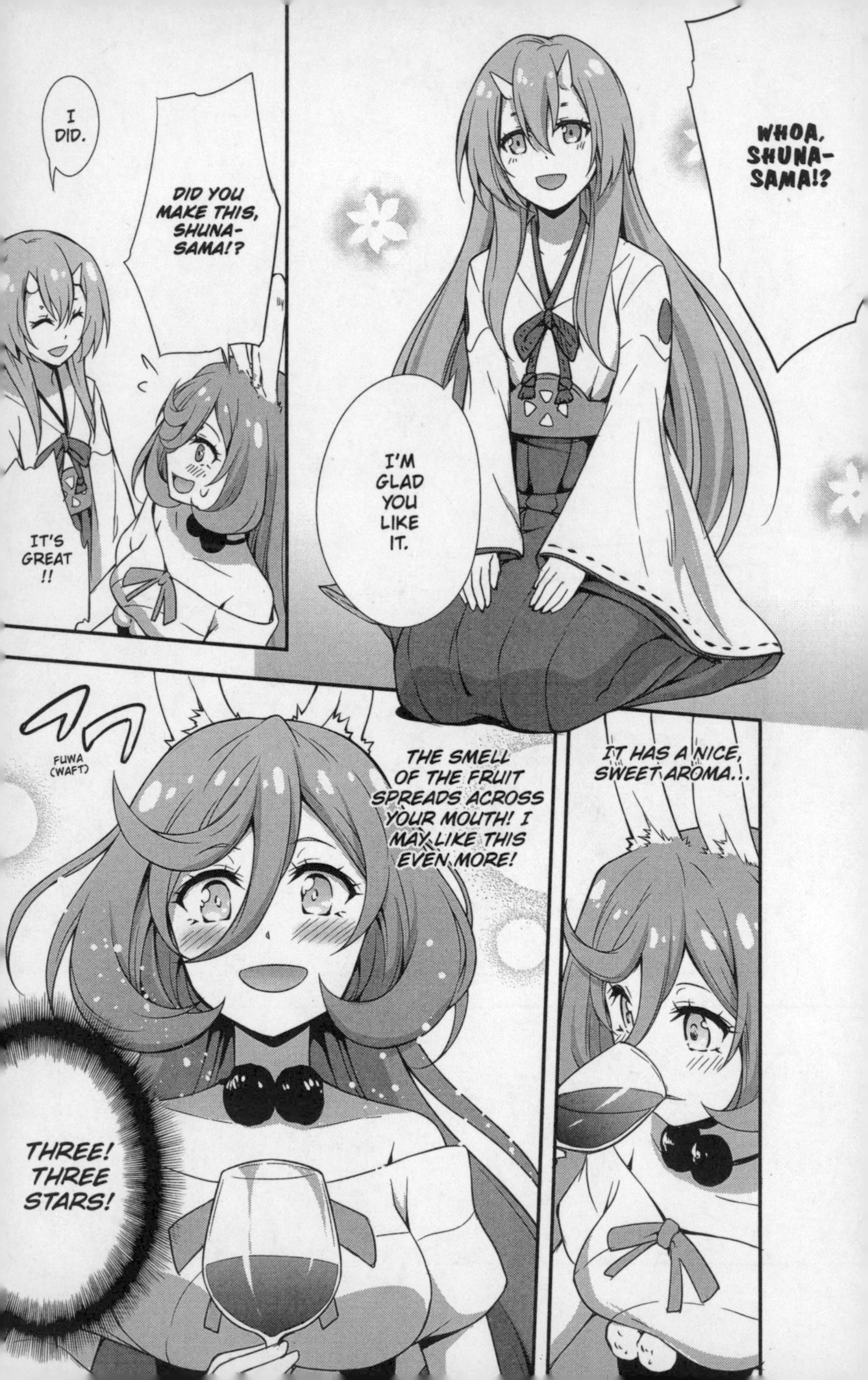
WHOA, SHUNA-SAMA!?
I'M GLAD YOU LIKE IT.
DID YOU MAKE THIS, SHUNA-SAMA!?
I DID.
IT'S GREAT!!
IT HAS A NICE, SWEET AROMA...
THE SMELL OF THE FRUIT SPREADS ACROSS YOUR MOUTH! I MAY LIKE THIS EVEN MORE!
FUWA (WAFT)
THREE! THREE STARS!

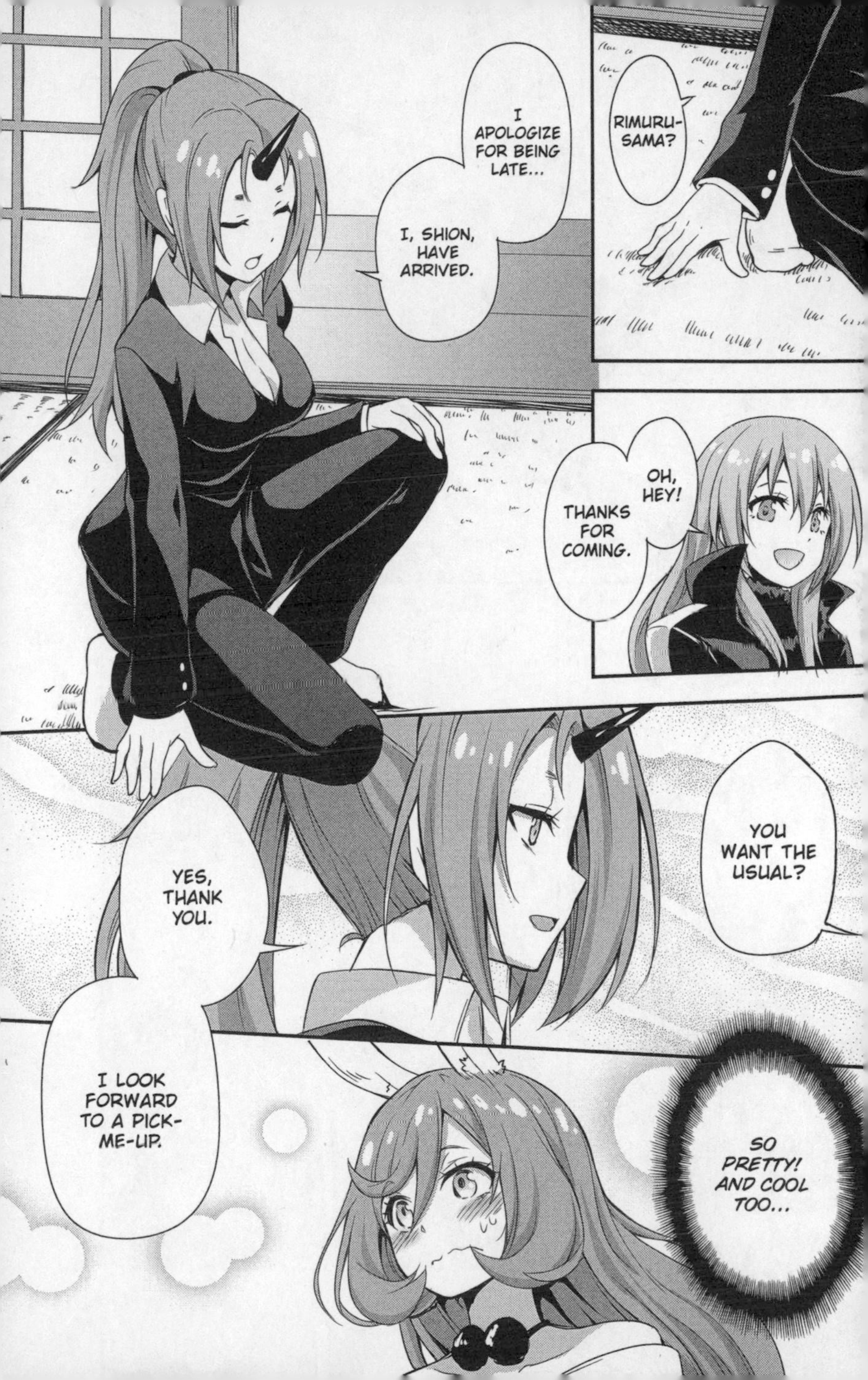
RIMURU-SAMA?
OH, HEY! THANKS FOR COMING.
I APOLOGIZE FOR BEING LATE...
I, SHION, HAVE ARRIVED.
YOU WANT THE USUAL?
YES, THANK YOU.
I LOOK FORWARD TO A PICK-ME-UP.
SO PRETTY! AND COOL TOO...

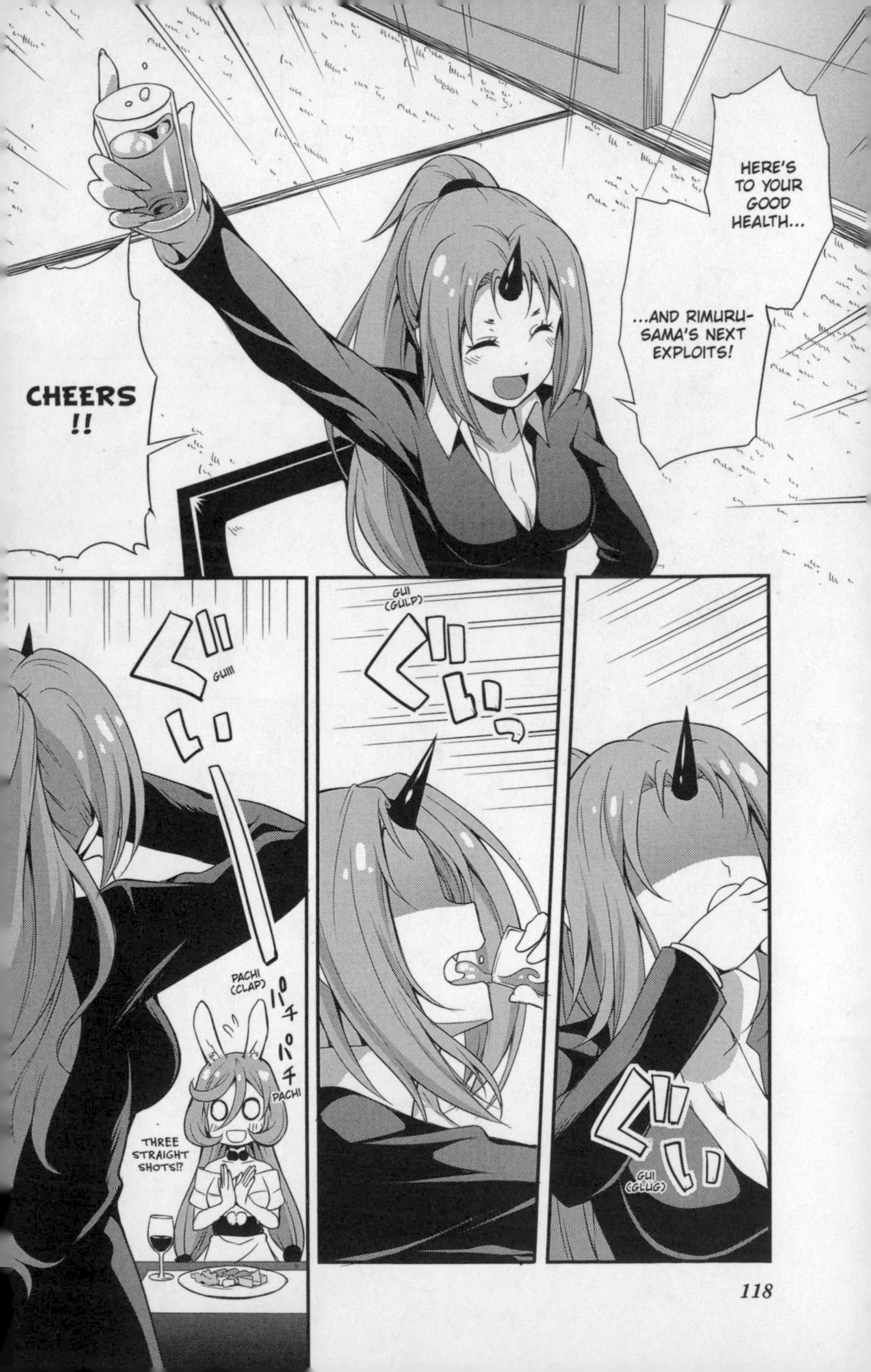
HERE'S TO YOUR GOOD HEALTH...
...AND RIMURU-SAMA'S NEXT EXPLOITS!
CHEERS!!
GUI (GLUG)
GUI (GULP)
GUIII
PACHI (CLAP)
PACHI
THREE STRAIGHT SHOTS!?

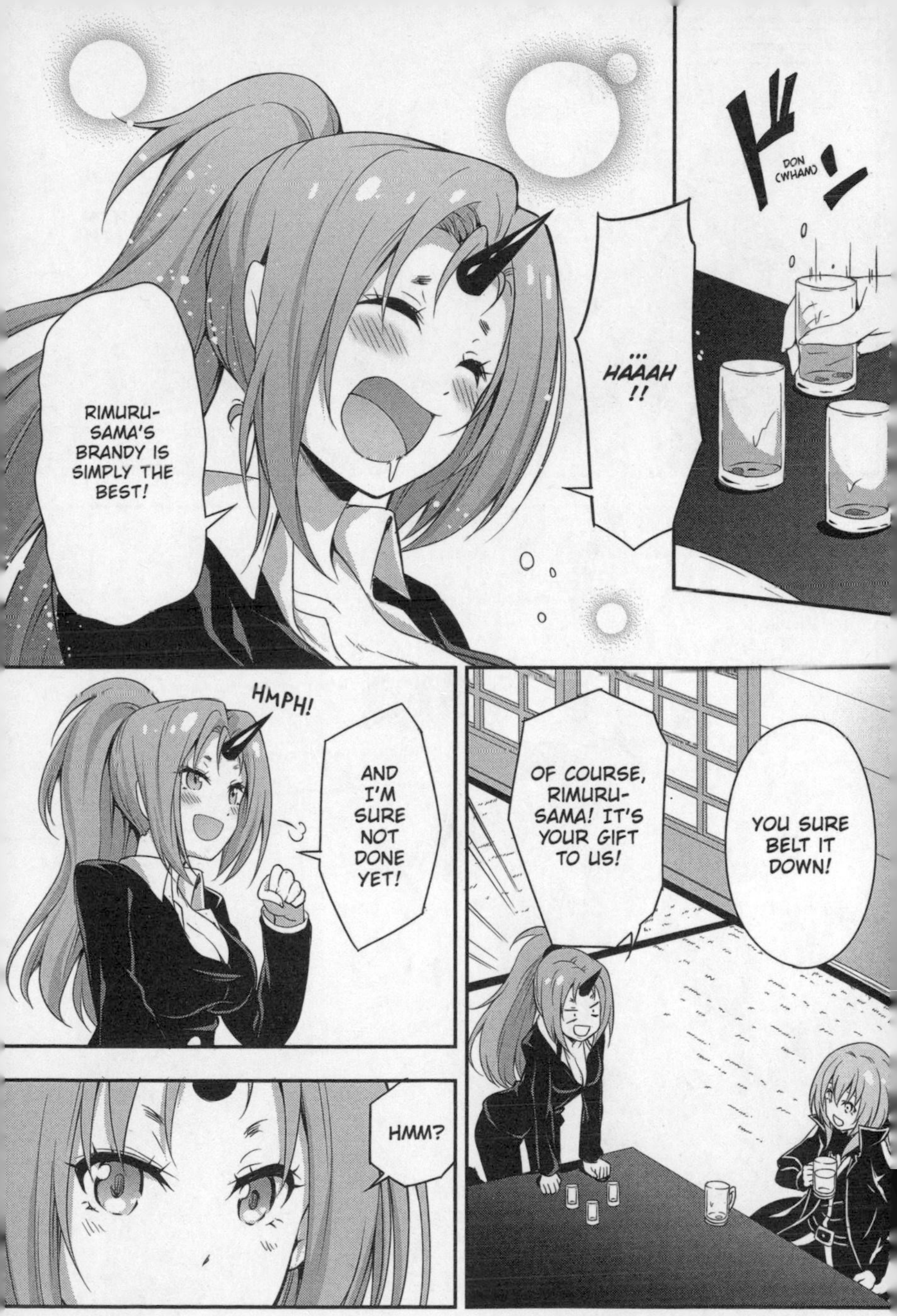
DON (WHAM)
...HÄÄAH!!
RIMURU-SAMA'S BRANDY IS SIMPLY THE BEST!
YOU SURE BELT IT DOWN!
OF COURSE, RIMURU-SAMA! IT'S YOUR GIFT TO US!
HMPH!
AND I'M SURE NOT DONE YET!
HMM?

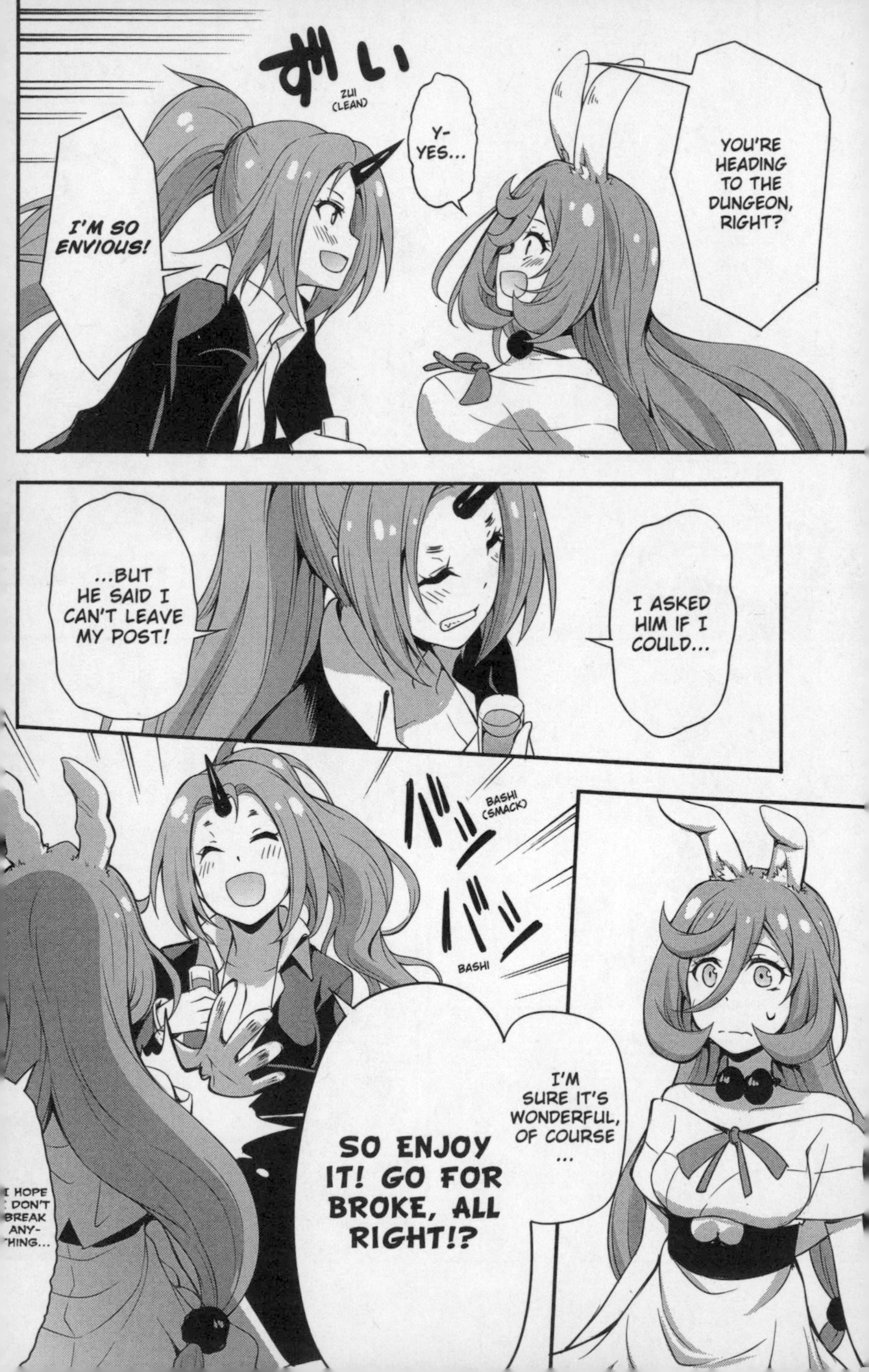
YOU'RE HEADING TO THE DUNGEON, RIGHT?
ずい
ZUI (LEAN)
Y-YES...
I'M SO ENVIOUS!
I ASKED HIM IF I COULD...
...BUT HE SAID I CAN'T LEAVE MY POST!
I'M SURE IT'S WONDERFUL, OF COURSE ...
BASHI (SMACK)
BASHI
SO ENJOY IT! GO FOR BROKE, ALL RIGHT!?
I HOPE DON'T BREAK ANY- HING...

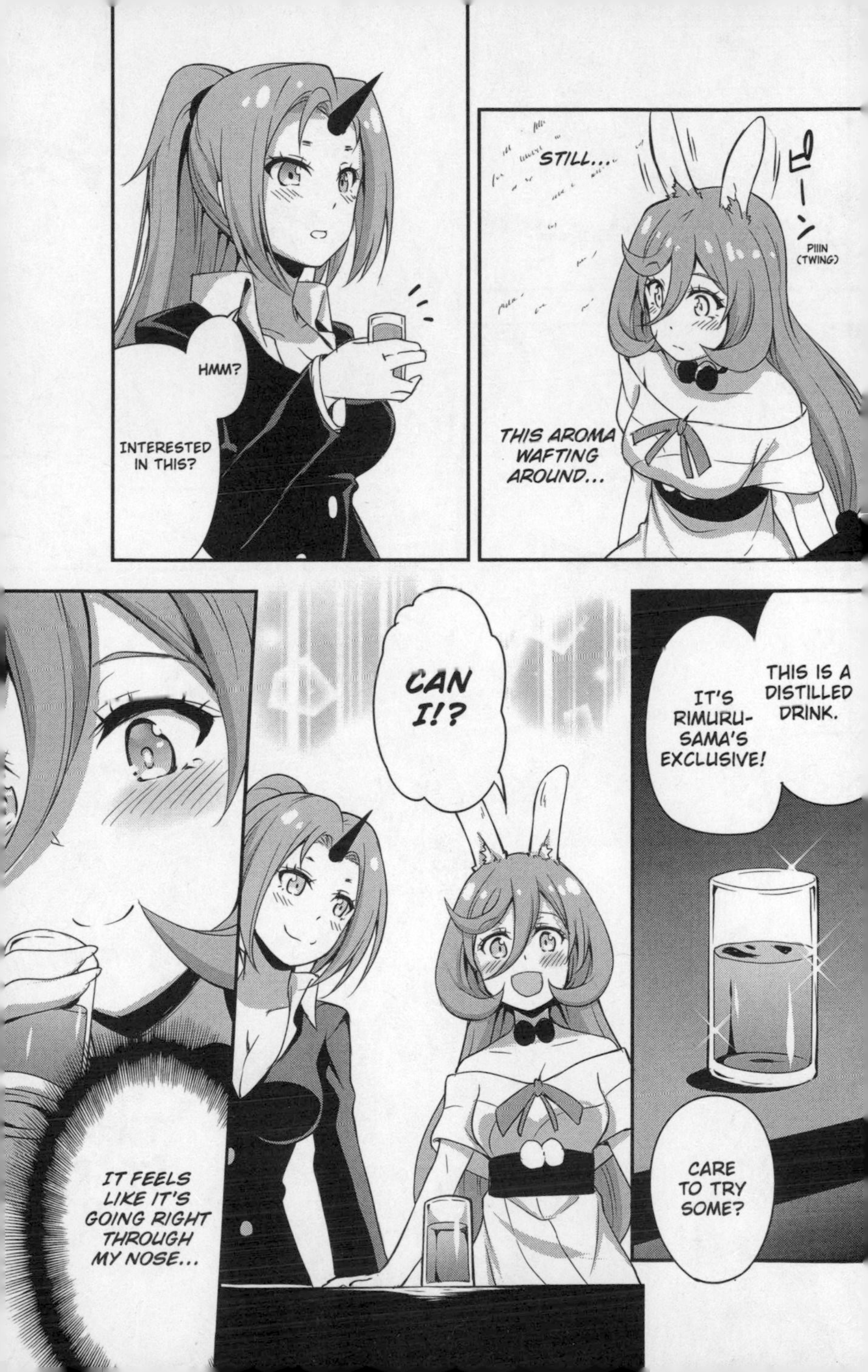
ピーン
PIIN (TWING)
STILL...
THIS AROMA WAFTING AROUND...
HMM?
INTERESTED IN THIS?
THIS IS A DISTILLED DRINK.
IT'S RIMURU-SAMA'S EXCLUSIVE!
CARE TO TRY SOME?
CAN I!?
IT FEELS LIKE IT'S GOING RIGHT THROUGH MY NOSE...

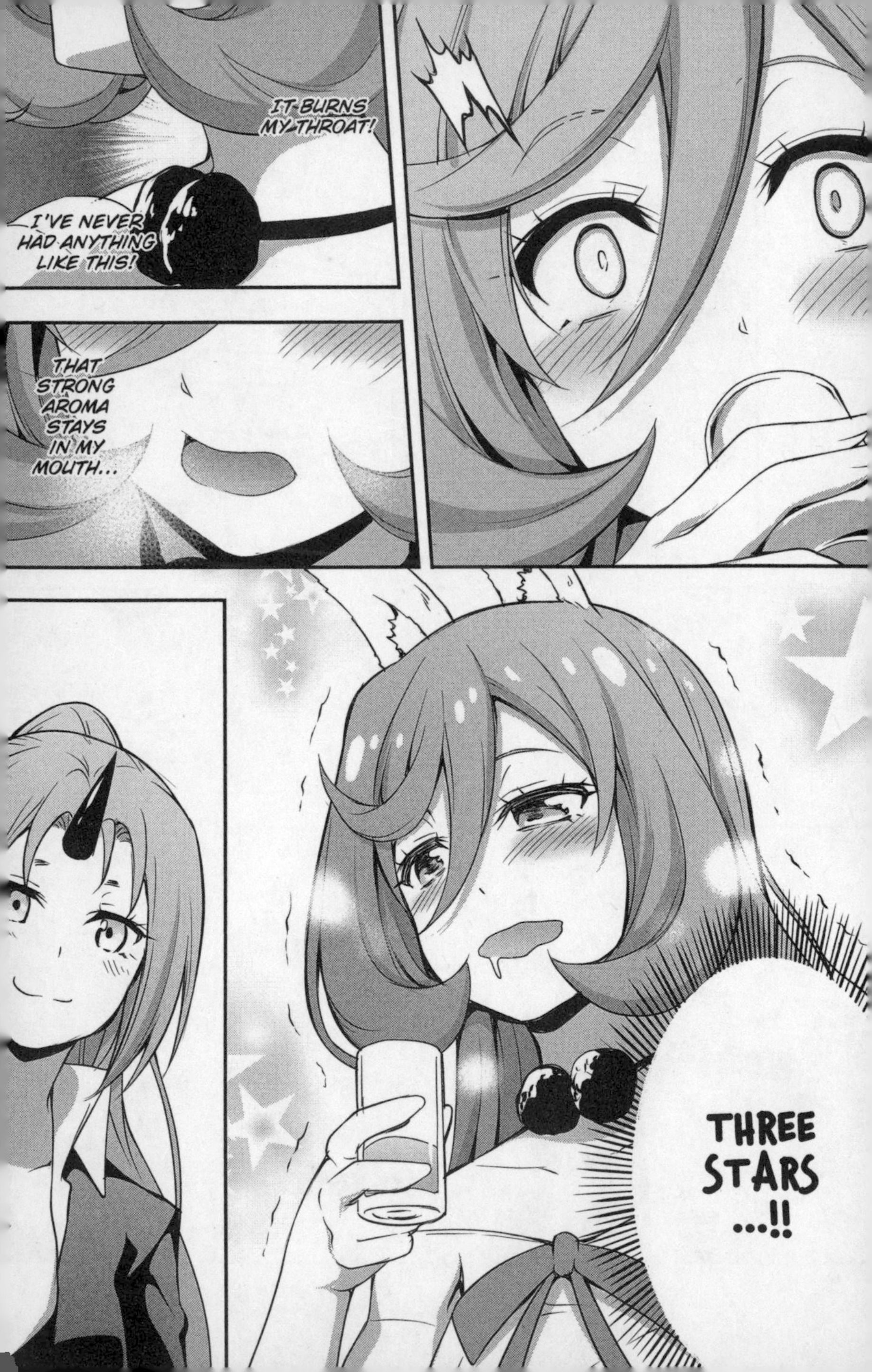
IT BURNS MY THROAT!
I'VE NEVER HAD ANYTHING LIKE THIS!
THAT STRONG AROMA STAYS IN MY MOUTH...
THREE STARS ...!!

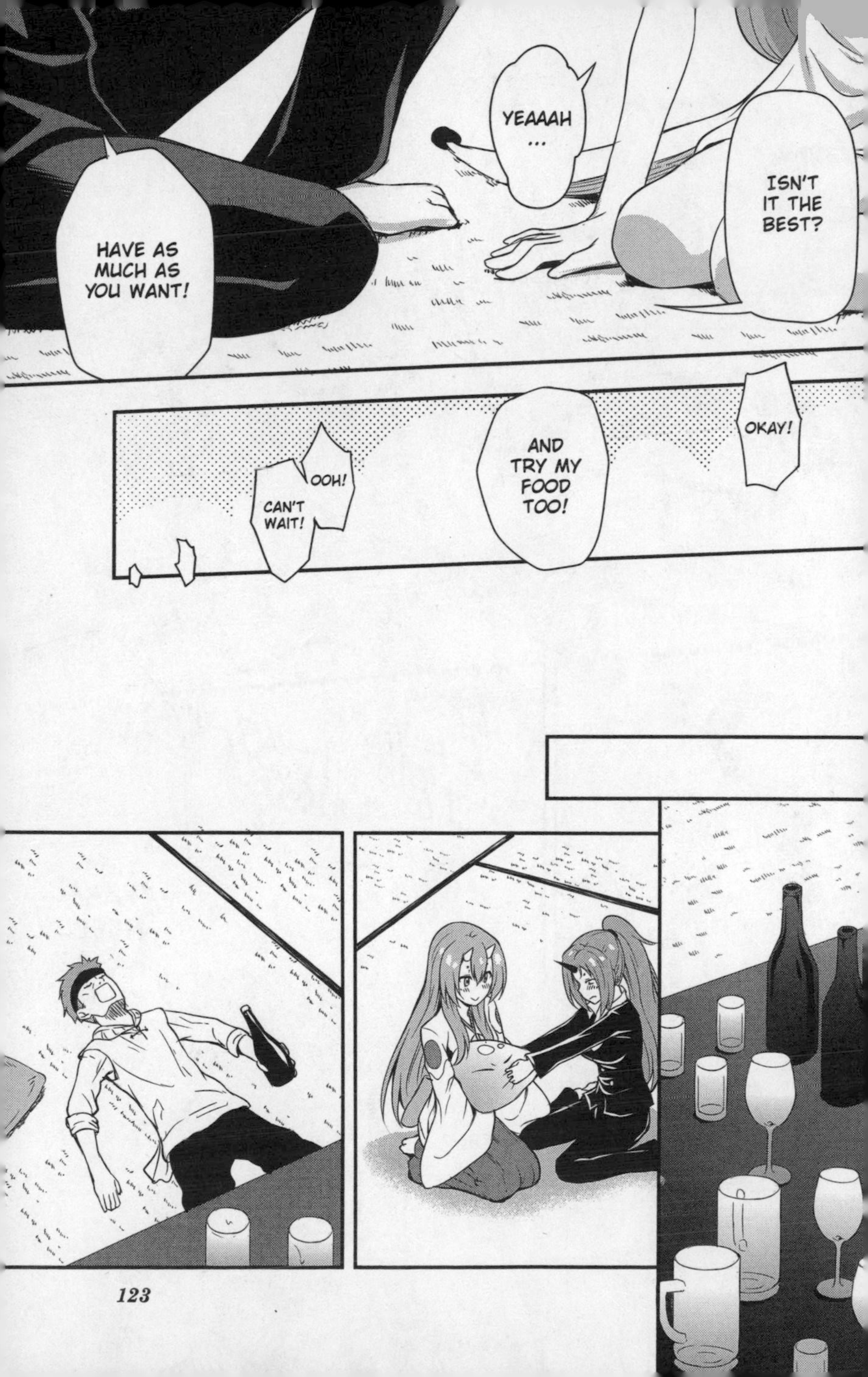
ISN'T IT THE BEST?
YEAAAH ...
HAVE AS MUCH AS YOU WANT!
OKAY!
AND TRY MY FOOD TOO!
OOH!
CAN'T WAIT!

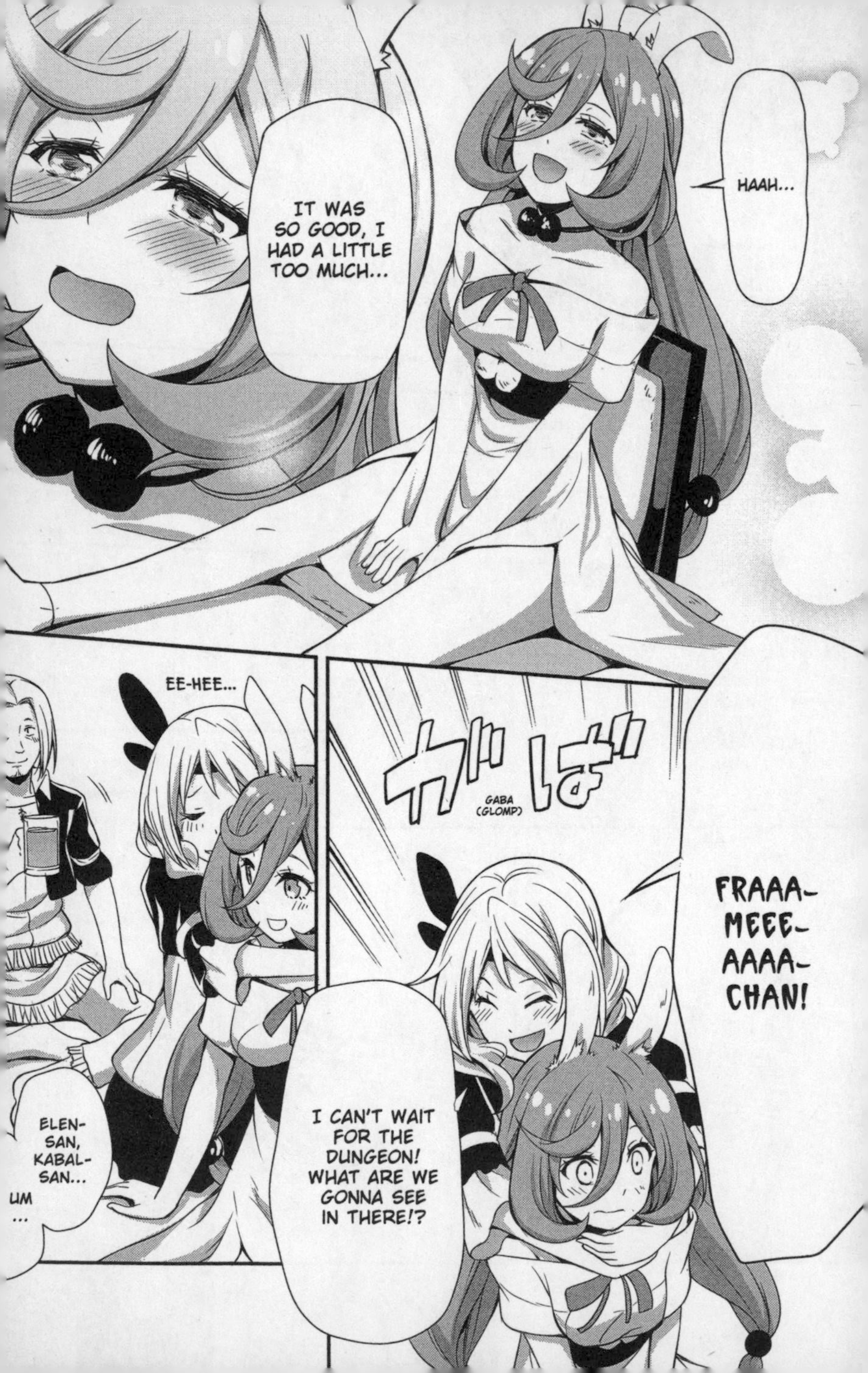
HAAH...
IT WAS SO GOOD, I HAD A LITTLE TOO MUCH...
FRAAA-MEEE-AAAA-CHAN!
GABA (GLOMP)
I CAN'T WAIT FOR THE DUNGEON! WHAT ARE WE GONNA SEE IN THERE!?
EE-HEE...
ELEN-SAN, KABAL-SAN...
UM ...

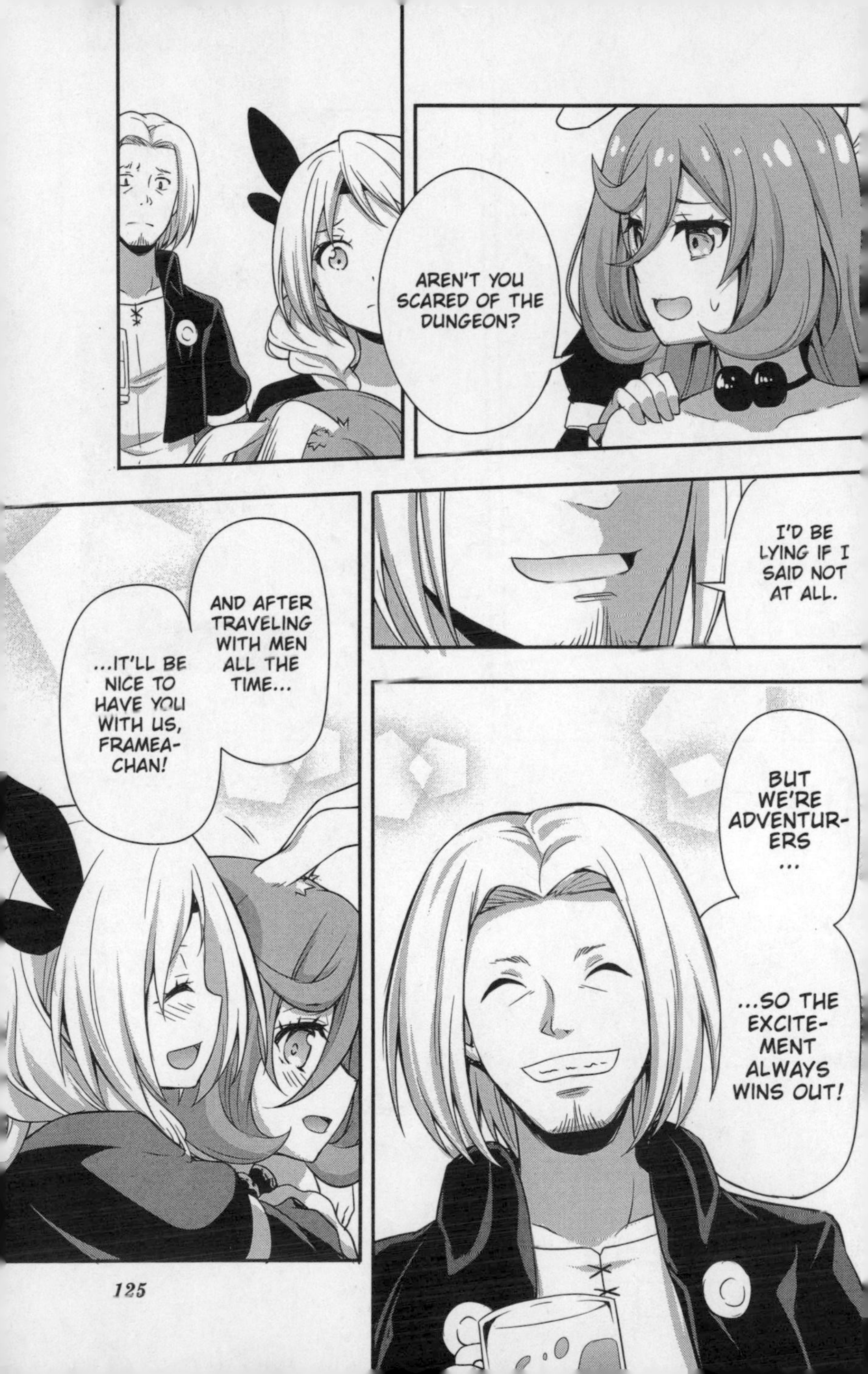
AREN'T YOU SCARED OF THE DUNGEON?
I'D BE LYING IF I SAID NOT AT ALL.
BUT WE'RE ADVENTURERS...
...SO THE EXCITEMENT ALWAYS WINS OUT!
AND AFTER TRAVELING WITH MEN ALL THE TIME...
...IT'LL BE NICE TO HAVE YOU WITH US, FRAMEA-CHAN!

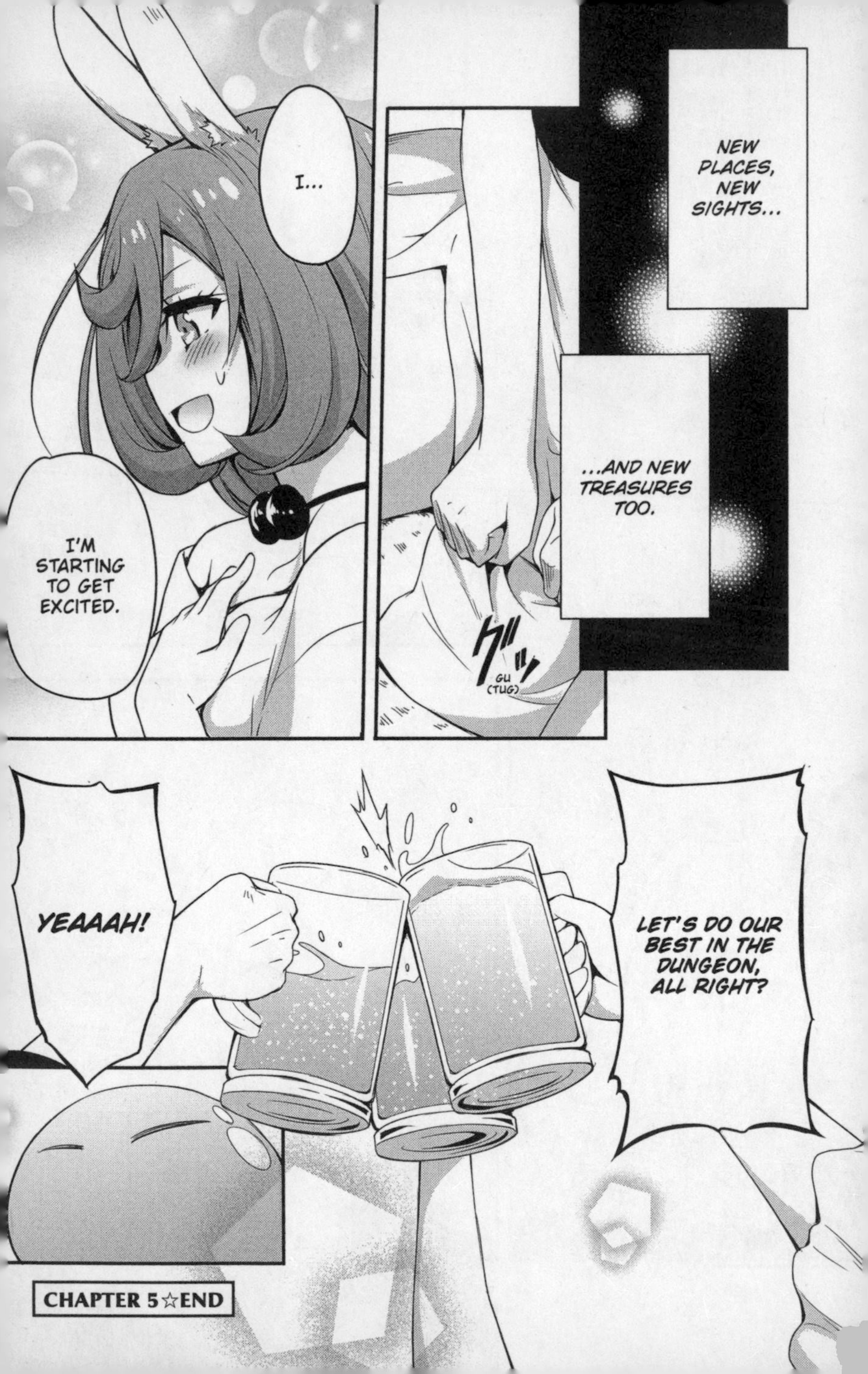
NEW PLACES, NEW SIGHTS...
...AND NEW TREASURES TOO.
グッ
GU (TUG)
I...
I'M STARTING TO GET EXCITED.
LET'S DO OUR BEST IN THE DUNGEON, ALL RIGHT?
YEAAAH!
CHAPTER 5☆END

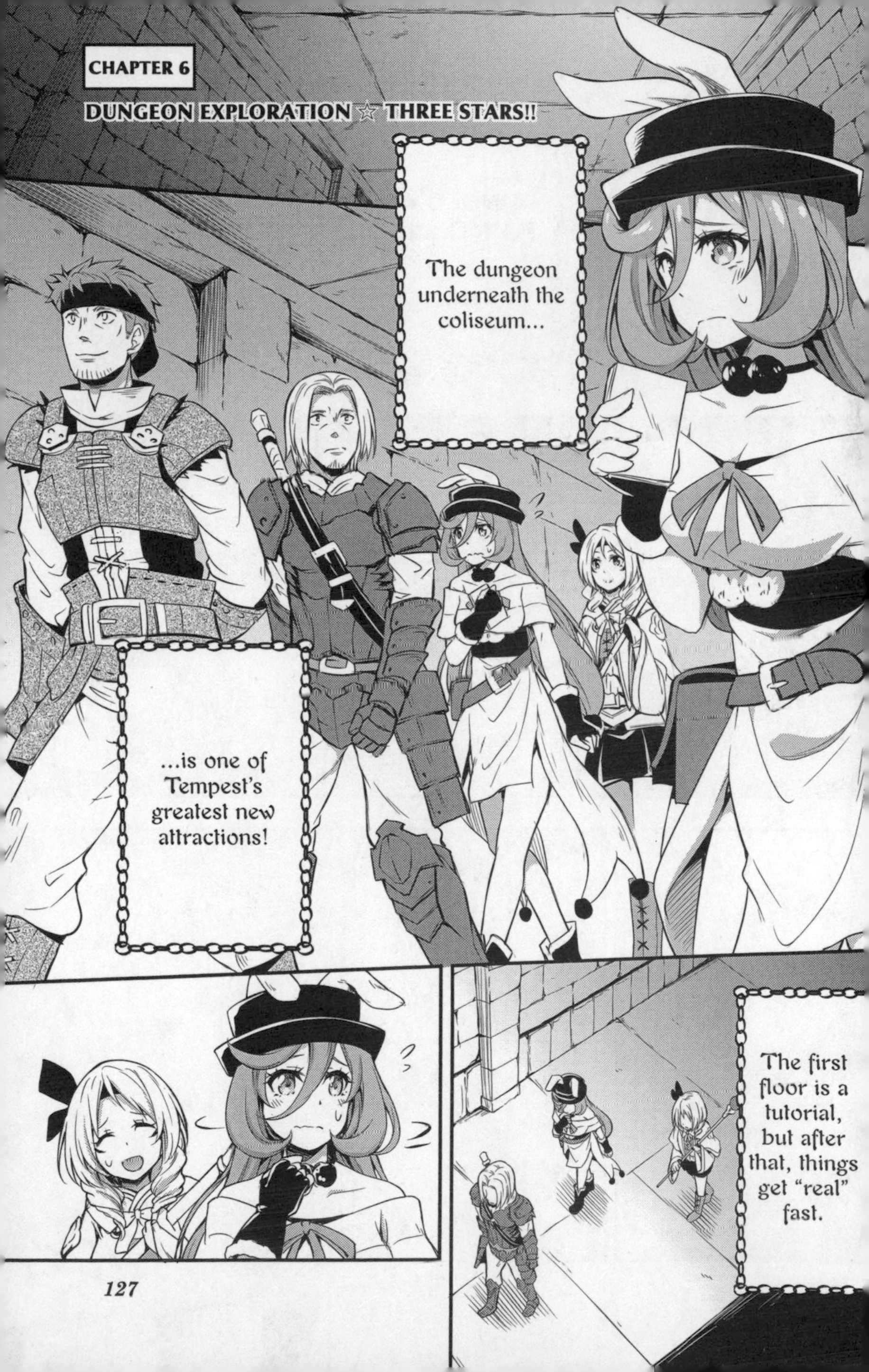
CHAPTER 6
DUNGEON EXPLORATION ☆ THREE STARS!!
The dungeon underneath the coliseum...
...is one of Tempest's greatest new attractions!
The first floor is a tutorial, but after that, things get "real" fast.

DUNGEON POINTERS

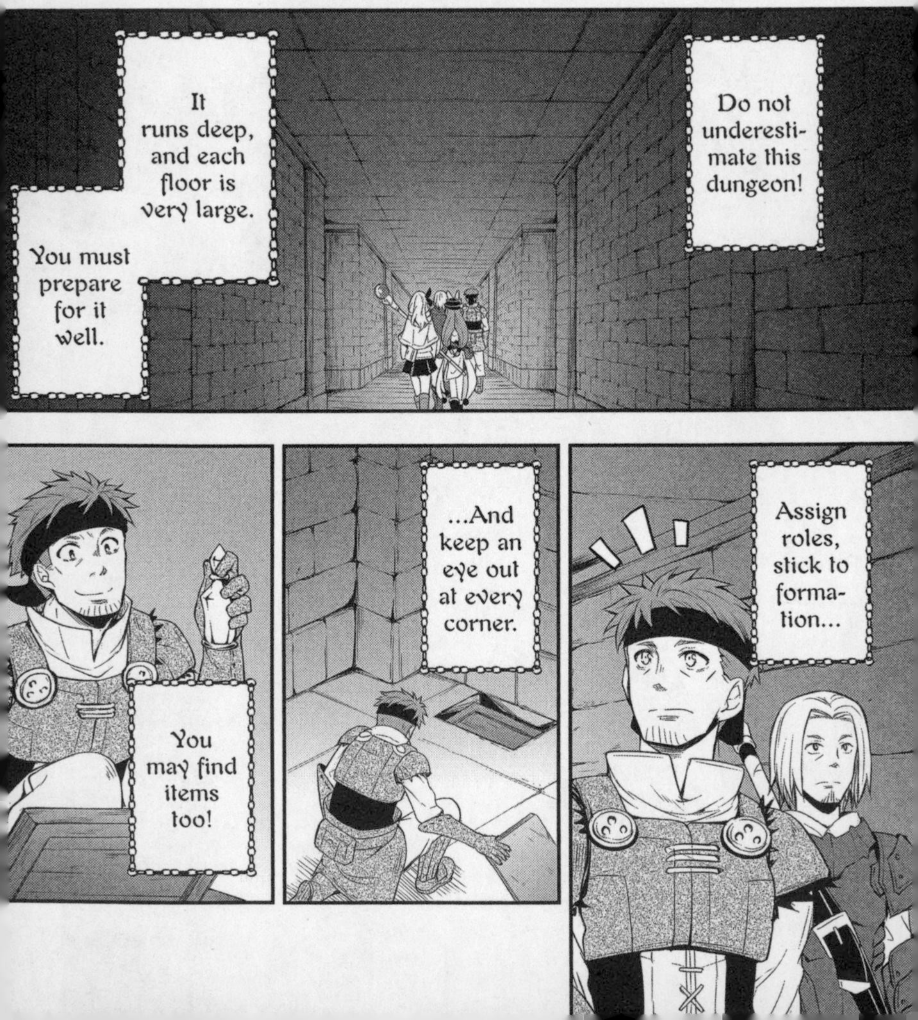
Do not underestimate this dungeon!
It runs deep, and each floor is very large.
You must prepare for it well.
Assign roles, stick to formation...
...And keep an eye out at every corner.
You may find items too!

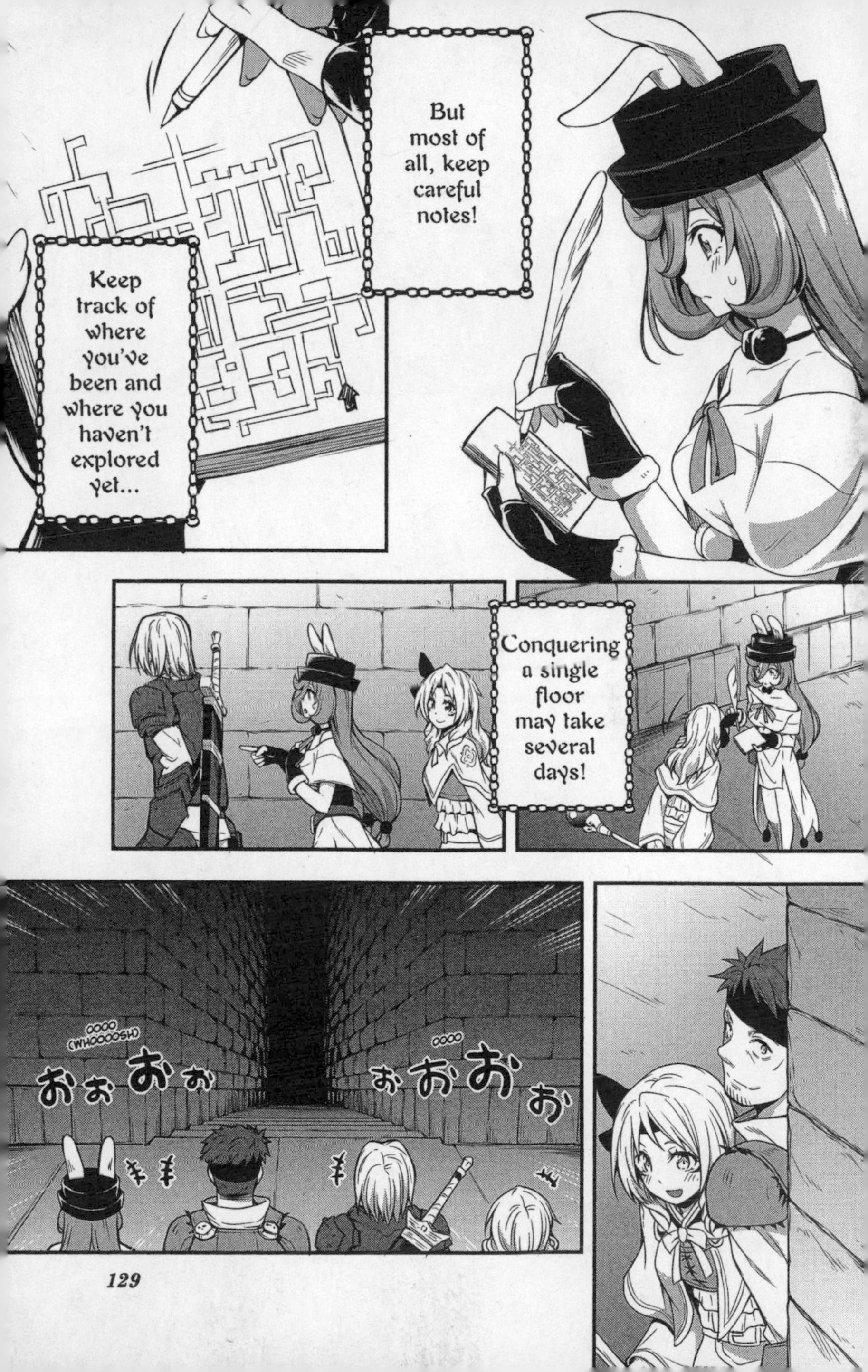
Keep track of where you've been and where you haven't explored yet...
But most of all, keep careful notes!
Conquering a single floor may take several days!
oooo
ぉおおぉ
oooo (WHOOOOSH)
おぉおぉ

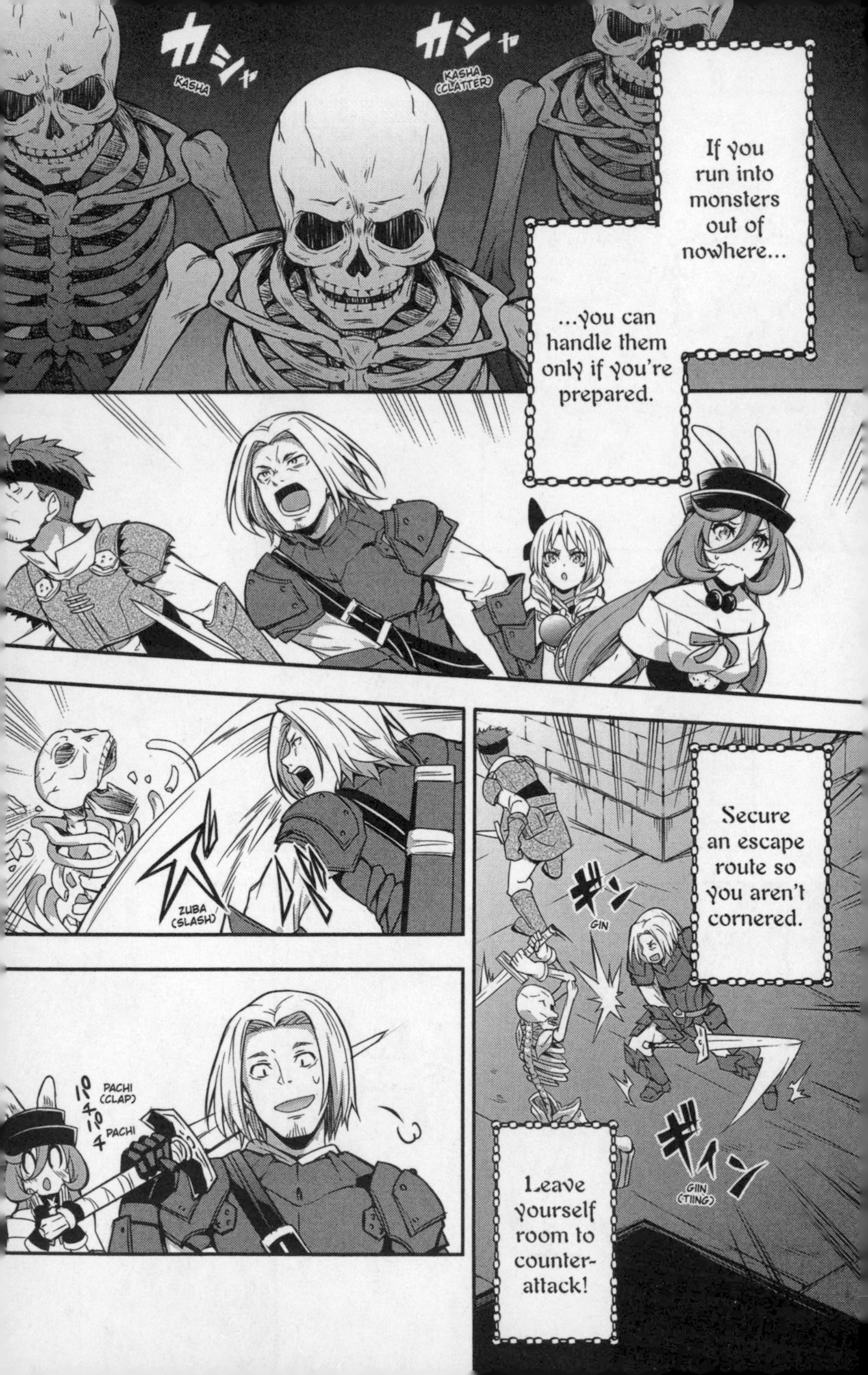
カシャ
KASHA (CLATTER)
カシャ
KASHA
If you run into monsters out of nowhere...
...you can handle them only if you're prepared.
Secure an escape route so you aren't cornered.
ギン
GIN
ギィン
GIIN (TIING)
Leave yourself room to counter-attack!
ZUBA (SLASH)
パチ
PACHI (CLAP)
パチ
PACHI

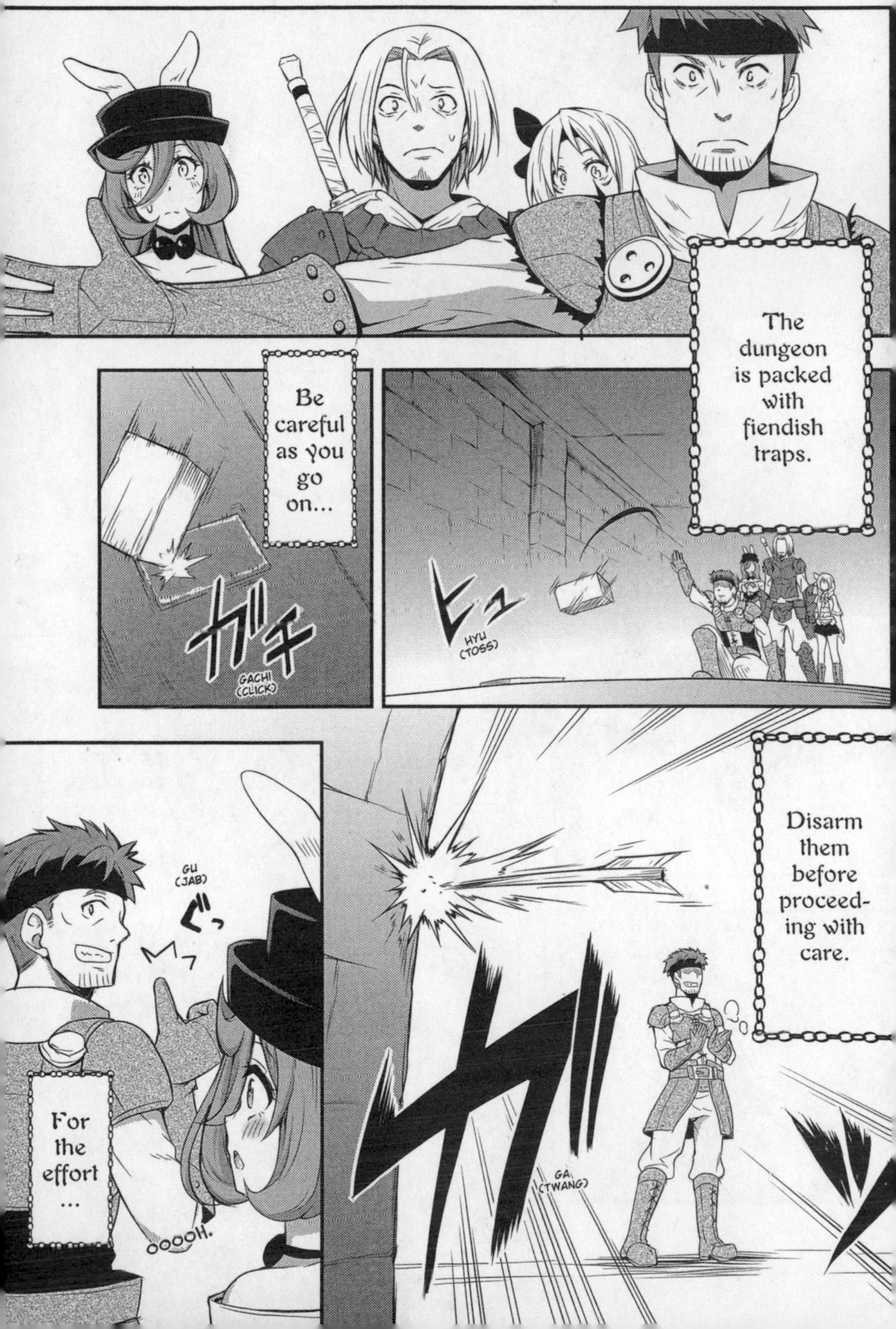
The dungeon is packed with fiendish traps.
ヒュ
HYU (TOSS)
Be careful as you go on...
ガチ
GACHI (CLICK)
Disarm them before proceeding with care.
GA (TWANG)
GU (JAB)
ぐっ
For the effort...
OOOOH.

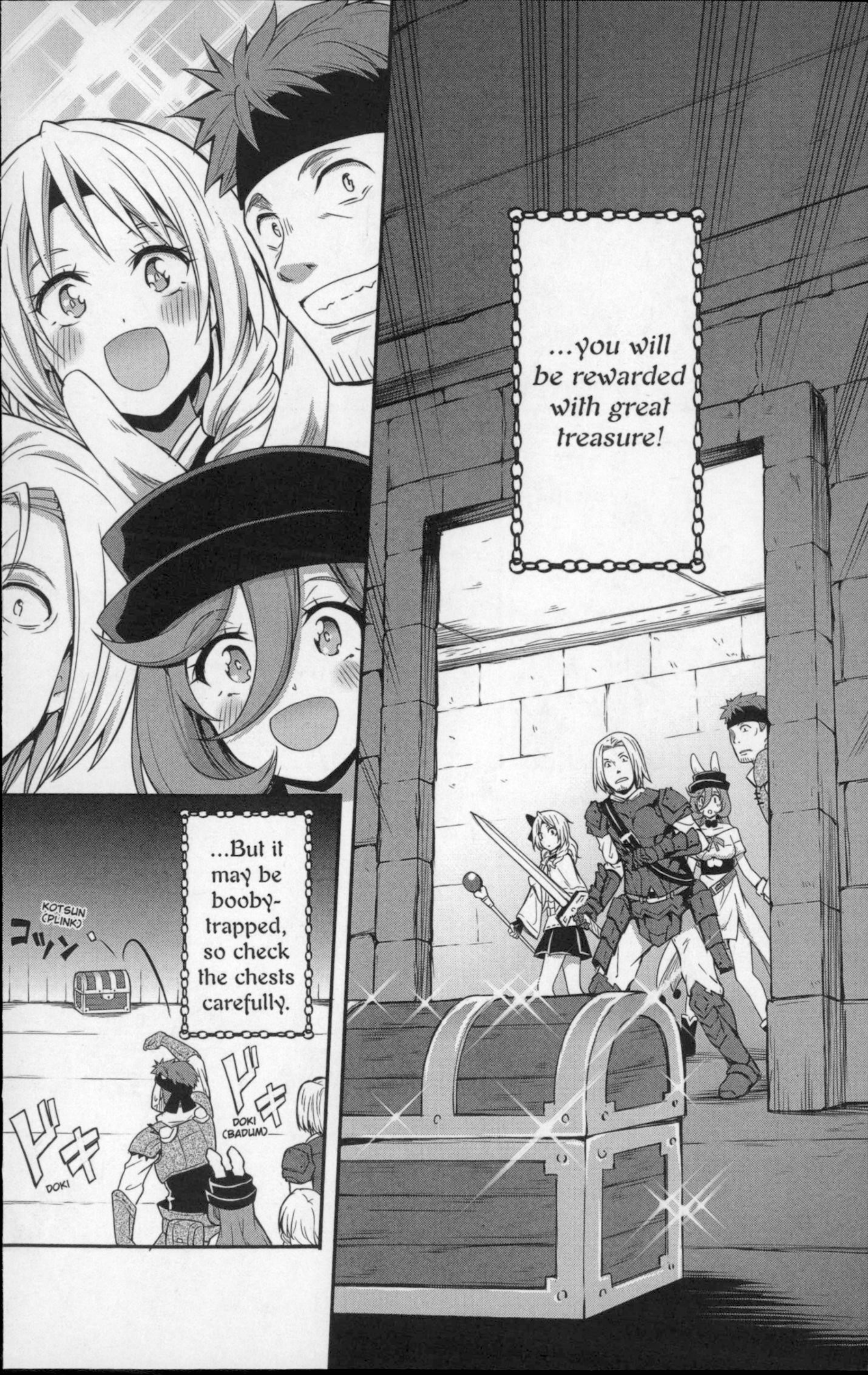
...you will be rewarded with great treasure!
...But it may be booby-trapped, so check the chests carefully.
コツン
KOTSUN (PLINK)
ドキ ドキ
DOKI (BADUM)
DOKI

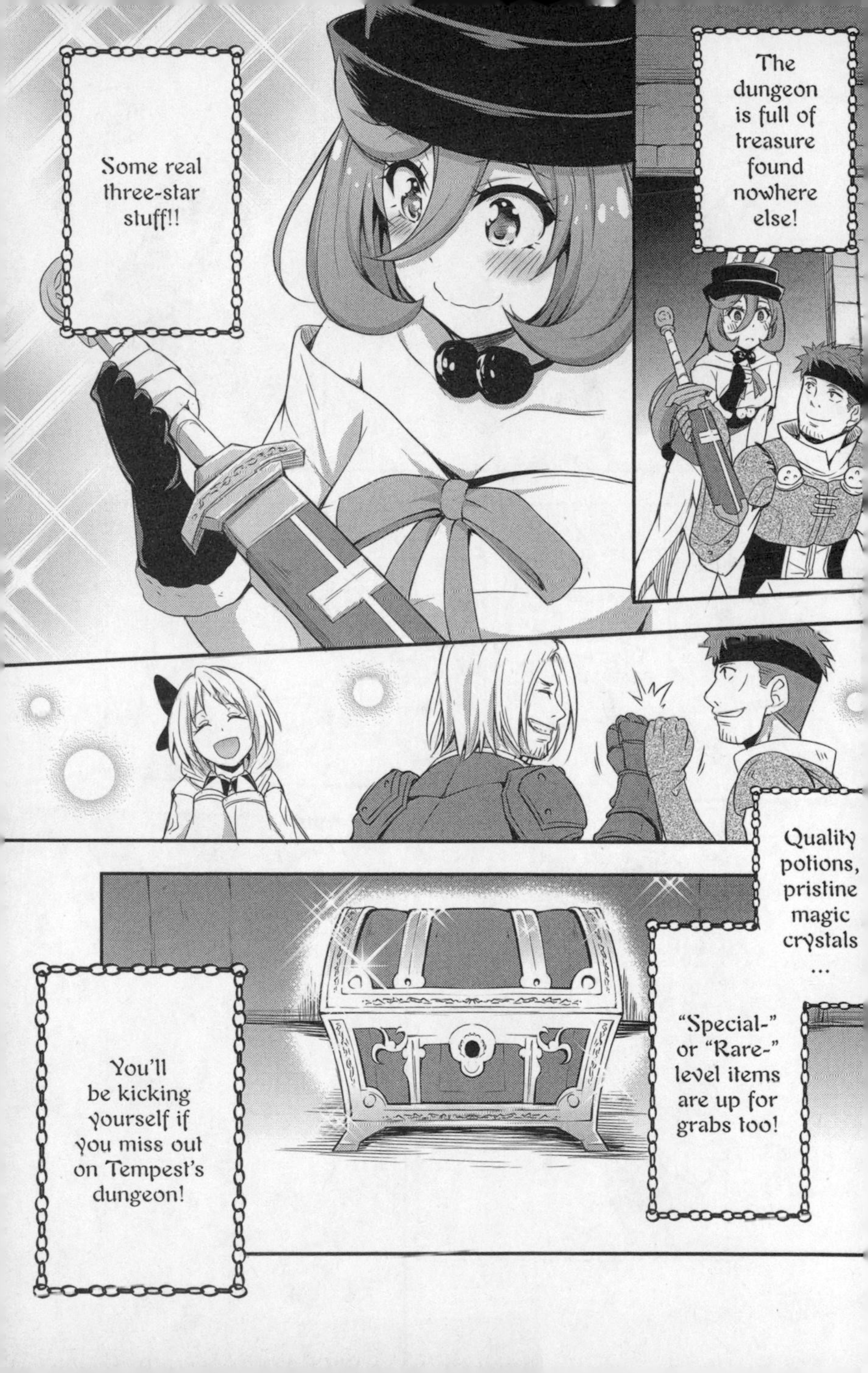
The dungeon is full of treasure found nowhere else!
Some real three-star stuff!!
Quality potions, pristine magic crystals…
"Special-" or "Rare-" level items are up for grabs too!
You'll be kicking yourself if you miss out on Tempest's dungeon!

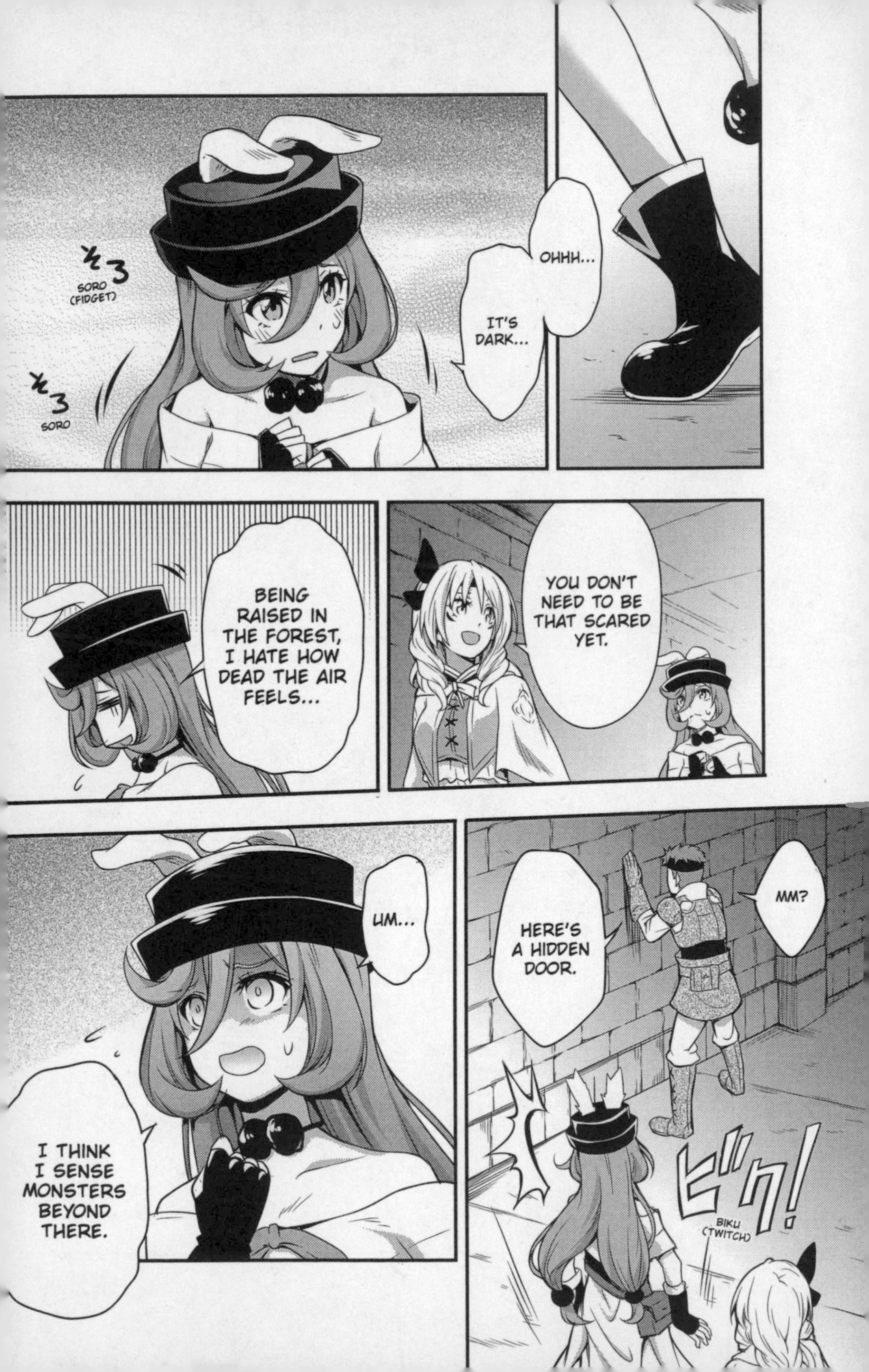
OHHH...
IT'S DARK...
そろ
SORO (FIDGET)
そろ
SORO
YOU DON'T NEED TO BE THAT SCARED YET.
BEING RAISED IN THE FOREST, I HATE HOW DEAD THE AIR FEELS...
MM?
HERE'S A HIDDEN DOOR.
ビク!
BIKU (TWITCH)
UM...
I THINK I SENSE MONSTERS BEYOND THERE.

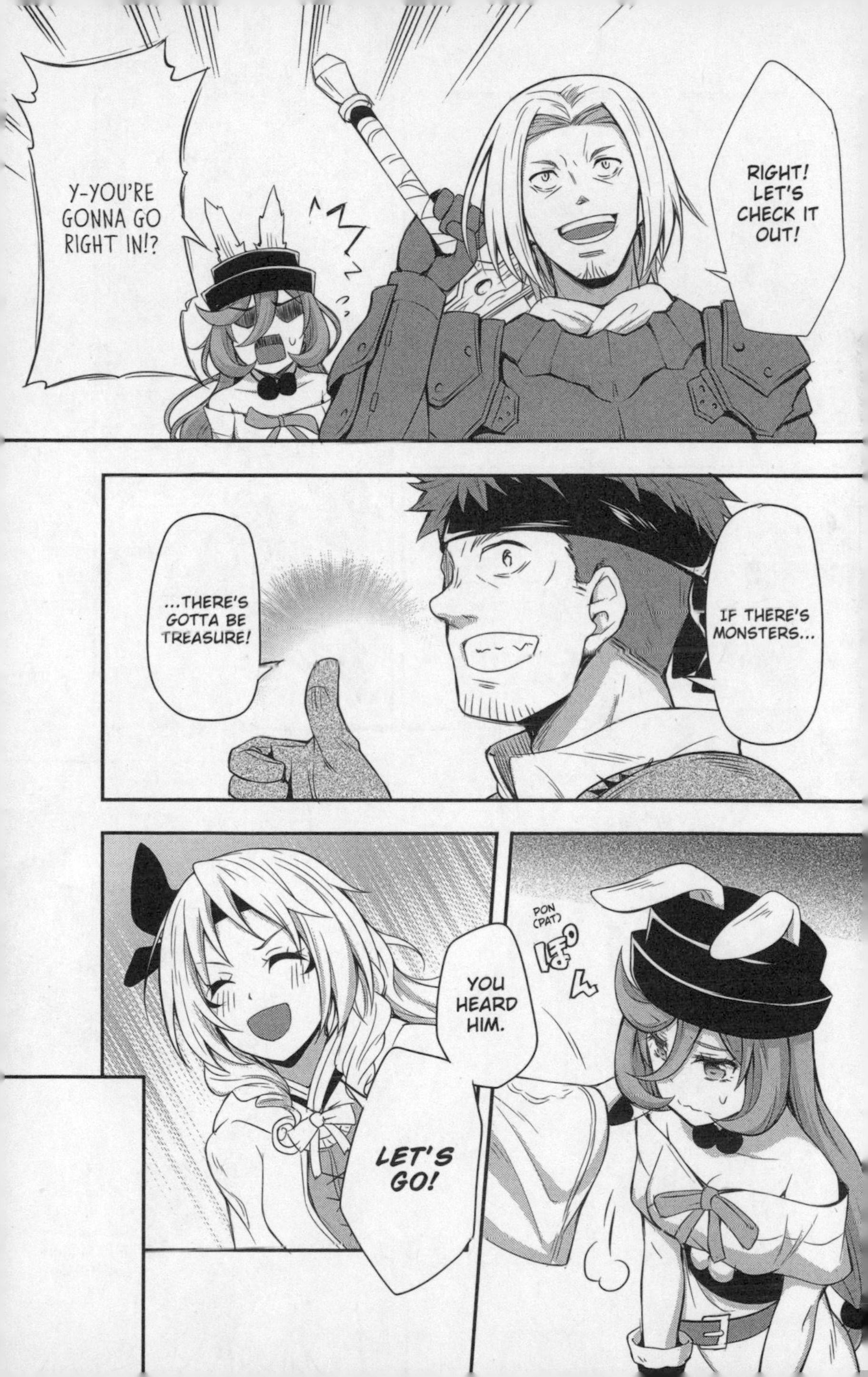
RIGHT! LET'S CHECK IT OUT!
Y-YOU'RE GONNA GO RIGHT IN!?
IF THERE'S MONSTERS...
...THERE'S GOTTA BE TREASURE!
PON (PAT)
YOU HEARD HIM.
LET'S GO!

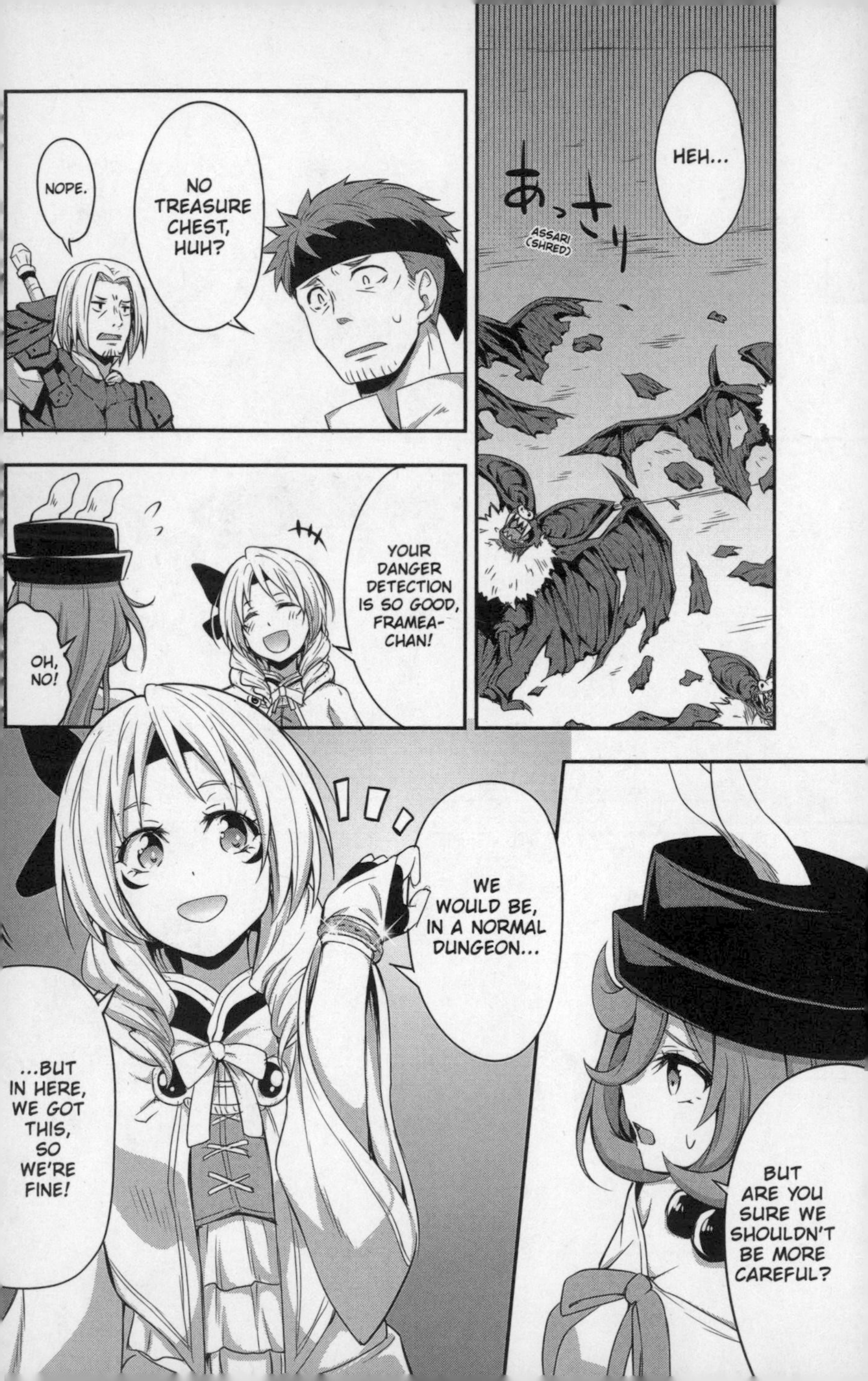
HEH...
あっさり
ASSARI (SHRED)
NO TREASURE CHEST, HUH?
NOPE.
YOUR DANGER DETECTION IS SO GOOD, FRAMEA-CHAN!
OH, NO!
BUT ARE YOU SURE WE SHOULDN'T BE MORE CAREFUL?
WE WOULD BE, IN A NORMAL DUNGEON...
...BUT IN HERE, WE GOT THIS, SO WE'RE FINE!

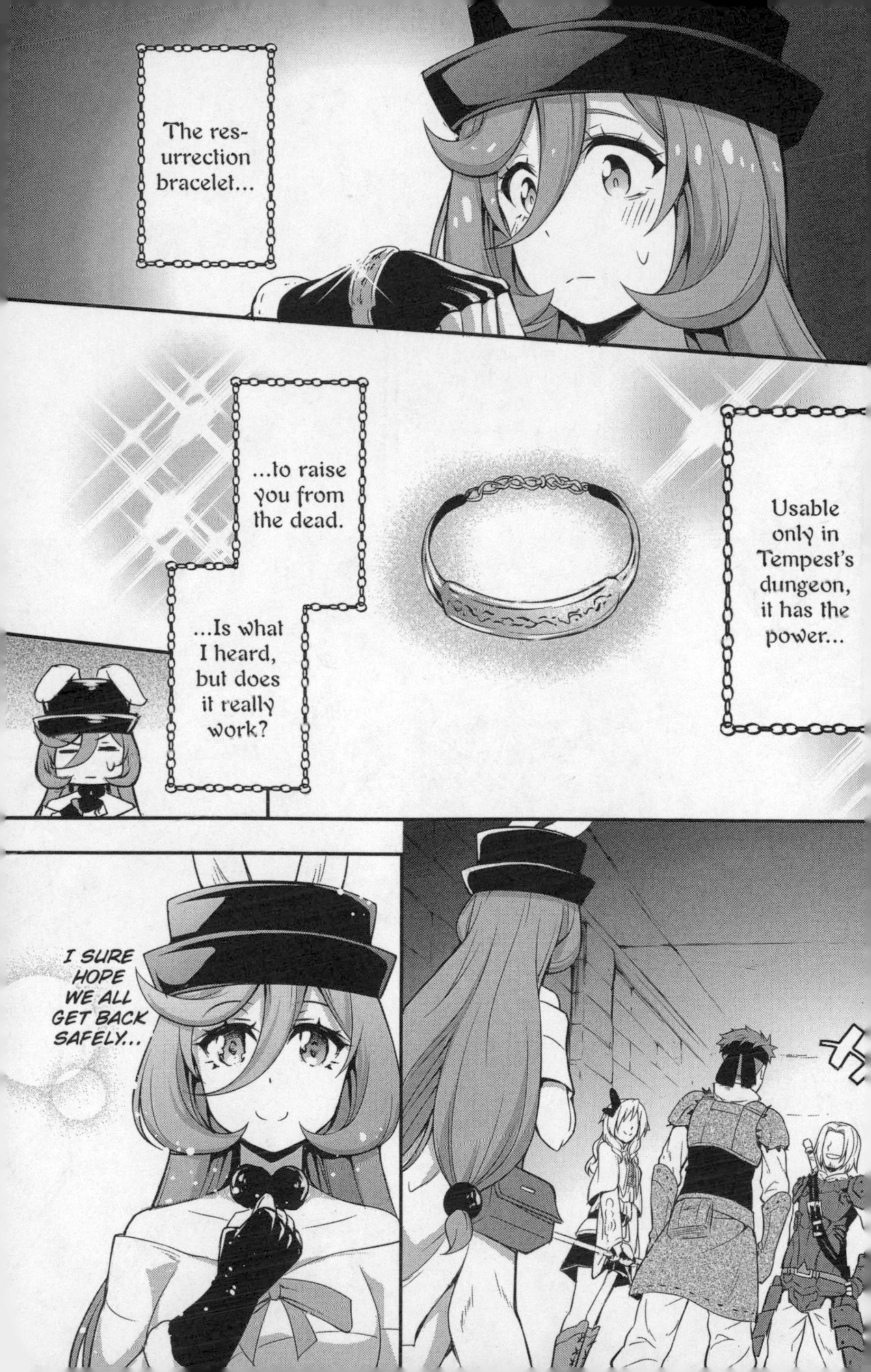

The resurrection bracelet...
Usable only in Tempest's dungeon, it has the power...
...to raise you from the dead.
...Is what I heard, but does it really work?
I SURE HOPE WE ALL GET BACK SAFELY...

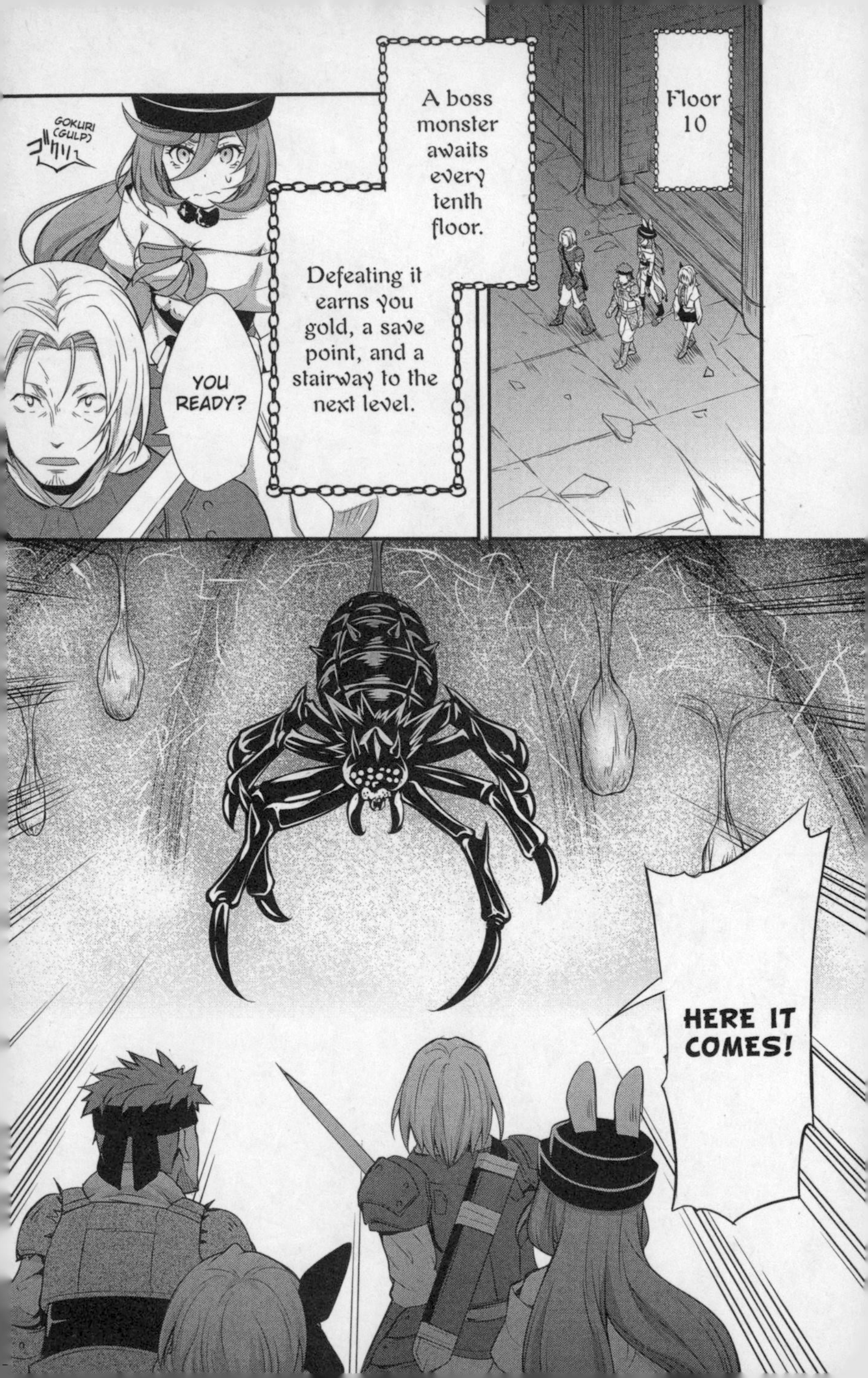
Floor 10
A boss monster awaits every tenth floor.
Defeating it earns you gold, a save point, and a stairway to the next level.
GOKURI (GULP)
YOU READY?
HERE IT COMES!

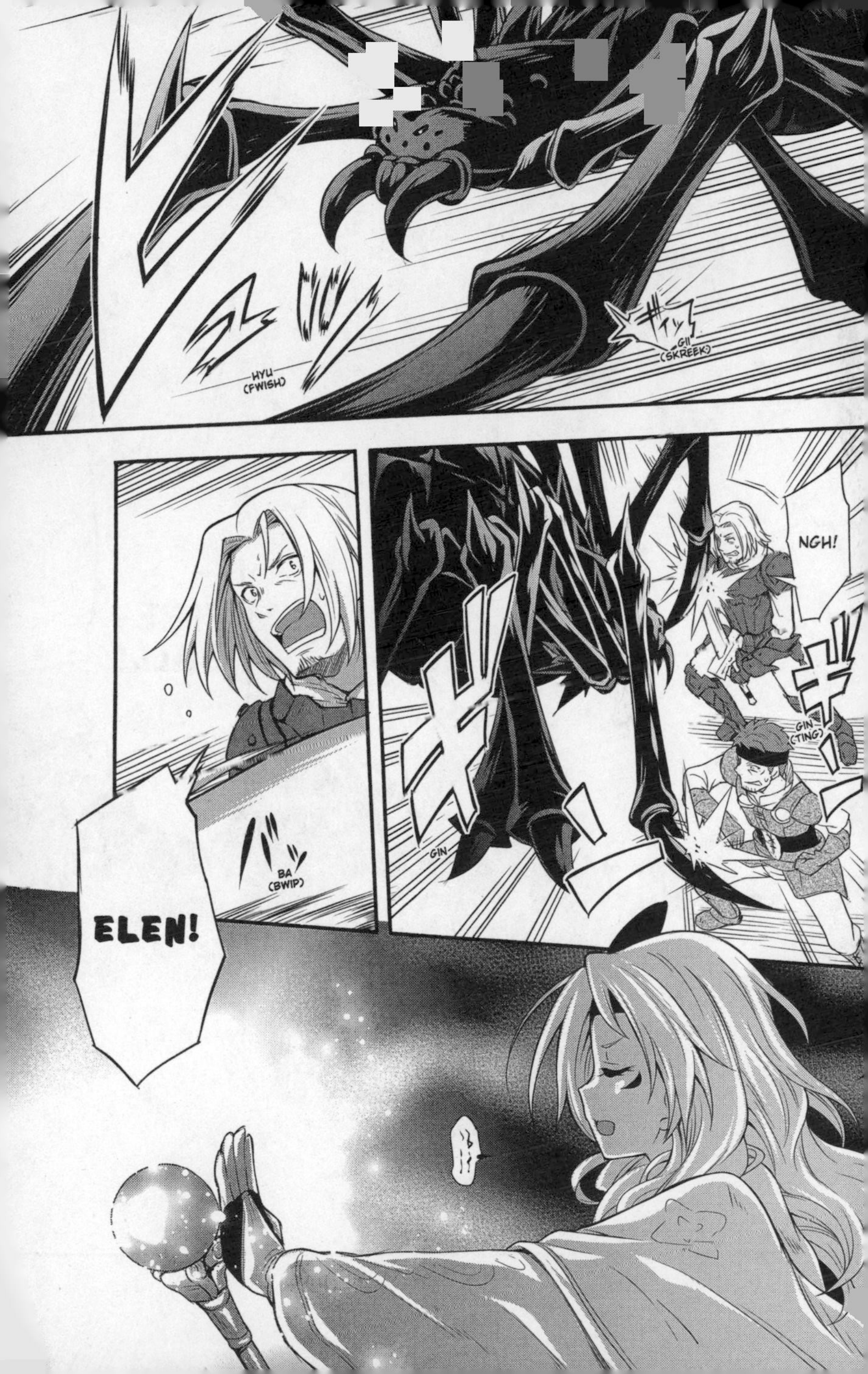
GII
(SKREEK)
HYU
(FWISH)
NGH!
GIN
(TING)
GIN
BA
(BWIP)
ELEN!

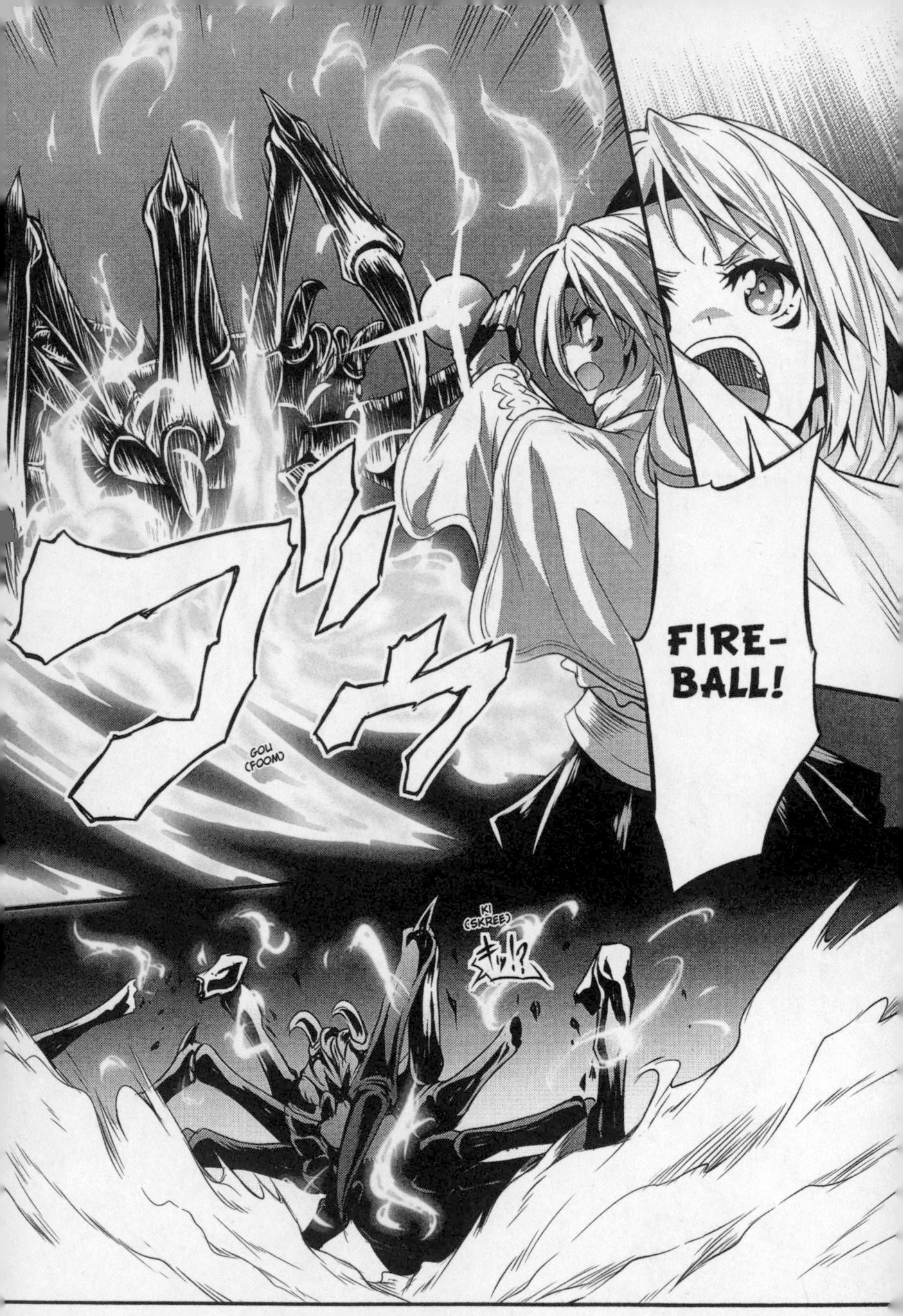
FIRE-BALL!
GOU (FOOM)
KI (SKREE)

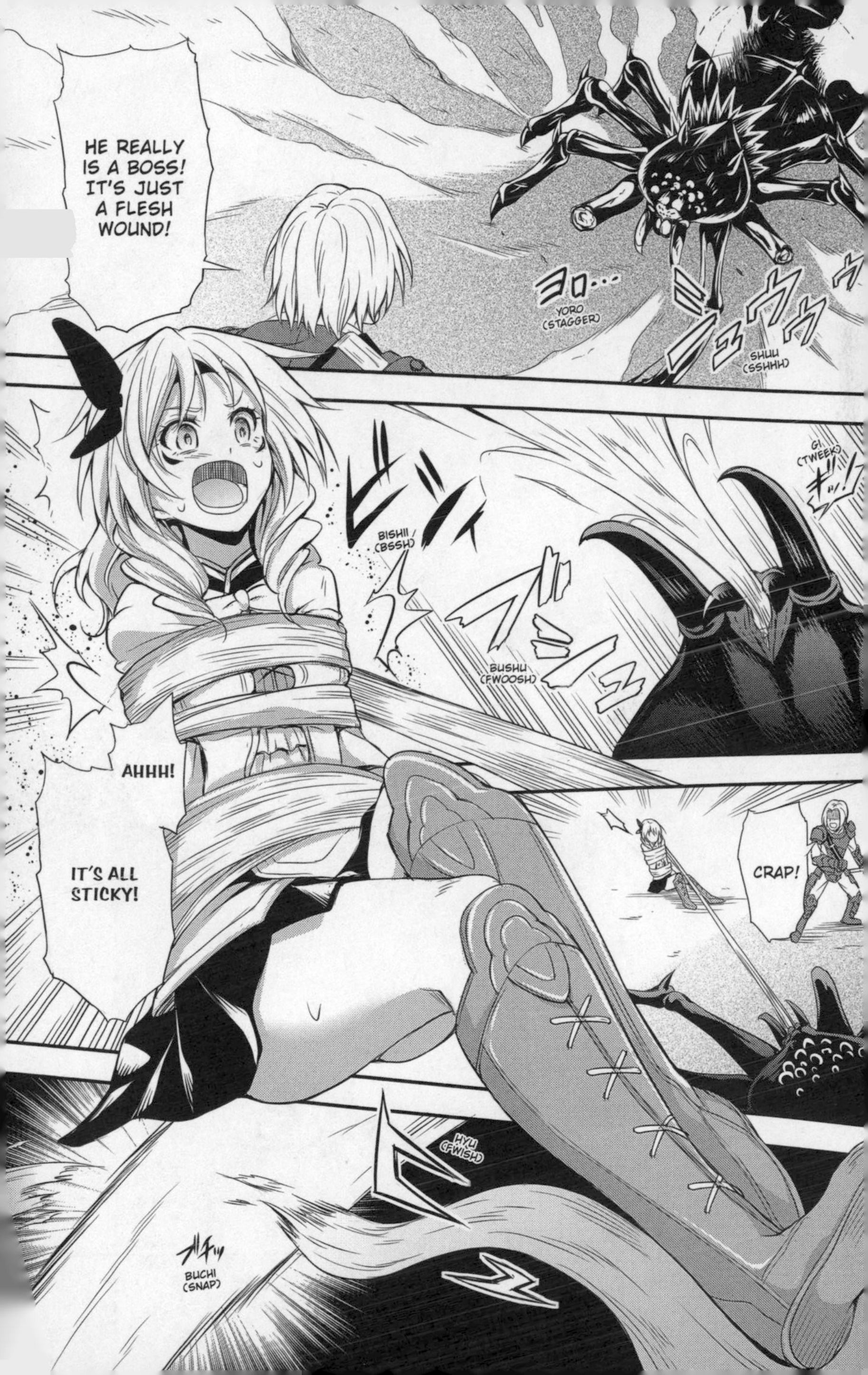
HE REALLY IS A BOSS! IT'S JUST A FLESH WOUND!
YORO (STAGGER)
SHUU (SSHHH)
GI (TWEEK)
BISHU (BSSH)
BUSHU (FWOOSH)
AHHH!
IT'S ALL STICKY!
CRAP!
HYU (FWISH)
BUCHI (SNAP)

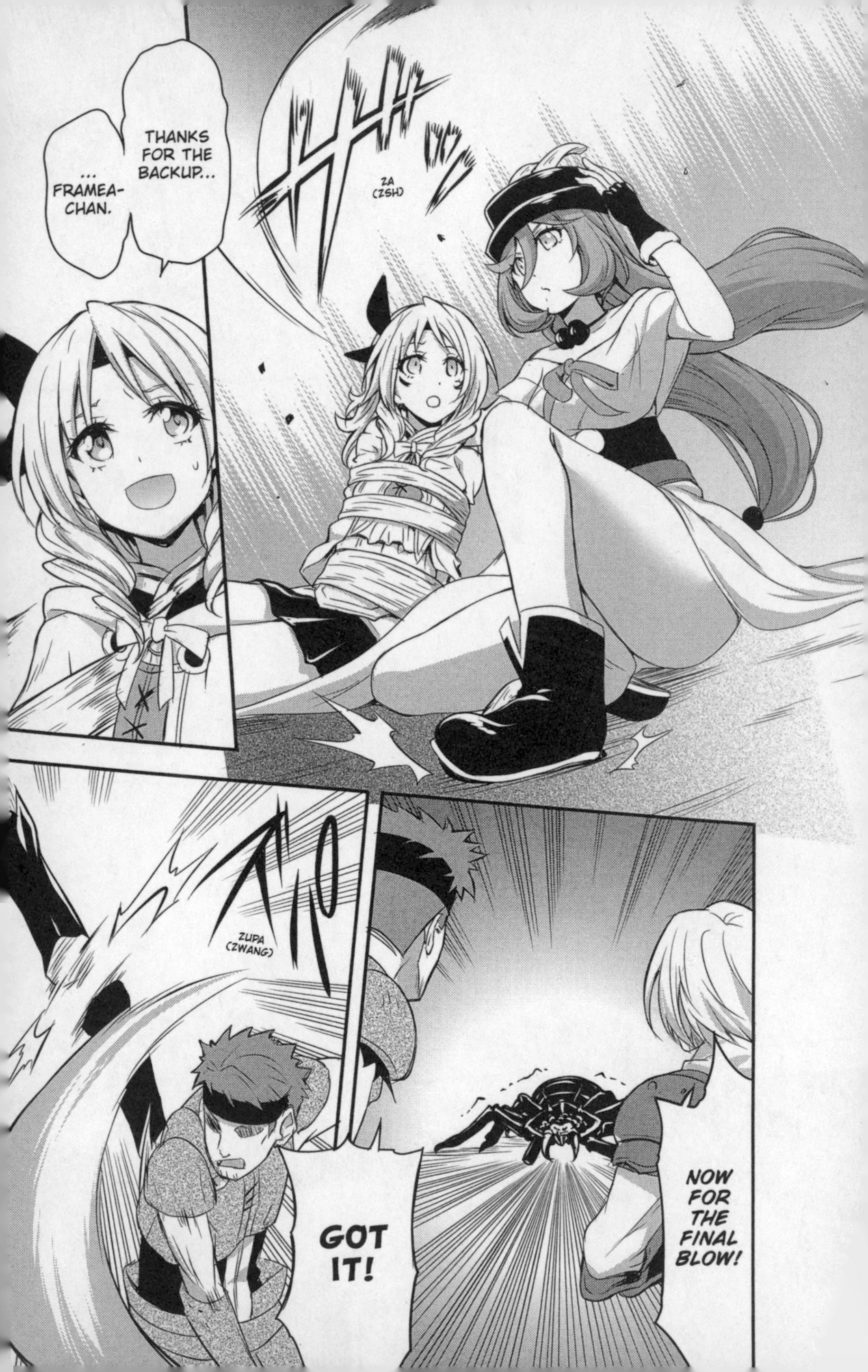
ZA (ZSH)
THANKS FOR THE BACKUP...
... FRAMEA-CHAN.
NOW FOR THE FINAL BLOW!
ZUPA (ZWANG)
GOT IT!

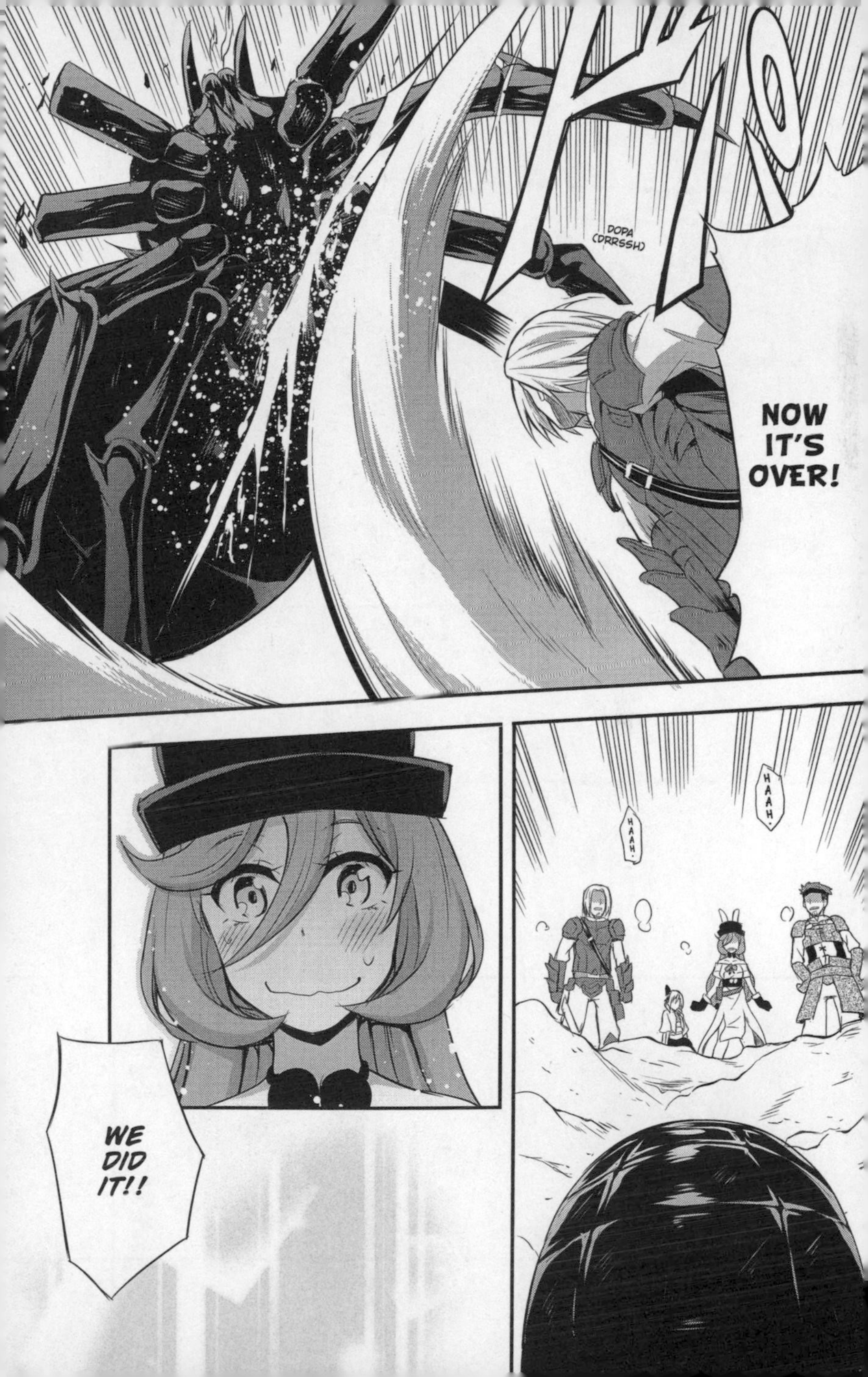
DOPA (DRRSSH)
NOW IT'S OVER!
HAAH.
HAAH.
WE DID IT!!

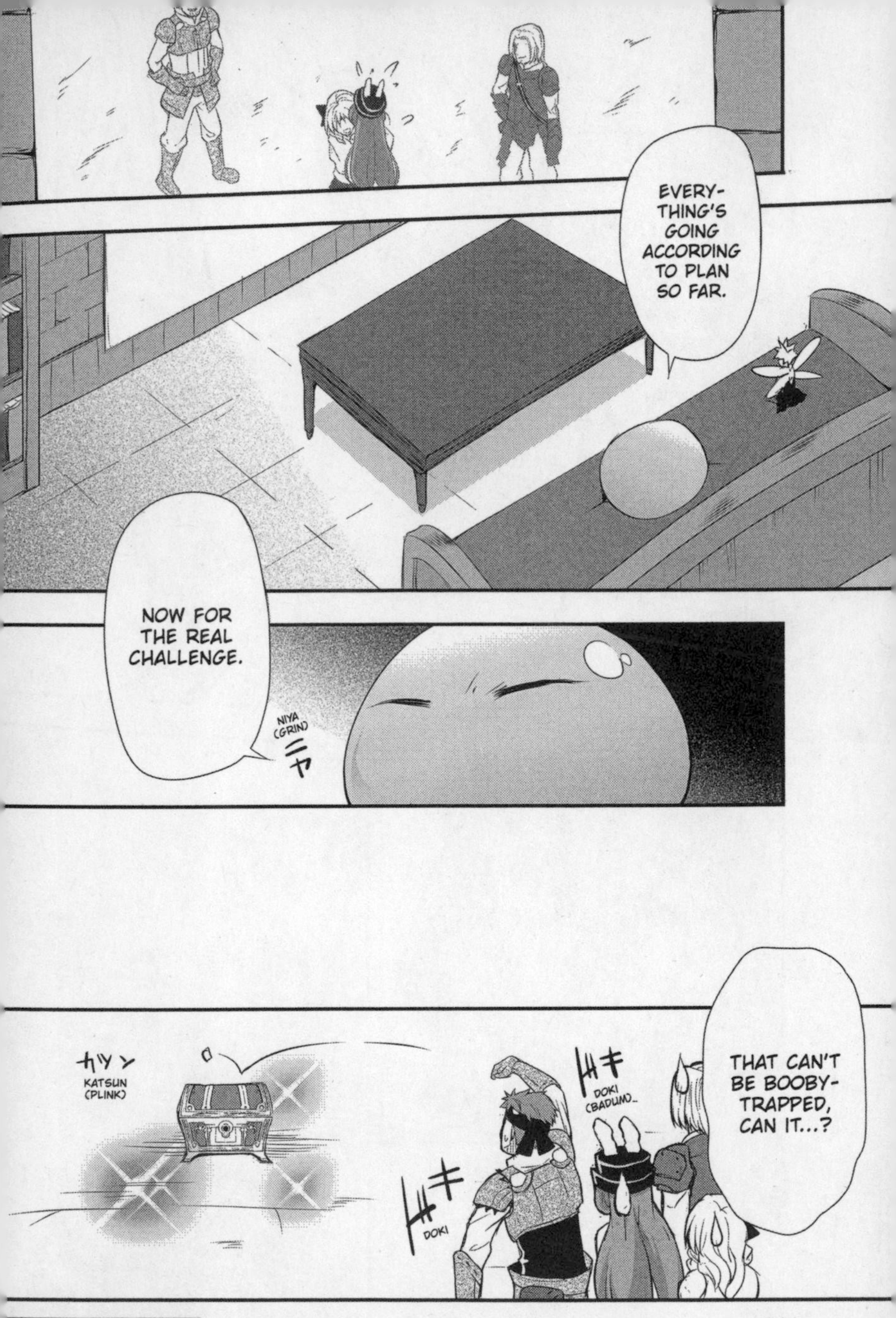
EVERY-THING'S GOING ACCORDING TO PLAN SO FAR.
NOW FOR THE REAL CHALLENGE.
ニヤ
NIYA (GRIN)
THAT CAN'T BE BOOBY-TRAPPED, CAN IT...?
ドキ
DOKI (BADUM)...
ドキ
DOKI
カツン
KATSUN (PLINK)

CHAPTER 6☆END

CHAPTER 7

DUNGEON EXPLORATION ☆ THREE STARS!! (PART 2)

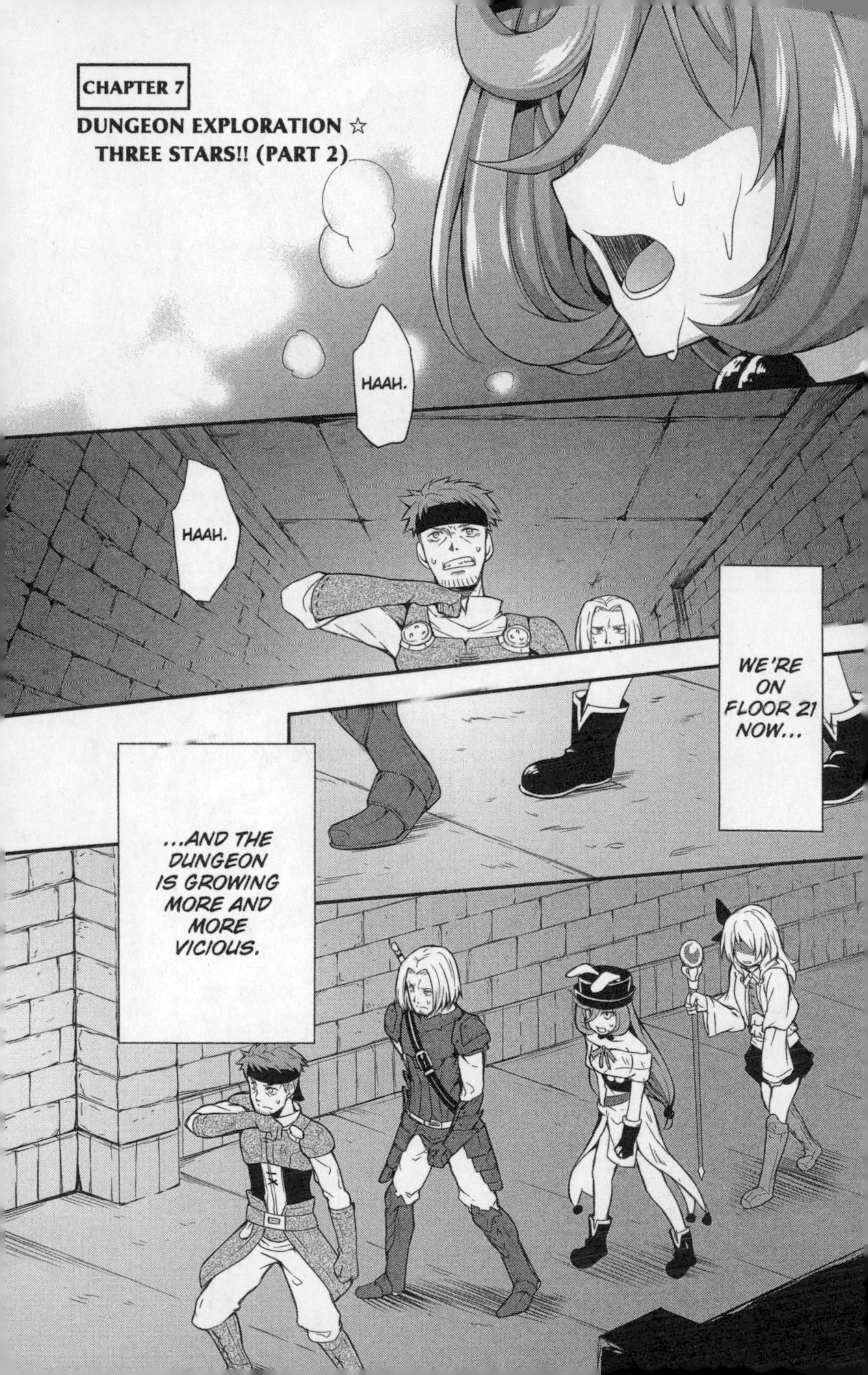
HAAH.
HAAH.
WE'RE ON FLOOR 21 NOW...
...AND THE DUNGEON IS GROWING MORE AND MORE VICIOUS.

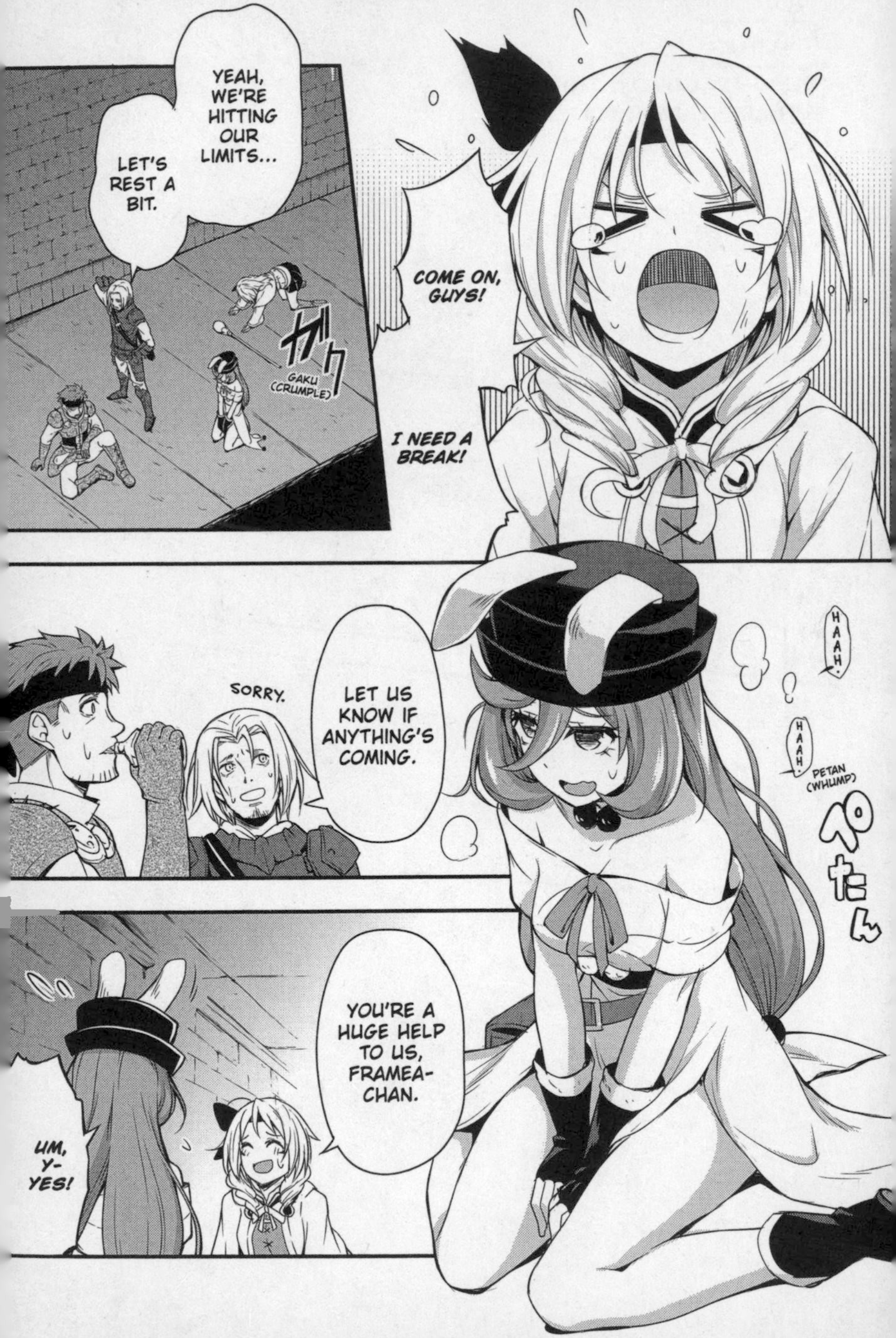
COME ON, GUYS!
I NEED A BREAK!
YEAH, WE'RE HITTING OUR LIMITS...
LET'S REST A BIT.
ガク
GAKU (CRUMPLE)
HAAH.
HAAH.
PETAN (WHUMP)
ぺたん
LET US KNOW IF ANYTHING'S COMING.
SORRY.
YOU'RE A HUGE HELP TO US, FRAMEA-CHAN.
UM, Y-YES!

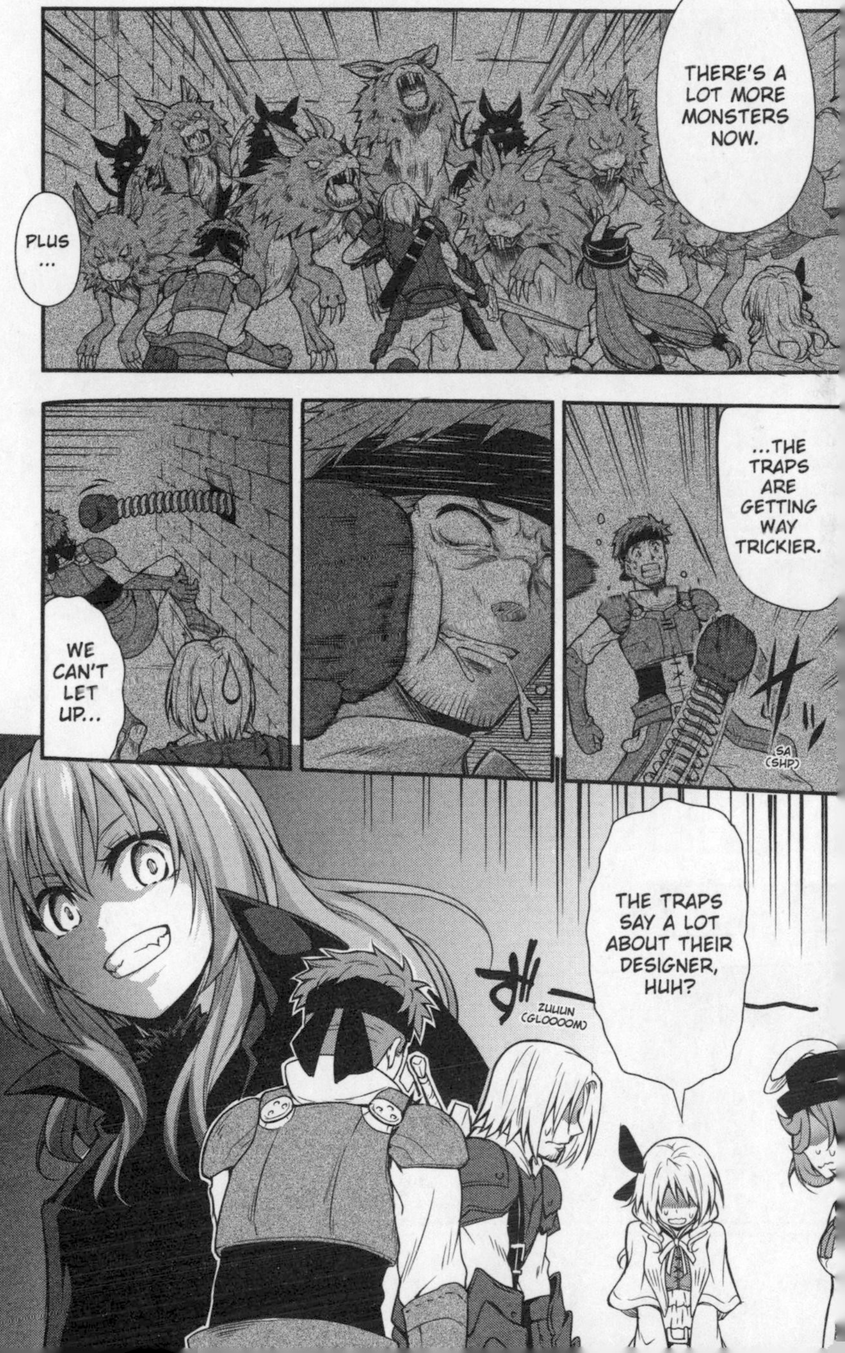
THERE'S A LOT MORE MONSTERS NOW.
PLUS...
...THE TRAPS ARE GETTING WAY TRICKIER.
SA (SHP)
WE CAN'T LET UP...
THE TRAPS SAY A LOT ABOUT THEIR DESIGNER, HUH?
ZUUUN (GLOOOOM)

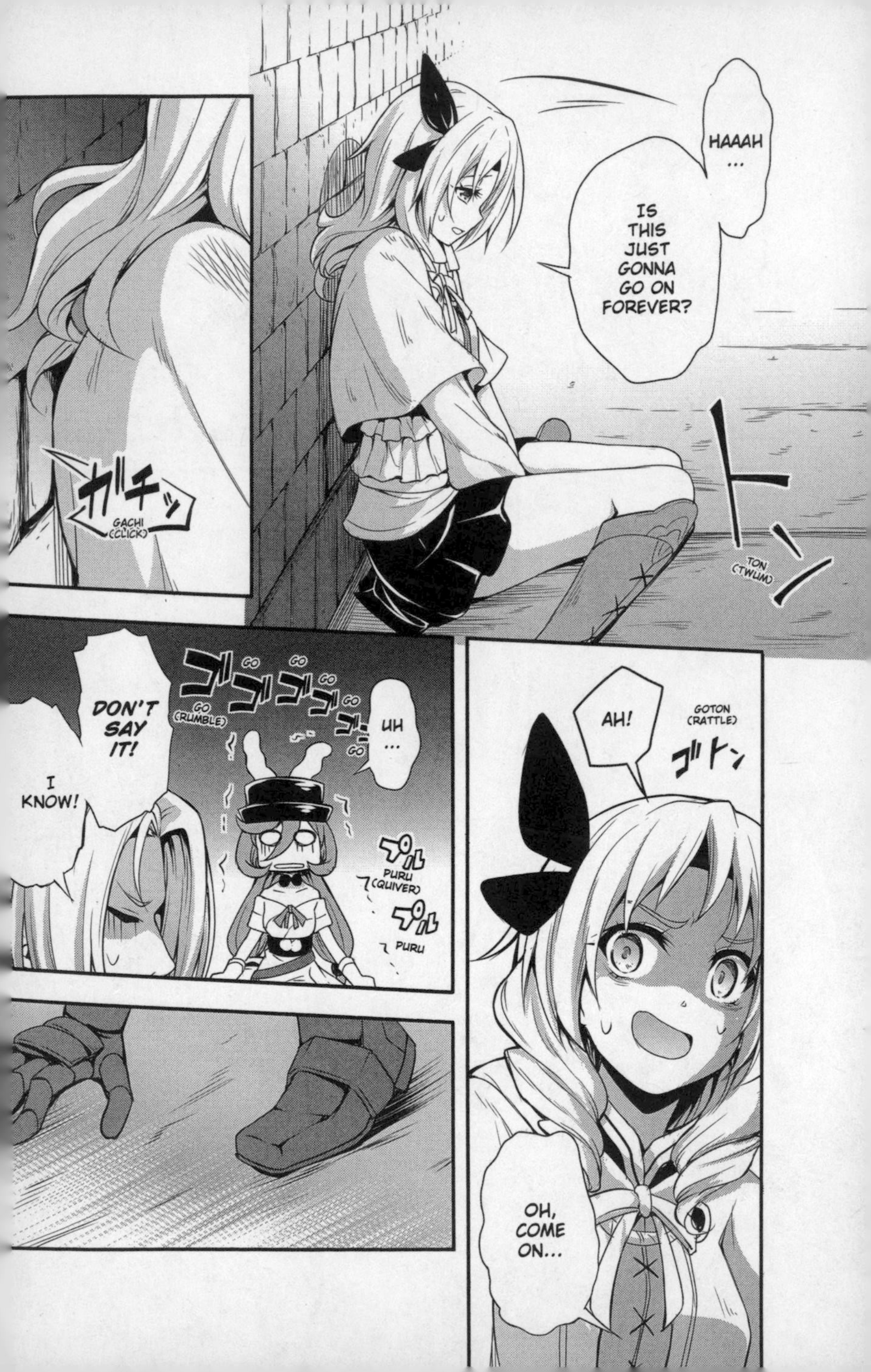
HAAAH ...
IS THIS JUST GONNA GO ON FOREVER?
TON (TWUM)
GACHI (CLICK)
AH!
GOTON (RATTLE)
OH, COME ON...
UH ...
GO GO GO GO GO GO (RUMBLE)
DON'T SAY IT!
I KNOW!
PURU (QUIVER)
PURU

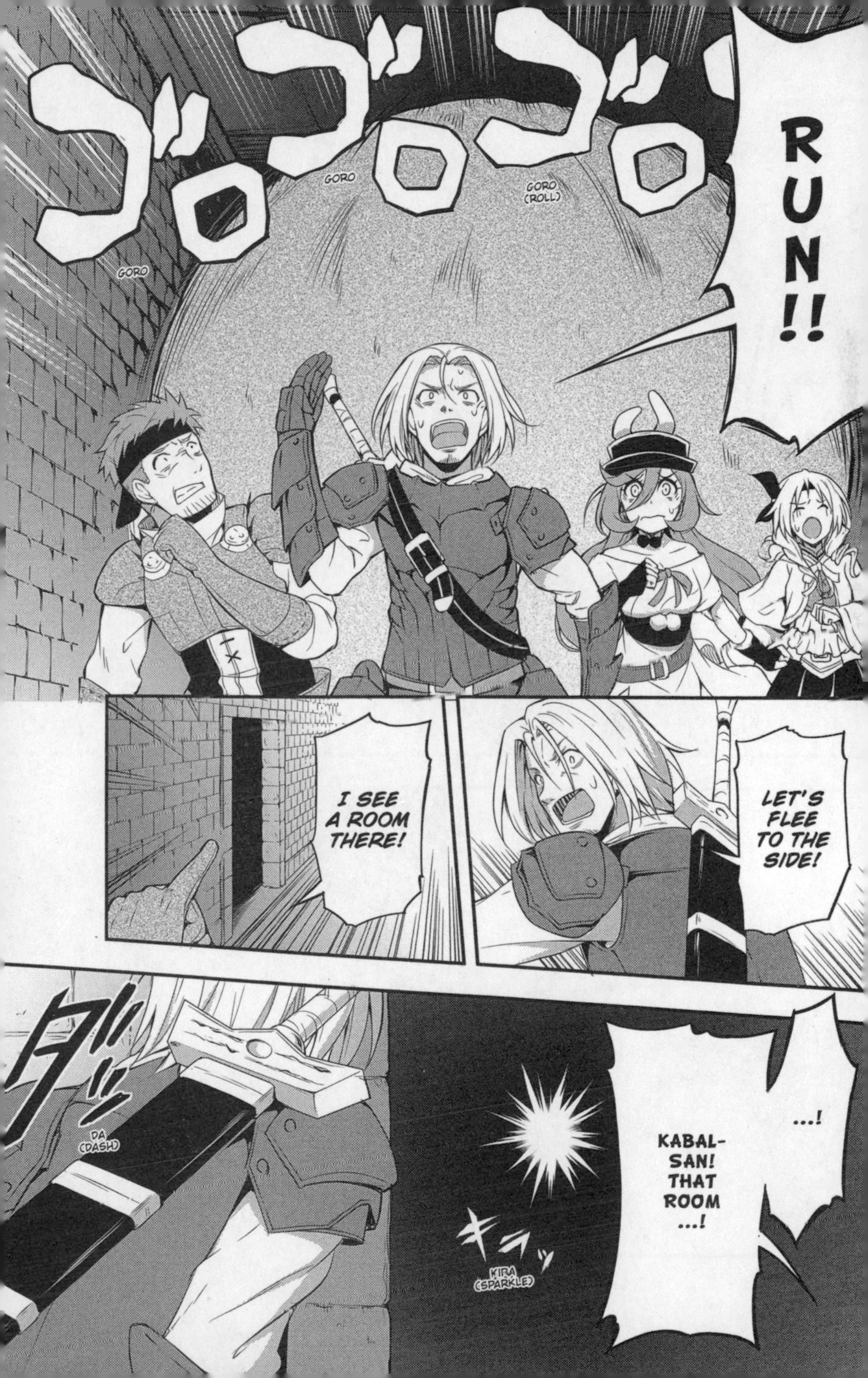

RUN!!
GORO (ROLL)
GORO
GORO
LET'S FLEE TO THE SIDE!
I SEE A ROOM THERE!
...!
KABAL-SAN! THAT ROOM ...!
KIRA (SPARKLE)
DA (DASH)

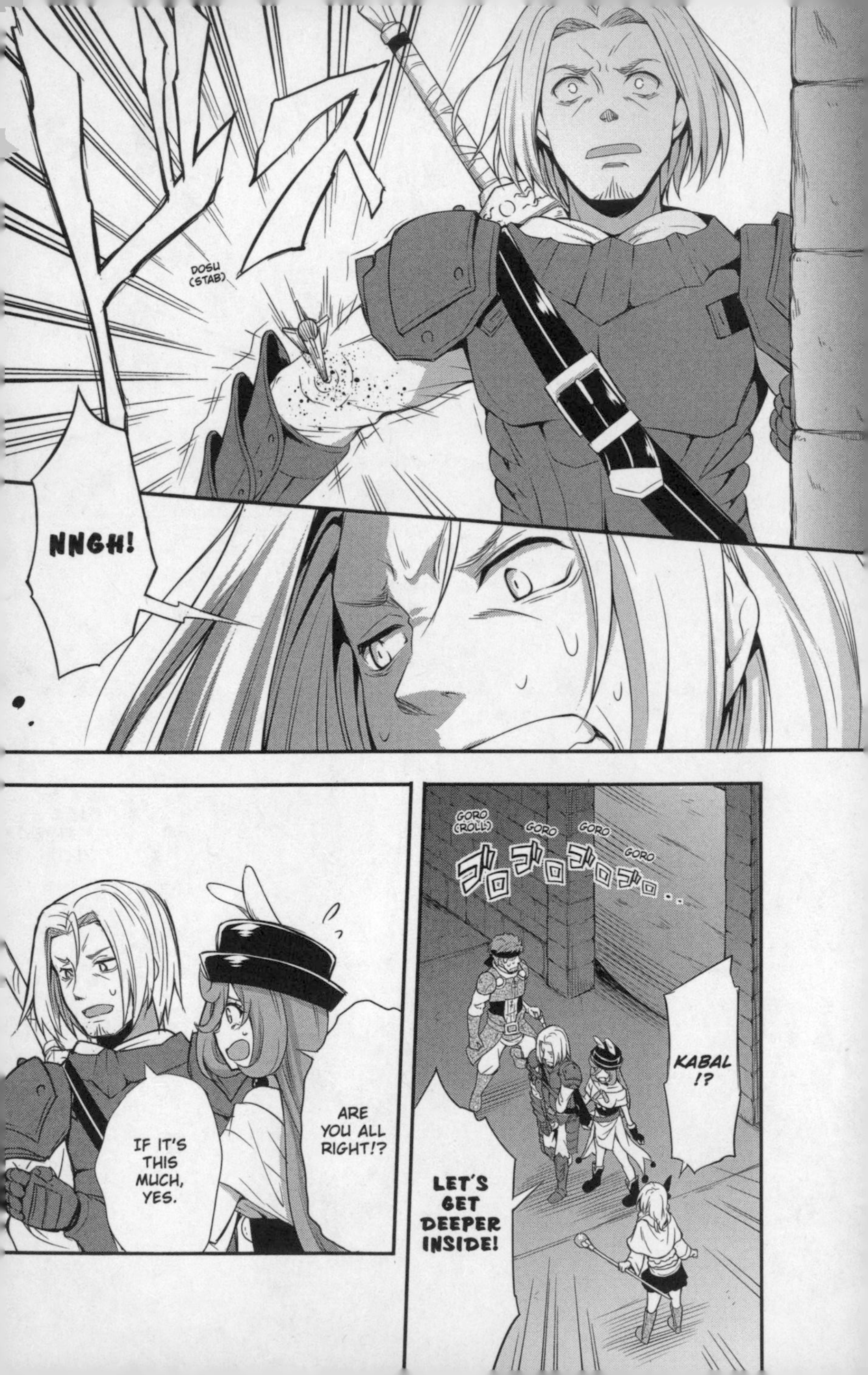
DOSU (STAB)
NNGH!
GORO (ROLL) GORO GORO GORO
ゴロゴロゴロゴロ‥
KABAL !?
LET'S GET DEEPER INSIDE!
ARE YOU ALL RIGHT!?
IF IT'S THIS MUCH, YES.

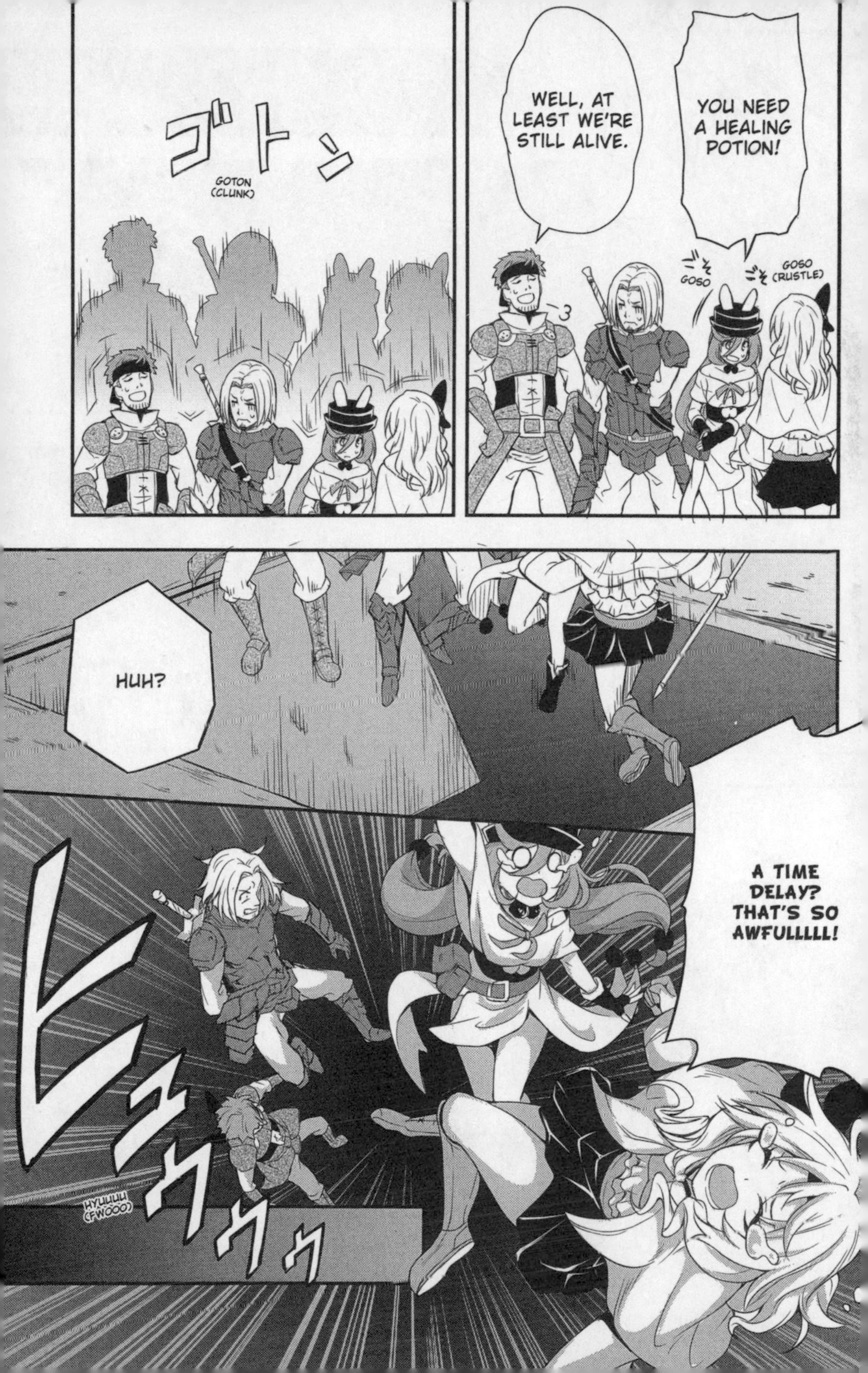
YOU NEED A HEALING POTION!
WELL, AT LEAST WE'RE STILL ALIVE.
ゴソ GOSO (RUSTLE)
ゴソ GOSO
ゴトン
GOTON (CLUNK)
HUH?
A TIME DELAY? THAT'S SO AWFULLLLL!
ヒュウゥゥ
HYUUUU (FWOOO)

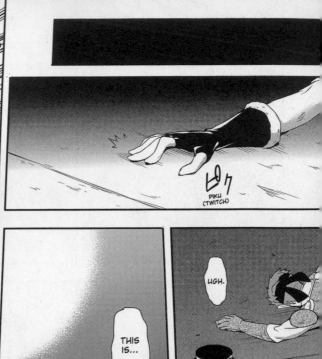

GROOOWL~

PIKU
(TWITCH)

NO...
WAY...

THIS IS...

UGH.

WHA...?

152

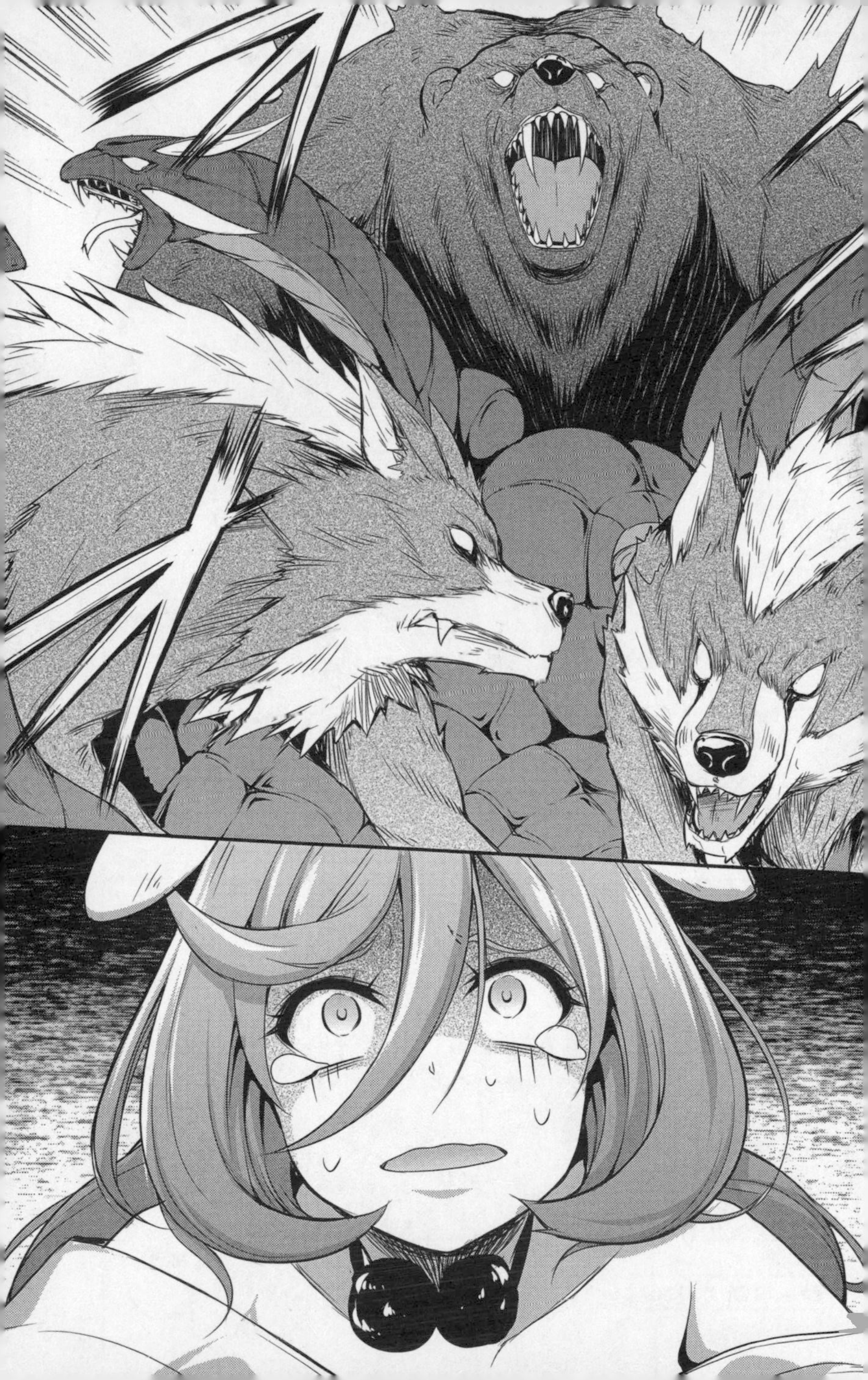

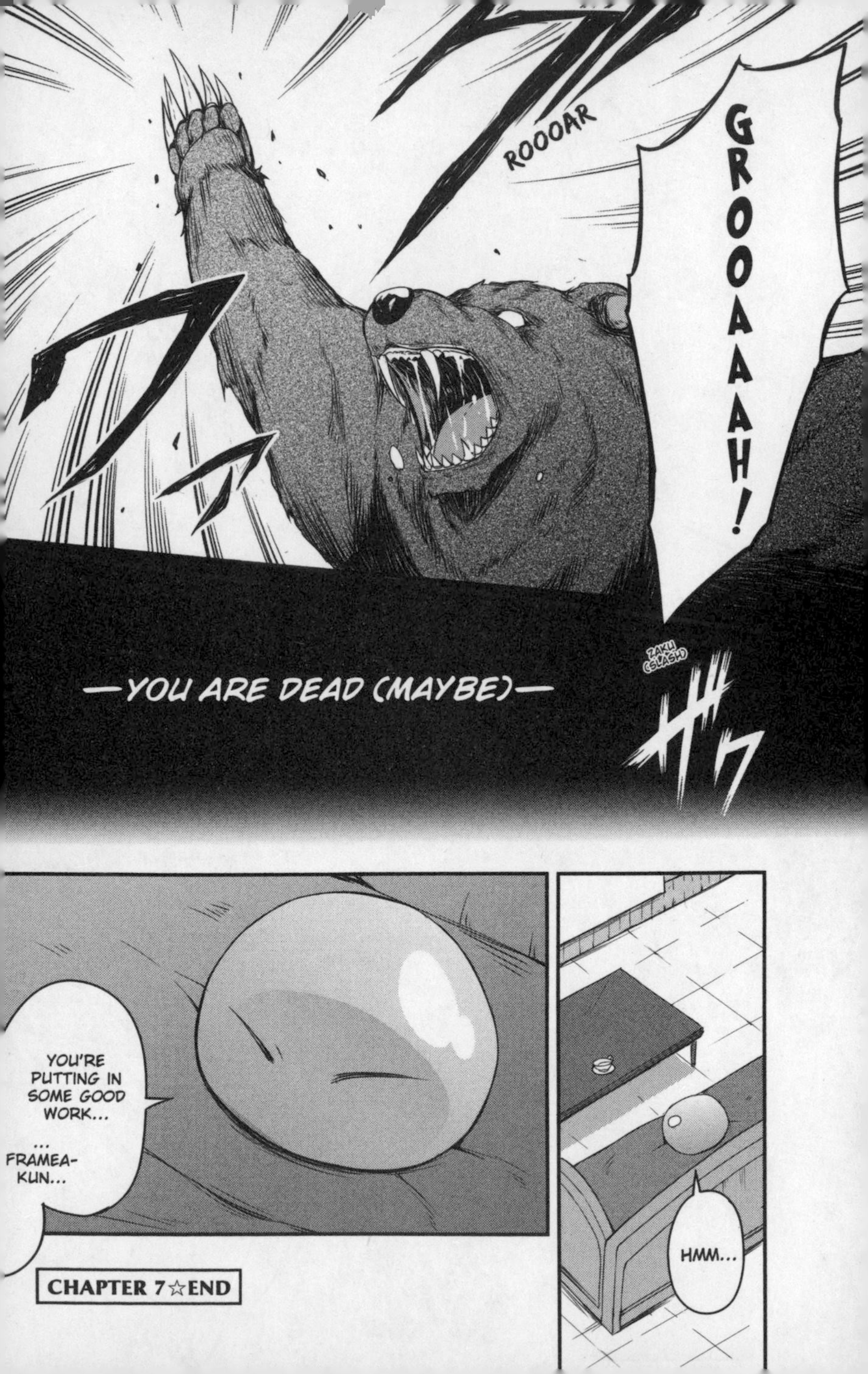
GROOOAAAH!
ROOOAR
—YOU ARE DEAD (MAYBE)—
ZAKU (SLASH)
HMM...
YOU'RE PUTTING IN SOME GOOD WORK...
... FRAMEA-KUN...
CHAPTER 7☆END

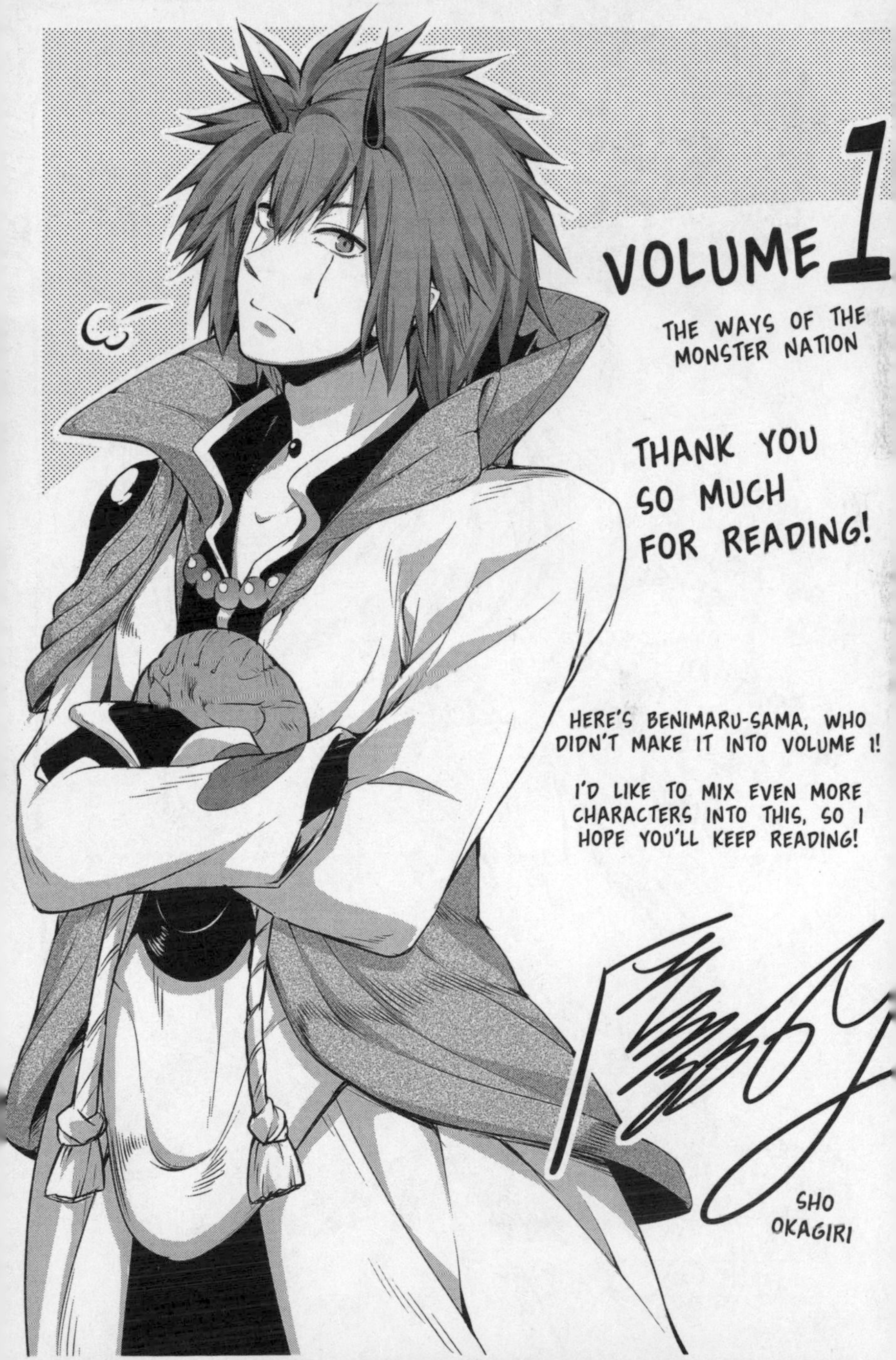
VOLUME 1
THE WAYS OF THE MONSTER NATION
THANK YOU SO MUCH FOR READING!
HERE'S BENIMARU-SAMA, WHO DIDN'T MAKE IT INTO VOLUME 1!
I'D LIKE TO MIX EVEN MORE CHARACTERS INTO THIS, SO I HOPE YOU'LL KEEP READING!
SHO OKAGIRI

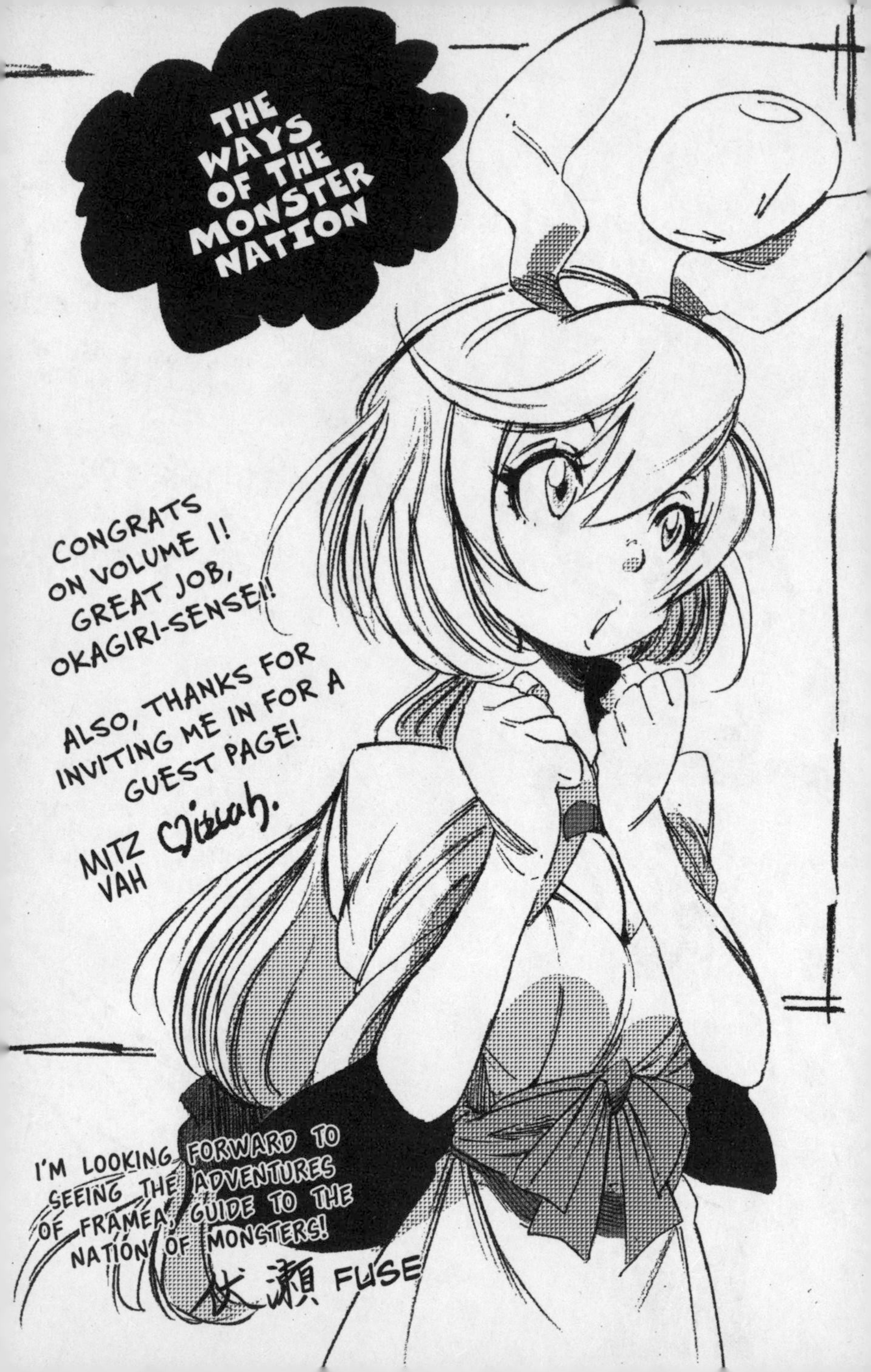
THE WAYS OF THE MONSTER NATION
CONGRATS ON VOLUME 1! GREAT JOB, OKAGIRI-SENSEI!!
ALSO, THANKS FOR INVITING ME IN FOR A GUEST PAGE!
MITZ VAH
I'M LOOKING FORWARD TO SEEING THE ADVENTURES OF FRAMEA, GUIDE TO THE NATION OF MONSTERS!
伏瀬 FUSE

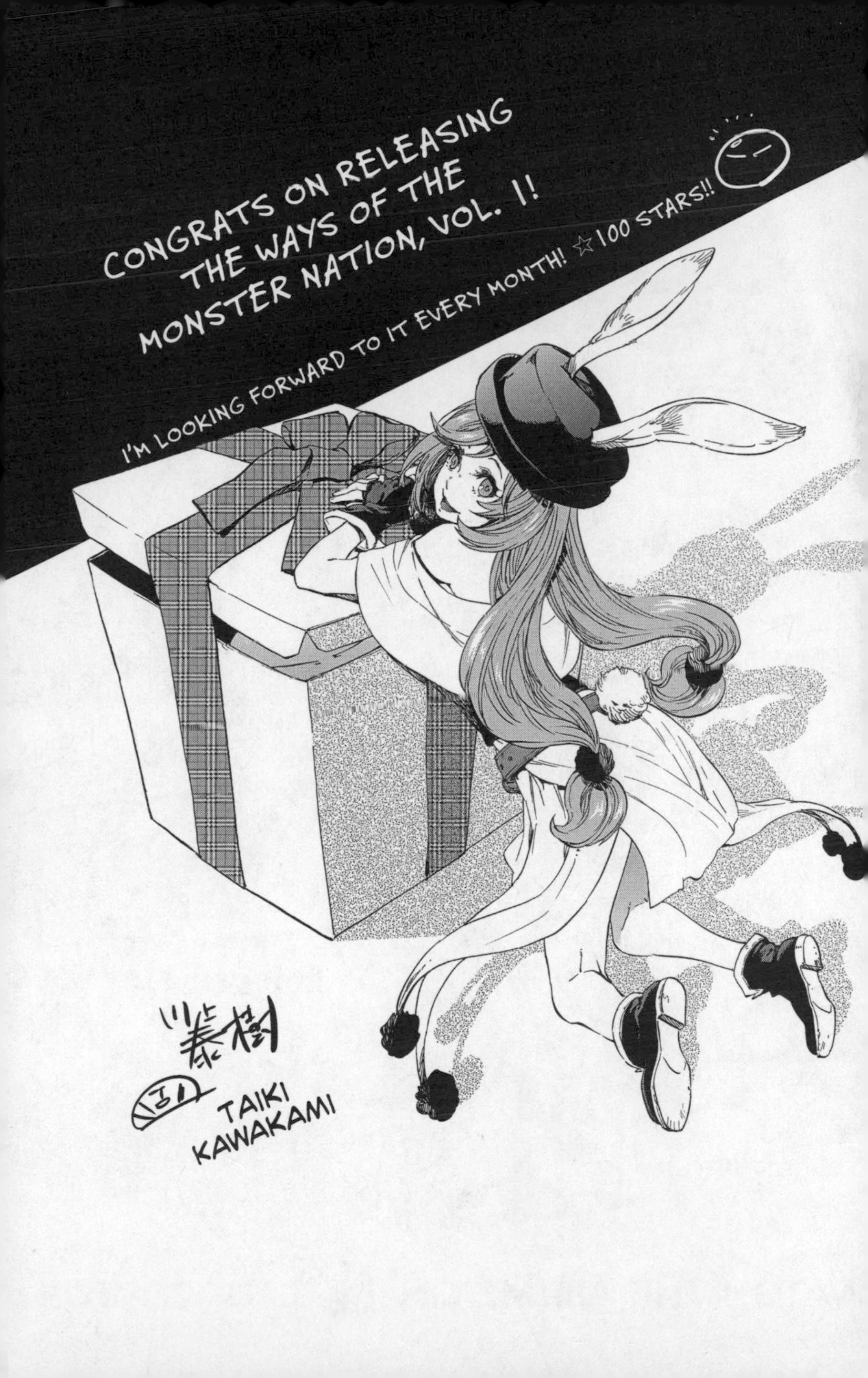
CONGRATS ON RELEASING THE WAYS OF THE MONSTER NATION, VOL. 1!
I'M LOOKING FORWARD TO IT EVERY MONTH! ☆100 STARS!!
TAIKI KAWAKAMI

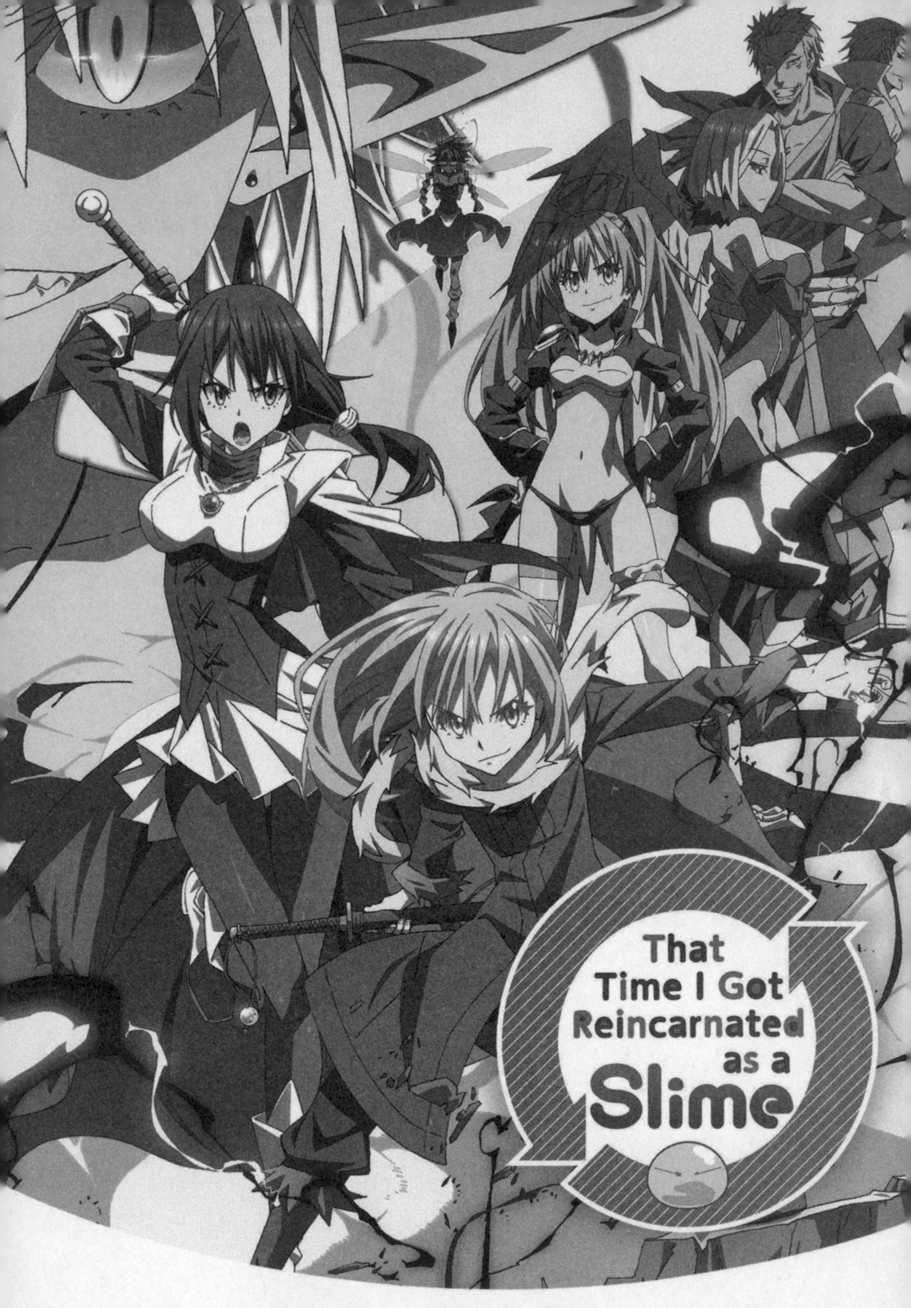
That Time I Got Reincarnated as a Slime

That Time I Got Reincarnated as a SLIME
The Ways of the Monster Nation

Translation: Kevin Gifford • Lettering: Barri Shrager

TENSEI SHITARA SURAIMU DATTA KEN ~MAMONO NO KUNI NO ARUKIKATA~ Vol. 1
©Fuse 2017
©Sho Okagiri, Mitz Vah 2017
First published in Japan in 2017 by MICRO MAGAZINE, INC.
English translation rights arranged with MICRO MAGAZINE, INC.
through Tuttle-Mori Agency, Inc., Tokyo.

English translation © 2020 by Yen Press, LLC

Yen Press
150 West 30th Street, 19th Floor
New York, NY 10001

Visit us at yenpress.com
facebook.com/yenpress
twitter.com/yenpress
yenpress.tumblr.com
instagram.com/yenpress

First Yen Press Edition: July 2020

Yen Press is an imprint of Yen Press, LLC.
The Yen Press name and logo are trademarks of Yen Press, LLC.

Library of Congress Control Number: 2020936422

ISBNs: 978-1-9753-1350-0 (paperback)
978-1-9753-1351-7 (ebook)

10 9 8 7 6 5 4 3 2 1

BVG

Printed in the United States of America